AF482139

WHITE NILE ARABS

Political Leadership and
Economic Change

LONDON SCHOOL OF ECONOMICS
MONOGRAPHS ON SOCIAL ANTHROPOLOGY

Managing Editor: Ioan Lewis

The Monographs on Social Anthropology were established in 1940 and aim to publish results of modern anthropological research of primary interest to specialists.

The continuation of the series was made possible by a grant in aid from the Wenner-Gren Foundation for Anthropological Research, and more recently by a further grant from the Governors of the London School of Economics and Political Science. Income from sales is returned to a revolving fund to assist further publications.

The Monographs are under the direction of an Editorial Board associated with the Department of Anthropology of the London School of Economics and Political Science.

LONDON SCHOOL OF ECONOMICS
MONOGRAPHS ON SOCIAL ANTHROPOLOGY
No. 53

WHITE NILE ARABS

Political Leadership and Economic Change

BY

ABBAS AHMED MOHAMED

THE ATHLONE PRESS
NEW JERSEY: HUMANITIES PRESS INC.
1980

Published by
THE ATHLONE PRESS
90-91 Great Russell Street
London WC1

USA and Canada
Humanities Press Inc.
New Jersey

© *Abbas Ahmed Mohamed* 1980

British Library Cataloguing in Publication Data
Abbas, Ahmed Mohamed
  White Nile Arabs – (London School of
  Economics and Political Science. Monographs
  on social anthropology; 53; 0077–1074).
  1. Hassaniya – Social Life and customs
  2. Hissinat – Social life and customs 3. Ethnol-
  ogy – Sudan – White Nile Province
  I. Title   II. Series
  301.29′629′3   GN652.H/
  UK SBN 0 485 19553 4
  USA SBN 0 391 00969 9

Printed in Great Britain by
T. & A. CONSTABLE LTD
EDINBURGH

PREFACE

This book is an account of the changing social and political structure of the Hassaniya and Hissinat, two Sudanese Arabic-speaking tribes inhabiting the northern part of the White Nile Province in the Sudan. The account is based on field research over 15 months, between June 1969 and November 1970, among these groups. The original plan was to give major consideration to the working of the Native Administration but this was abolished as soon as I arrived in the field by the new government that came to power in May 1969. Only certain native courts under the tribal chiefs were allowed to function, and these only for a very short period. For a long time afterwards the administrative machinery was highly chaotic. In mid-1970, the villages' Magistrates Courts were established to replace the former tribal courts while administrative services were performed directly by the local government.

Other upheavals in the area have also interrupted the course of this study. March 1970 witnessed the Mahdists' revolt at Aba Island and the government counter-action to crush that revolt. Many of the White Nile Arabs are devout followers of the Mahdist Sect and the people whom I came to study were directly involved in the incident. Thus, even in the small village I lived in, some people were interrogated and one or two were taken to Khartoum pending investigations. This put me in a critical position, for it meant that I had to make great efforts to gain the confidence of the people and overcome a rising feeling among some suspicious individuals that I might be a spy for the government. This situation is no doubt common for social anthropologists, who in many circumstances have learned how to overcome, or at least to bear, such problems.

In the field, I conducted my interviews and gathered most of the information in Arabic. I made use of some Hassaniya assistants, most of whom were secondary school pupils. They were very helpful especially when I conducted a household census and a questionnaire about agricultural production and relations between the scheme and tenants. Only a very small part of the questionnaire is used in this book. In addition, I have collected a mass of data relating to oral traditions, folk tales, songs, case-histories, genealogies, sources of wealth and so on.

During most of my time in the field, I lived at Es-Sufi village. I selected this place for a number of reasons. Firstly, it lies in the centre of Dar Hassaniya, roughly half-way between Dueim and Jebel Awliya. Secondly, it lies in the centre of a concentration of agricultural schemes that is not found in other parts of the territory. Thirdly, it lies on the west bank where I could easily gain access to the pastoral groups inhabiting the western interior, for these groups have become highly involved in the riverain economy. Fourthly, it lies very near to Wad Nimir Village, the former headquarters of the deputy Nazirate, and to Naima across the river, the former headquarters of the Nazirate. This placed me near the Gushgushab lineage homeland and its ruling section, the Habbaniya.

In this work I deal with tribal politics before the abolition of the Native Administration, and I do not take into consideration the fact that all private agricultural schemes are today taken over by the government – a factor which has affected the economic foundation of the former ruling élite, the Habbaniya. My work here deals mainly with general sorts of relationship that existed in the past and still exist today among the Hassaniya Arabs. I take the inauguration of the Jebel Awliya Dam development scheme in 1937 as a dividing point between the traditional and the new emerging institutions. Among other things, I focus on the relationship between the tribal rulers and the people they ruled, and trace the development of political domination in that relationship. As such, this study complements recent studies on the tribal élite, especially that which exists among the close neighbours of the Hassaniya – the Kabbabish Arabs.

ACKNOWLEDGMENTS

I am most grateful to the University of Khartoum for financing the fieldwork on which this book is based.

During my fieldwork I had the willing co-operation of Shaikh Yusuf Habbani (the former Nazir), Omer Idris Habbani, Mahdi Abdel Gadir Habbani, Ibrahim Habbani (former Minister of Dar Hassaniya), Farouk Idris Haj Muhammad Habbani, Abdallah Idris Habbani, Sayed Abdel Gadir Habbani, Ismail Ibrahim Nimir and Osman Idris Habbani. I owe a special debt to Omer Idris Habbani, the former Deputy-Nazir and Principal of the Executive Rural Council, for giving me detailed impartial information. I cannot imagine how I could otherwise have gained access to it.

I wish to thank Ahmed El Rayah Hussein, Abdel Rahman El Nadi, Muhsin El Nadi and Mukhtar El Asem, for making initial arrangements and providing accommodation for me for some time.

At Es-Sufi village, I found many sincere and faithful friends. I wish to express my deep gratitude to all of them, especially Abdel Tam El Tayib and his family, without whose help I should have encountered many difficulties. Massalam and El Tayib Camilallah of the *Garnab* Amriya and Muhammed Yusuf Fadlallah, Bilal Awadallah and Yusuf Hamid of the *Ribaihab* Amriya, and Muhammed Mugawir are among those I wish to mention by name.

In writing this book I have received considerable help and guidance from Professor I. M. Lewis, who had always stimulating suggestions to offer. I wish to express my gratitude for his patience, co-operation and encouragement.

To Professor Ian Cunnison and Dr Talal Asad I owe a special debt of gratitude for their encouragement and for reading the draft and making criticisms and recommendations.

Gill Shepherd, Dr Pamela Constantinides and Mrs Ruth Beaglehole have saved me time by correcting the grammatical mistakes in the various chapters.

I would like to record my thanks to Professor Lucy Mair, Dr

Peter Loizos and Dr Pamela Constantinides who undertook the task of rearranging and correcting the final draft.

Finally it is only fair to mention my wife, Suad, and to express my gratitude for her patience and sustained encouragement.

Note on Transliteration

In transliteration of Arabic words I have avoided any complex system of diacritical marks and have written the words in a simple way, which can easily be grasped by anyone who knows Arabic. I have also attempted to render the words as they are pronounced by the Hassaniya and other Kawahla. With the exception of a few Arabic plurals, most plural forms are indicated by adding an 's' to the singular form. Italics are not used for those terms and titles, such as nazir, amir, ummar, and meglis, which occur throughout the text.

CONTENTS

MAPS

FIGURES

TABLES

Introduction

For a long time social anthropologists have tended to over-emphasize the significance of kinship and other normative or ideological systems in the analysis of social structure at the expense of ecology and economy. It is only during the last decade or so that new trends in anthropological writing have given systematic and detailed analyses of the ecological and economic forces behind the organization of human relationships. Leach's study of Pul Eliya (1961a) is one example. It is, however, the new emphasis on change and diachronic analysis *vis-à-vis* the earlier 'static' synchronic analysis that has made provision for ecological and economic factors absolutely essential, for, as Leach among others has argued, over-emphasis on the priority of kinship, descent, and normative rules makes the analysis of social change virtually impossible (Leach op. cit.). The priority of kinship and normative rules within the structural-functional tradition of analysis, may be seen as only one problematic aspect of the issue of individuals seen as individuals, rather than as helpless entities within a deified society. The main problem facing this type of structural-functionalism is to find a conceptual framework in which both individuals, as well as the nature and function of the groups and institutions within the system, are given satisfactory consideration. Some illuminating attempts to resolve this problem have been put forward by Emmet (1960) and Lewis (1968) among many others.

Lewis has offered an interesting suggestion by pointing out that 'function has meaning and utility less in its *status quo* maintenance aspects than in referring to the actual engagement and interests of people in different roles and positions' and that 'to understand how a given structure works, or rather how it is worked, it seems more profitable to pose our questions in terms of the extent to which the individual's commitment to a given pattern, or set of social relations and obligations serves his interests in a fashion which, in the circumstances, he regards as most advantageous' (op. cit., p. xxii). This is why in describing and analysing the social and political change that has taken place among the Kawahla, I have emphasized the element of individual interest. Thus I have proceeded first to answer the question: what principles generated the corporate groups that existed before the Jebel Awliya Dam? The answers are to be found in the environmental, ecological and economic factors that necessitated co-operation and close and exclusive attachments to wider groupings such as herding partnerships and camping units. These groupings emerge as a result of individuals' attempts to maximize their interest and to secure a living in a basically insecure and unpredictable environment. It is only by considering this element of individual interest that we can possibly understand the change that has taken place today which has directed that interest towards the agricultural scheme and its management: hence the foundation of the earlier corporate groups as mutual aid groups.

The role of corporate groups together with their differentiated structure, reflected in the institution of the ummar,[1] has influenced the sociological character of the tribal polity. This polity took the form of a confederacy. The most important body was the meglis, the tribal council, in which representatives of the various lineages took the major decisions which could affect the entire region.

The post-dam economic and agrarian development has undermined the lineage corporation and differentiation while at the same time consolidating the power of the tribal chiefs. As a result the tribal chiefs have acted beyond the limits of the jurisdiction allowed to federal units and have become tyrannical in policy-making. They formulate policies without reference to the people mostly affected. Thus they make major appointments such as nazirs and deputies, and also control the omdas and shaikhs.

One of the main aims of this book is to try to relate the administrative and political changes at the higher levels of organization to grass-roots changes in the ecology and economy that accompanied the inauguration of the Jebel Awliya Dam development scheme in 1937. Therefore it gives equal consideration to pre-dam and post-dam social structures and describes their relevance to the major pattern of change.

Chapter 1 provides basic information about the region – the territorial setting, the tribal population and its distribution. It includes a detailed discussion of the ecological and economic

---

[1] Ummar (sing. amir), i.e. big men in terms of achieved wealth or power.

setting in the pre-dam period. This takes into consideration various physical and environmental factors such as rain, river-flood, pests and animal diseases, and examines the critical bearing of these factors on the modes of livelihood of the White Nile Arabs. The highly insecure environment characterized by famine and occasional scarcity has in turn dictated certain risk-reducing devices which are expressive of a highly rational and organized view of life. This exhibited itself in the way people came together to satisfy certain needs or to maximize specific interests. Accordingly, the functional nature of such groupings as herding partnerships and camping units is discussed briefly. The nature and function of these groupings are fairly similar to grazing and camping units among the Somali (Lewis 1961) and the Kababish (Asad 1970). The formation of such groupings on the basis of divisions of labour and its exchange is already demonstrated by these studies. Here close consideration is given to what may be called topographical and ecological zones. These are analysed as factors generating a high measure of economic diversification, which in turn necessitates various forms of what economists call 'horizontal integration' such as that between cattle and sheep herding, or between herding and cultivation. The ecological setting thus exhibited relatively discrete spheres of economic activity. Two of these spheres were concerned with animal husbandry (cattle and sheep grazing) and three with agricultural production (rain, river and *goz* cultivation). The deployment of resources in these various spheres necessitated exchange of labour between extended families so that it was in their own interests to emphasize the common bonds that united them.

In Chapter 2 I examine in more detail the common pattern of exchange between lineage members in two spheres of economic activity: those concerning labour and consumption goods. In the sphere of labour detailed examples are given of herding partnerships, while the kinship relations between the different partners are shown and explained. Herding partnerships were formed between people having the same lineage name who consequently considered themselves as very close kin. I examine other institutions in which lineage solidarity in the pre-dam era was reflected and/or promoted, such as co-residence, endogamy and homicide. The corporate character of the lineage was exemplified by its emergence as a vengeance group. With regard to marriage, the exchange of women within an entire lineage was considered to be an expression of lineage solidarity and power on the one hand, and a measure to control property such as land and animals which were transferred at marriage on the other.

Chapter 3 discusses and analyses the pattern of social differentiation that provided two categories of people, the ummar and religious shaikhs, with special sources of power over other categories. Here I argue that these sources of power were a function of the insecure environment and consequently emerge inevitably as part of it. The source of power altered as that environment changed. This occurred in the post-dam period which I shall discuss later.

Both the religious shaikhs and ummar acted in general as foci for the solidarity of their groups. But the shaikhs in particular were also inter-lineage and inter-tribal functionaries because they emerged as mediators between rival groups and individuals. As such they stood above the sectional interests of any one group. Their role was similar to that of the Somali holy men (Lewis 1965), the Sanusi shaikhs (Evans-Pritchard 1949), and other religious leaders such as those among the Pathans (Barth 1959) and the Atlas Berbers and, to a lesser degree, among the Hausa in West Africa (Cohen 1968).

The emergence of these two categories of leaders should not be seen as contradictory for, as Barth has demonstrated for the Pathans (1959), the religious and secular leaders have complementary roles; one exhibits qualities of modesty, piety and reasonableness, the other has qualities of manliness, courage and dominance. Each role presupposes the other.

The Kawahla congeries consisted of various religious shaikhs and ummar, each with his own group of followers comprised mainly of lineage mates. The lineage may be described in this sense as a centralized group in a way more or less similar to Barth's designation of groupings of leaders and followers as centralized (Barth 1954). The amalgamation of these centralized groups into the Kawahla polity affected its sociological character with its many acephalous features. The Kawahla polity, roughly speaking, was a confederacy rather than a unitary state. This is shown clearly in Chapter 4 in the discussion of the pattern of tribal and administrative politics during the early part of the Condominium (1900–37). Here the interaction between what might be distinguished as lineage politics and higher level politics is demonstrated by the emergence of the ummar and religious shaikhs as delegates or representatives for the various lineages in the meglis or tribal council in which *nas-el-shura* or 'people of consent' sit to decide upon major issues such as senior appointments or the settlement of disputes. It was extremely difficult for any major decision which could affect the whole tribal population to be made without summoning the meglis. Three sectional roles were important in the meglis: the tribal chiefs, the government, and the representatives. Thus one can speak about the meglis as an institutional complex which displayed features of representative politics or politics of consent, or perhaps of compromise – to borrow Lewis's usage, 'Republican Politics' (Lewis 1971).

Chapters 5 and 6 give an account of the salient effects of the dam upon the ecological and economic setting and describe the basic features of the post-dam economy's agrarian development. Here the story of the dam is given together with its impact on the semi-sedentary, semi-pastoral mode of livelihood. The radical effects on the ecology, the attraction of cotton cultivation while the bases of animal rearing were undermined, have resulted in a gradual transformation of these semi-pastoral groups into sedentary cultivators growing cotton as a cash crop, together with their incorporation into a regional as well as a national economy. The discussion emphasizes the significance of the national trends and the international factors, such as the Second World War and the Korean War, on the local economy and considers these historical facts within a sociological perspective.

The second part of the argument here offers detailed consideration of the introduction and the cumulative increase in the acquisition of modern farm machinery, such as tractors, sprayers and pumps. It goes on to show to what extent the mechanization of agricultural activities has resulted in changes in the environment and to what extent it has provided new sources of economic security for the individual and his family, which has created new social relationships with significant social repercussions. Chapter 7 considers these repercussions with a special focus on the present-day lineage. In particular, it examines the effects of the post-dam economy, especially the new dependence of the people on the scheme, on the traditional spheres of exchange. It argues that these spheres have been narrowed or have been eliminated in certain

B

cases which has led to the breakdown of the horizontal relationships that formerly promoted the viability and corporate character of descent groups. The problem of social differentiation and the position of the ummar and religious shaikhs is then considered. It is shown that this differentiation has had its basis in the insecure, unpredictable pre-dam environment and that the elimination or at least the reduction of this insecurity has affected the foundation of this differentiation and has contributed to the formation of an egalitarian lineage structure. Some case studies indicate that these leaders no longer have the backing of their previous groups and it has become difficult for them to mobilize such groups for common and effective political action. Some cases illustrate the way in which individualization of action and lack of corporate unity have become the dominant social principles. Earlier (Mohamed 1971), I accounted for certain significant changes which are only hinted at in this discussion, such as the changing strategy of the religious shaikhs who acted as mediators and peace-makers in the pre-dam period but today are becoming increasingly personally involved in competition over such valued prizes as administrative posts and other positions.

In Chapter 8 there is an outline of the new trends at the higher levels of administrative and tribal politics. The account given is sketchy and brief and deals with the taking-over of the power of the meglis as a decision-making body by the tribal chiefs, the Habbaniya. Today, the Habbaniya emerge as the primary decision-makers and policy-formulators, occupying the top positions in both local government and party politics. An important issue is the understanding of how and why the Habbaniya have been able to establish themselves and to consolidate their monopoly of power during the last two decades or so. The answer in my view lies in the recent development that weakened effective resistance and opposition to the Habbaniya by undermining the corporate nature of the lineages and limiting accordingly the influence of their leaders. Here I employ the insight of certain of the élite theorists, especially C. Wright Mills and Burnam, that 'horizontal contacts between members of the society break down and are replaced by vertical contacts between atomized individuals and the élite' (Parry 1959). The conclusion elaborates on this and considers the problem of social and political change in relation to early élite theorizing.

I

The Territorial and Tribal Setting: The Pre-Dam Ecological Framework and Traditional Economic Organization

THE TERRITORIAL AND TRIBAL SETTING

Dar Hassaniya denotes the area lying roughly between latitudes $13\frac{1}{2}/15$ north, and longitudes $33/31\frac{1}{2}$ east. It has an area of approximately 76,000 square miles, extending for about 100 miles from north to south and 76 miles from east to west.

The 1956 general census gives the figure of 386,000 for the human population in Dar Hassaniya; today it is approximately 500,000. So it is not a densely populated area – although, as we shall see later, the riverain section has become relatively densely populated in the last decade or so. National statistics divide Dar Hassaniya into two parts: that lying to the west of the White Nile with an approximate density of under two persons per square mile, and that to the east of the White Nile with an estimated density of 10 to 50 persons per square mile. This is because national statistics include the eastern part of Dar Hassaniya in the relatively densely populated Gezira area.[1]

There are no reliable statistics for the area prior to 1956, although the following figures are available from the local administrative files.[2]

(a) Economic Survey, 1927: Population: 229,613
(b) Annual Report, 1933: Population: 225,572
(c) Mr Owen's (D.C.) Population Check, 1931: Population: 165,481

The file says that 'probably the correct answer is 200,000'.

---

[1] See The Philosophical Society of Sudan: 'The Population of the Sudan', 1958.
[2] Administrative Files, North District, Dueim, 20/7/1934: No. N.D./66/K.4.

Dar Hassaniya is inhabited today by many tribes, the most important of which, in terms of numbers as well as power, are those of the Kawahla group. Among the Kawahla the most powerful and important are the Hassaniya. Since 1930 this Dar, or land, has been named after them. During that time Dar Hassaniya came into existence as an administrative unit under a policy of 'indirect rule', known as the 'Native Administration', according to which tribal authorities were created or officially recognized as rulers of their own tribes. Dar Hassaniya contains several tribes brought together under a Hassani Nazir, that is, a paramount chief.

When Dar Hassaniya was established in 1930, it formed part of the larger area, between Jebel Awliya in the north and Shawal village in the south, which was known as White Nile Province. The Province was divided into two parts: from about latitude $13\frac{1}{2}$ and north was known as Dar Hassaniya, while the southern part, from latitude $13\frac{1}{2}$ and south became Dar Baggara. The White Nile Province was organized administratively into a number of districts. These were called Geteina, Dueim and Kosti. The first two comprised Dar Hassaniya while the third district comprised Dar Baggara.

In the 1940s, the area known as the White Nile Province was administratively subsumed in the neighbouring Gezira Province which was later called the Blue Nile Province. The two administrative districts which were coincident with Dar Hassaniya merged to form the electorate for the 'North White Nile Rural Council' (NWNRC). The White Nile cuts Dar Hassaniya into two administrative sections known as Hassaniya East and Hassaniya West.

Crossing Dar Hassaniya from north to south by way of the river, the two Kawahla tribes first encountered to the south of Jebel Awliya are the Urwab and Muhammadiya. To the south of these lies the homeland of another Kawahla tribe called the Hissinat which extends to Wadi Afu on the west bank and Abu-Hugar on the east bank. Then comes the Hassaniya land which goes as far south as Khor Abu-Gasaba. After that, there is another Hissinat settlement as well as small settlements of various tribes such as the Ga'afra, Dueim, Kunuz, and Massalamiya extending to the north of Shawal village, the southern limit of Dar Hassaniya. To the south lies the Baggara Nazirate.

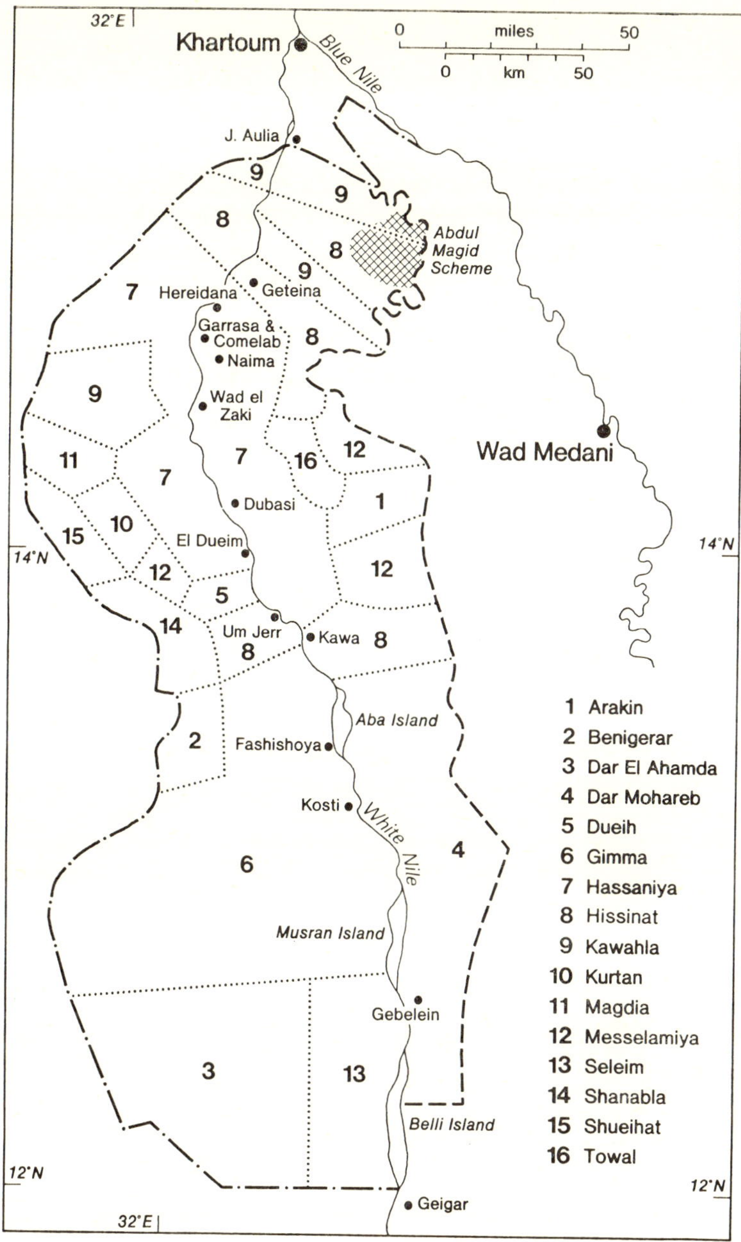

Map 1. North White Nile rural council

From east to west, the territorial and tribal setting is difficult to describe and can be better represented by a map (see Map 1). To the west of Dar Hassaniya is Dar Kababish while its eastern boundaries can be represented roughly by the villages of Ma'tuk and Abu Guta. In the south-east some part of Dar Hassaniya lies within the Managil extension of the Gezira scheme.

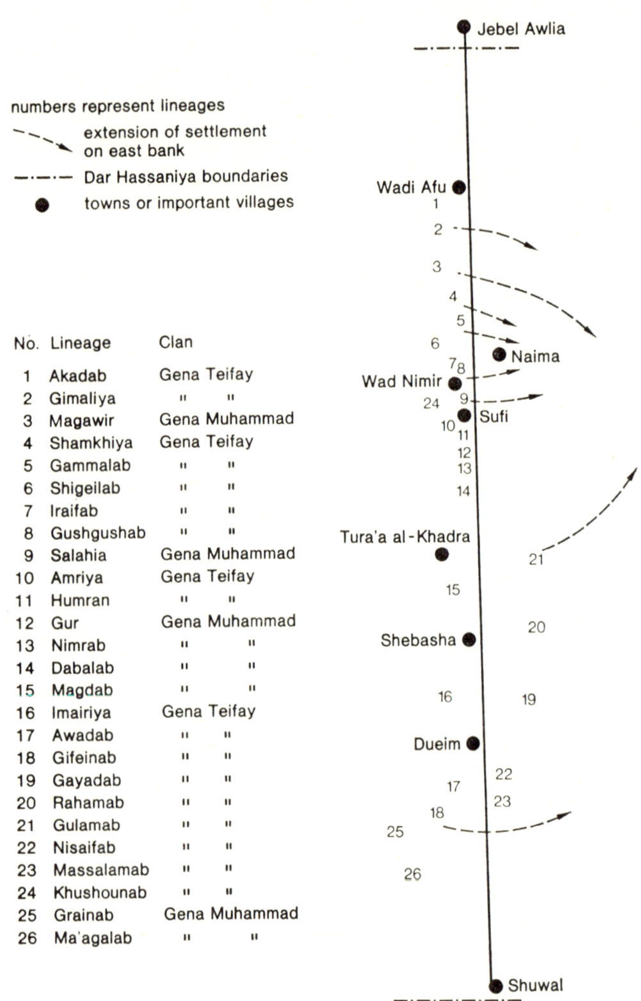

No.	Lineage	Clan
1	Akadab	Gena Teifay
2	Gimaliya	" "
3	Magawir	Gena Muhammad
4	Shamkhiya	Gena Teifay
5	Gammalab	" "
6	Shigeilab	" "
7	Iraifab	" "
8	Gushgushab	" "
9	Salahia	Gena Muhammad
10	Amriya	Gena Teifay
11	Humran	" "
12	Gur	Gena Muhammad
13	Nimrab	" "
14	Dabalab	" "
15	Magdab	" "
16	Imairiya	Gena Teifay
17	Awadab	" "
18	Gifeinab	" "
19	Gayadab	" "
20	Rahamab	" "
21	Gulamab	" "
22	Nisaifab	" "
23	Massalamab	" "
24	Khushounab	" "
25	Grainab	Gena Muhammad
26	Ma'agalab	" "

Fig. 1. Distribution of Hassaniya lineages

The distribution is such that the Kawahla tribes, and particularly the Hassaniya, dominate the riverland. This has had a vital bearing on the dominance of the Hassaniya and other Kawahla tribes in the White Nile throughout its political history, a matter which is discussed later. The politics of the White Nile may be seen to be largely the politics of the Kawahla. The intra-tribal distribution of the Kawahla and specifically the Hassaniya is represented by Figure 1. Each of the tribes is divided into a number of *furua* (literally, 'branches') which I shall call lineages.

Most of the inhabitants of the White Nile including the Kawahla are today sedentary cultivators who grow cotton and *dura*, a sorghum, in a number of governmental as well as private schemes. As tenants, in the terms of these schemes, they depend on *dura* as a staple food and derive income from the sale of the cash crop, cotton. Some Kawahla, however, and many other small tribes, lead a semi-nomadic or nomadic existence and depend mainly on the rearing of livestock for their subsistence.

Before 1937, when the Jebel Awliya Dam was built, all the Kawahla tribes were largely semi-nomadic practising both animal husbandry and subsistence cultivation. They used to grow *dura* as a staple food in both rain and river land. But the dam submerged most of the river land and consequently the government instituted a number of agricultural subsistence schemes which were administered later by the White Nile Schemes Board (WNSB) which had parallel social, agricultural and economic aims to the already existing Gezira Scheme. These schemes have had an enormous effect in changing the semi-nomadic life of the White Nile inhabitants to one of sedentary agriculture. The change in economy led to significant changes in the social and political organization of local people. The aim of this study is to investigate the social, economic and political repercussions of this change upon the White Nile Arabs, particularly among the Kawahla tribes and specifically the Hassaniya.

THE PRE-DAM ECOLOGICAL FRAMEWORK AND TRADITIONAL ECONOMIC ORGANIZATION

In this section I discuss the ecological setting and the different aspects of economic organization as they existed among the White Nile Arabs in the pre-dam period. The information was gathered from members of the Amriya lineage with whom I lived during the period of fieldwork. Its pattern of organization, however, was typical of all the other lineages, or *furua*, among the Hassaniya. By concentrating on one lineage the course of action that its members used to gain a living will be made clear together with the ecological and economic factors which had a crucial bearing upon that course of action.

ECOLOGY

The Northern White Nile area, co-terminous with Dar Hassaniya, lies within the geographical and climatic boundaries of the semi-arid zone. This is characterized by an essentially fluctuating pattern of rainfall with an annual average of 250–500 mm.[3] Rainfall is usually confined to the period between June and September. It is not so much the variability in intensity of annual rainfall which has a critical bearing upon the modes of living of the people as the variability in incidence and distribution within a specific year. For although there were occasional years without rain, the annual rainfall would remain roughly stable for some time. This may be illustrated by the annual rainfall for the years 1929–35, which are the years upon which I concentrate in the pre-dam period.

Year	Rainfall
1929/30	446.8 mm
1930/31	393.6 mm
1931/32	362.0 mm
1932/33	329.2 mm
1933/34	378.8 mm
1934/35	394.0 mm

These figures were taken at Dueim which was the district headquarters and the only place with a rain gauge in Dar Hassaniya at the time.[4] They may not, therefore, be representative of the whole area.

Rain is crucial for grazing and for cultivation. Rain allows the growth of various perennial grasses and herbs, the common form of natural vegetation in the region, upon which animals depend for grazing. Other forms of vegetation are thorny bushes and trees of the acacia type. The rains also fill the innumerable watercourses (*khairan*) and pools (*birak*) for brief periods during the

---

[3] See The Philosophical Society of Sudan, 1961, p. 37.
[4] I did not collect statistics on rainfall during my fieldwork.

rainy season. These are necessary to water animals and people, and some take a relatively long time to drain. In the past, when animal herding was a basic enterprise, both people and animals would be separated from their permanent dwellings near the river and would have to depend on these sources of water. Since the construction of the dam and the institution of agricultural schemes, the government has built modern wells throughout the region.

The inhabitants of the White Nile used to depend exclusively on rain for the irrigation of their rainland cultivation, known as *terus* (sing. *teras*) and *goz* or *adar* (sand dunes) (see below, p. 15). Since 1937 many artificial irrigation schemes have been implemented and today a great deal of the *terus* no longer depends on rain water. The introduction of artificial irrigation has greatly eliminated the element of uncertainty in agricultural production and has had wide socio-economic repercussions.

The variability and distribution of rainfall within any one specific year is more vital to cultivation than to grazing. The rainfall most favourable to cultivation occurs in two instalments: the first, a really heavy rain after the *rushash* (early showers) in the early part of the *kharif* (rainy season), during which the seeds are sown; the second, after the cultivator has taken advantage of a dry period to finish the task of clearing his land from weeds and grasses, to bring the growing plants on to bearing seeds. An administrative report on rain in the White Nile area says

Either it has not rained enough and the grain will not mature before it ripens, or else it has rained too much and cannot *hish* (be harvested). The latter is a misfortune which always accompanies good rains and makes the first clearing *murr* (hard work), so that some will give up in despair and explain moodily to the enquirer, 'we can't cope with it'.

The close interconnection between the variables of rainfall and agricultural production will be discussed further (see below, p. 21).

The year has four seasons: (a) *kharif*, or the rainy season, a warm, wet season falling between June or July and September; (b) *darat*, or post-rain, a warm, dry period occurring between the end of the rainy season in September and the beginning of winter in early December; (c) *shita*, or winter, a cool, dry season extending roughly from December to February; and (d) *saif*, or summer, a very hot, dry period between March and June.

PHYSICAL RESOURCES

The White Nile, the dominant feature of the region, flows from south to north dividing Dar Hassaniya into the two administrative segments of Hassaniya East and Hassaniya West. The area around the White Nile is a wide flat basin with a specially gradual slope on its west bank where, in the past, the river as it receded used to uncover large areas of clay soil which were utilized for cultivation. The slope is much steeper on the east bank except in certain places. Accordingly, nearly all cultivatable riverland was on the west bank. All this riverland, however, was submerged by the Jebel Awliya Dam in 1937.

Before the building of the dam, the river used to rise about early July and to recede gradually by the end of September or early October until it reached its original minimum level by December. After the building of the dam, the flooding of the river became technically controlled and changed considerably. Today, it rises early in July as before, but it falls at the end of April when the dam reservoir is opened. Before the building of the dam, the river flood was not so reliable. Although it might remain fairly stable for some years, there was always the threat of an extremely low flood which would be insufficient to produce much of a crop.

The area uncovered by the receding river on the west bank was dependent upon the flood level. Local people divided the riverland into four categories according to their relative exposure to river flood. This local classification, together with the approximate heights of the categories of land, is presented in Table 1.

Next to the riverland there is usually a strip of hard land ill-suited for cultivation and known as *shorab* (lit. 'watering passages', see Fig. 2). These are paths used by animals approaching the river to drink. Traditionally, they were areas where permanent settlements were established. These settlement areas were submerged by the dam.

Beyond the *shorab* lies the rainland known as *terus*. This is generally fertile clay soil known as *tin* (mud, clay). Today the greater part of this has become the sites of irrigation schemes. For ecological and geographical reasons, riverland lay mostly on the west bank while most of the rainland was on the east side of the

Table 1. Classes and height of river land

Name	Description	Approx. metres above sea-level
Bugur	The highest which is seldom reached by the river but produces crops when it is.	375.70–376.50
Feteib	The second highest some part of which is generally watered.	374.20–375.70
Kabab	Always watered and the most valuable for this reason. Sufra grown on it in most years if it is not fallowed.	373.20–374.20
Fasda	The lowest level which is submerged too long to grow grain. Certain vegetables are grown on it.	Below 373.20

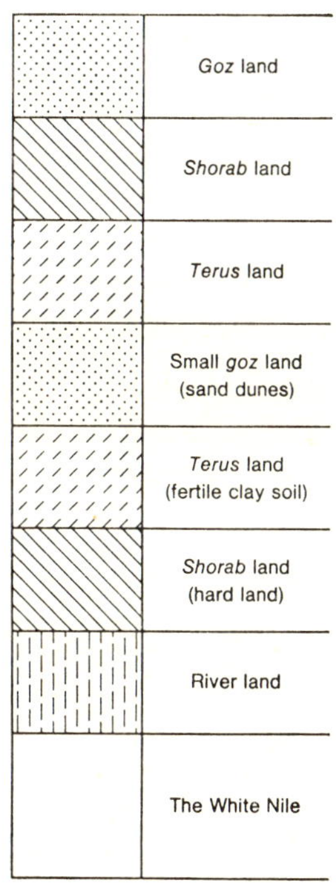

Fig. 2. Ecological and topographical belts in the White Nile

river and was inhabited by the non-Hassaniya Kawahla. In the north White Nile, the *goz* (sand dunes) of Central Kordogan come close to the river bank like waves spreading onto the beaches so that very little of the clay rainland is left. On the east side of the river, however, the bank extends into the relatively fertile and rich Gezira clay soil much of which has been used for cultivation, watered in the past by rain and today by irrigation schemes.

Because the riverland and rainland lie for the most part on different sides of the river, many people on both sides of the river divided their economic activities equally between the two types of land. This had the effect of transcending the barrier imposed by the river and made feasible the social and cultural homogeneity of Dar Hassaniya.

The river bed was originally about 1 to $1\frac{1}{2}$ miles wide. During the summer, particularly, it became so narrow that people could speak to each other across it. Since then the east bank has been known as *al-hoy*, an Arabic word for addressing or calling someone relatively far away but within earshot. Today, the river extends for five miles or more and symbolizes the separation of the two banks which has developed since the establishment of the Jebel Awaliya Dam. Since then the whole of the riverland has disappeared. Some of those who lost their riverland have been given holdings on the east bank where they have settled permanently and become spatially separated from their relatives on the west bank. The District Commissioner at Dueim, the headquarters of Dar Hassaniya, commented in 1940 on the implications of the construction of the dam:

the tribal connections between the people on the east and west banks will gradually diminish until they will finally disappear. . . . I have no doubt that the formidable barrier of the high Nile under final Dam conditions must result in the east and west banks becoming separate units of administration. Moreover this barrier will be such that one of these units cannot remain economically dependent on the other (Dueim, district files DD/SCR/91.a.1. 1 May 1940).

The forecast has been borne out. The reference to Hassaniya East and West which was formerly no more than a matter of administrative convenience has since then acquired social, economic and political significance.

Beyond the clay, rainland areas is a strip of hard land similar to the *shorab* and ill-suited to cultivation. It is, however, important grazing ground especially for sheep and goats. Short and minor perennial grasses and weeds of a type easily grazed and browsed by smaller animals are grown here. In the past this was the main area for the *shogara* of sheep and goats, that is, the westerly movement of animals which took place in the rainy season.

Finally, there is the wide and westerly-spreading area of *goz*, or sand dunes, which may also be called *adar*. These *goz* in the White Nile are of generally firm sand, not shifting like the ones found in the western interior. They were and still are used as areas for grazing as well as for limited rain cultivation. Major perennial grasses and thorny bush and trees grow in the *goz* which are well suited for cattle and camel herding. Innumerable water-courses (*khairan*) and pools (*birak*) which are usually filled with water during the rainy season are found on them and used for watering both animals and human beings.

OTHER NATURAL FACTORS AFFECTING AGRICULTURE

There were other crucial variables in economic production in the pre-dam period besides rainfall and riverflood. The most important of these were the endemic animal pests and plant diseases. These were sometimes serious enough to jeopardize the economy of the White Nile even without the threat of deficient rains or river flood.

The local inhabitants of the White Nile used to grow *dura* (sorghum) of a certain type called *sufra* on the riverland while they grew *fetereit* (another sort of *dura*) on the clay rainlands. In the case of *sufra* there were two serious pests. First, there was *himoyir*, a beetle which used to attack and eat the young shoots in their early stages of growth; secondly, there was a stem-borer, a white grub which bored into the roots and attacked the plant later on. *Fetereit*, on the other hand, was preyed on by birds and locusts both of which sometimes did widespread damage. It was also affected by *suweid*, a sort of blight which was not uncommon but did not cause serious loss.

There still exist some endemic as well as epidemic animal diseases. Among the epidemics is *garab* (mange) for camels and goats. Another disease afflicting camels is called *guffar* (trypanosomiasis). Sheep suffered from occasional outbreaks of smallpox.

With the development of veterinary services, these animal

diseases have been largely conquered. Traditional pre-dam native treatment was in two forms: namely, the use of local medicines of various types which were tested by experience; and also, and most significantly, spiritual treatment by religious shaikhs in the form of *mihaya* (draughts of water containing ink in which Quranic or other forms of religious blessings have been written). This religious treatment was rather less common with the small animals such as sheep and goats. *Higbat* (sing. *hugab*, meaning charms) were also used for camels both for protection from and treatment of diseases.

In addition to these epidemic diseases, there were and still are other threats to animal health. Certain wild grasses or weeds known as *simmit* or *adarib*, especially, grow near the river and are deleterious to animals. They cause digestive trouble which may result in serious illness or death.

The White Nile region is characterized by high temperatures and high rates of evaporation especially in the summer. The humidity around the river threatens the health of stock. In the mornings, the grass and herbs are covered with dew which has two effects: it makes the grass damp so that animals grazing suffer from digestive troubles, and also the dew may camouflage the weeds, *simmit* and *adarib*. When the grass is not damp it is relatively easy to keep the stock off the areas where these weeds are spotted.

Dew has limited the capacity for herding by lessening the period in which grazing can take place. People generally start herding their animals only towards midday to avoid the dew. Most of these bad grasses, however, are far less common in the interior west of the river. But dwellers near the White Nile have always been inhibited in their movement of livestock owing to their practice of combining pastoralism with cultivation. This limitation on movement has made their animals relatively more susceptible to disease than those belonging to nomadic pastoralists to the west, such as the Kababish. This susceptibility has become more serious with the establishment of the Jebel Awliya Dam and the settling of people in permanent village communities close to the river. The consequent limitation on both quality and quantity of grazing opportunities affects not only the animals' health, but also their breeding capacity. Animals on the relatively rich grazing areas to the west breed twice a year, while those kept on river-grazing breed only once a year.

Exposure of their animals to disease has always meant that the White Nile Arabs have had to expend more care and labour upon grazing and breeding livestock than do the neighbouring tribes to the west. These problems of grazing and breeding were intensified by sanitary conditions in the post-dam period and have caused, among other effects, some of the owners of large herds to become completely nomadic. Agricultural production was traditionally of two types: river cultivation and rain cultivation. River cultivation was carried out all along the river belt, although mostly on the western bank. Rain cultivation was of two types: *terus* and *goz*; but the Kawahla were mainly *terus* and not *goz* cultivators. The potential of these types of cultivation will now be examined.

RIVER CULTIVATION

The White Nile used to rise by June or July each year covering a more or less wide strip of land depending on the level of its annual flood. By the end of September or the beginning of October, it would start to recede leaving behind land which was available for cultivation. The Kawahla Arabs used to grow a special sort of *dura* called *sufra* in these naturally flooded plains. Cultivation started with sowing as soon as the highest levels of riverland were exposed, and continued until November or December when the river reached its final limit of retreat. Seeds were sown using a *turiya* (a digging tool) to make small holes into which four or five seeds were dropped which were then covered by *tin* (mud). As soon as the plant rose above the ground it was liable to attack by the *himayir* beetle and the husbandman might have to re-sow the crop in the hope that it would not be attacked again. This pest attacked in early September and October. The stem-borer usually appeared later, towards December.

If the owners of relatively high land had sown their seeds early, and succeeded in escaping the *himayir* infestation, by the time the stem-borer attacked in winter their crops would be sufficiently mature not to be seriously affected. Thus those who owned higher plots, while more vulnerable to any variability in the river flood, were less affected by pests. Vulnerability to external natural factors was thus equally shared by most people as was economic security. This promoted what economists call 'horizontal integration', that is integration between those who conduct similar economic activities and who combine to make their productive machinery, among other things, more efficient or economically viable. The harvest of the *sufra* crop usually took place in January or early February. The crop was then taken and stored in storage pits (known as *matamir*) at the permanent settlements.

River cultivation was a relatively easy enterprise physically, since no effort was required for irrigation and other agricultural activities such as land-clearing were less laborious than those involved in rain cultivation. Nevertheless, it was a very vulnerable enterprise because of the pests and the river flood. Although the river flood level might be fairly stable for some years (see Table 2)

Table 2. Annual river flood levels at Dueim

Year	River flood level (in feet)
1929/30	376.01
1930/31	375.36
1931/32	375.56
1932/33	375.64
1933/34	375.75
1934/35	375.15

Source: Administrative Files at Dueim, reference: ND/66.K.4 – 20/7/34.

there was always the threat of a difficult year when the flood was too low to raise any significant crop. There are no long-term statistics or figures relating to variability in river flood to show this, but from informants' accounts of various incidents, this can be inferred. One of the sources of information was found in the way that natives had of recording dates by certain important events. Appendix 2 is reproduced from a larger compilation by Reid of many dates and events so designated among the White Nile Arabs. They show clearly the dependence of crop cultivation upon occasional failures in river flood and/or other natural factors.

RAIN CULTIVATION

Rain cultivation involved relatively more laborious work than river cultivation. It started with *sanad*, or levelling the *terus*, in about mid-summer. This levelling was done in a certain pattern for irrigation. All the edges around the *terus* were levelled, the lower part called *hugna* (literally 'reservoir') was levelled more than the other sides as this part was to hold the *terus* water. Water would flow down the field to the *hugna* where it was held for some time.

The *terus* was levelled by *nafir* (collective work) performed by close relatives and neighbours. The recruitment of the group among whom this free labour was exchanged will be discussed later. Levelling the *terus* was laborious so it was a group and not an individual activity. It was achieved with a wooden tool called *wasuq* which needed three men to work it: one to push the vertical pole holding the leveller firmly to the ground while the other two men pulled the ropes tied to the leveller. In return for this work, a small feast was given and *marisa* (local beer) was served. But this immediate, tangible return was not by any means so substantial as to separate those who could afford to offer it from those who could not. The important aspect of the *nafir* was the 'deferred payment' represented by the mutual help given by kinsmen to each other in their respective *nafir*.

Nafir were mainly summoned during the levelling of *terus*, for it was only during that time that people were relatively idle and relaxing in their permanent settlements. By the end of summer and the advent of the rainy season, everyone would be heavily engaged in their own activities, both cultivation and animal rearing. The limit to the land cultivated was set by the degree to which a man was capable of performing the necessary activities with the aid either of a large family or of slaves.

The second step in rain cultivation occurred at the beginning of the rainy season. This was called *ziraa*, or the sowing of the seeds, and would start with the heavy rains marking the end of the *rushash* (early showers). The third step was the *nash*, the clearing of grass and weeds. It started after the crop rose above the ground. Clearing grass was again very laborious and might continue throughout the growth period if there was especially heavy rain. Too much rain would enable the weeds to grow very quickly, and an exceptionally wet season might be as disastrous as having no rains at all for people would find it extremely difficult to cope with weeding. Rain cultivation was vulnerable to variabilities in rain frequency as well as intensity. This made production extremely unpredictable, a fact which in turn promoted a high degree of economic interdependence and co-operation between people in a nexus of elaborate risk-reducing devices. Main

C

cultivation finally ended with the harvest of the crop in about October. The crop was then taken and stored in the *matamir*.

LIVESTOCK REARING

The Hassaniya and other Kawahla Arabs were mainly cattle, sheep and goat herders. The listing of animals for Dar Hassaniya showed the following figures in 1934:

Camels	13,282
Cattle	47,656
Sheep	301,076
Goats	152,161

The camels were owned mainly by non-Kawahla, although a few Kawahla sections owned some camels. The Hassaniya were not great camel enthusiasts and regarded them merely as beasts of burden. The slight emphasis on camel-rearing, however, should be seen as a result of ecological and geographical factors. The White Nile, especially the belt east and west of the river, was ill-suited to regular camel-herding. Unless a man was ready to move with his animals to the extent of good grazing grounds, camel-rearing would not be easy. The Hassaniya and other Kawahla were not prepared to undertake an enterprise of this sort.

Unlike the Kababish and the Baggara, for instance, the seasonal movements of the Hassaniya were of an intensive type. They moved within a limited range of the river and as far as possible within reasonable distance of their river and rain cultivation. Their urge to cultivate constrained the degree of mobility with the animals while their urge to move as far as they actually did had already set a limit to what might be said to be a roughly optimal agricultural production.

Camels, together with donkeys, were used mainly for transport. Cattle, sheep and goats were used both for subsistence and the acquisition of cash. All types of stock provided milk which formed the staple food in addition to grain. Goats were easy to keep, bred easily and derived sustenance where no other animals could. The Hassaniya were as famous for the number of their goats as they were for the fertility of their women. It was sung of them *'ahl allanz al-zarga, wa awlad al-bit al-mankhura'*, that is, 'owners of the black goat, and children of the penetrated girl'.

Sheep earned more cash than other animals because mutton was generally in much greater demand than other meat in the Sudan.

The Hassaniya used to sell their animals to get cash to buy market goods such as sugar, tea, salt, perfumes, clothes and occasionally furniture, as well as for settling their tax accounts with the government.

The ownership of livestock was highly valued, and the more animals one had the more social and political influence could be assumed. Those who owned a large stock of animals were known as *ummar gabila*, literally, 'wealthy men of their tribes'. The more animals a man owned, the more secure his economic position and hence, the more he would be expected to provide security for others. The position of the ummar is discussed in detail in Chapter 3. In a basically precarious environment such as that of the Hassaniya and other Kawahla before the construction of the dam, the ummar, whose role comprised the provision of security, attained considerable influence over those who were pressured by the vicissitudes of the environment and sought security.

LIVESTOCK HERDING AND CYCLICAL MIGRATION
(see Fig. 3)

As soon as the rainy season started with the first early showers (*rushash*), the White Nile inhabitants recognized the beginning of a new cycle for them and for their animals. From their permanent dwelling centres (*dumur*) in which they had been spending the summer, apart from levelling the *terus*, they began moving west-ward toward traditional grazing centres known as *shogara* or *azeib*. These last two terms denote the places of settlement as well as the seasonal movement towards them.

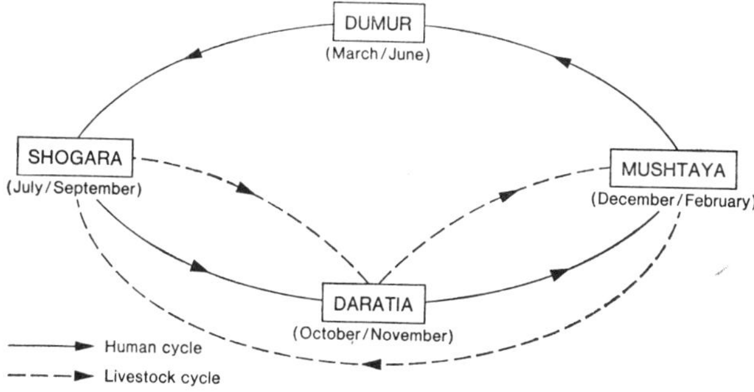

Fig. 3. Annual livestock and transhumance cycles

As I have mentioned, each lineage had its own grazing grounds which generally lay beyond the *dumur* and cultivation centres. All lineages had a roughly identical pattern of movement and settlement. The following account applies to the Amriya lineage with whom I resided during the course of my fieldwork. All the evidence, however, suggests that the Amriya pattern was typical of movements and organizational arrangements among other Kawahla lineages.

As I have mentioned, there was great variability in the grazing potentialities of *shogara* centres. The *shorab* had special short perennial grasses and weeds (*haskanit*) which were suited only to the grazing of sheep and goats whereas the *goz* were marked by tall perennial grasses, short bushes and trees that were well suited to grazing cattle. To exploit these resources more effectively, the Amriya kept separate the grazing of cattle and sheep. For convenience I will refer to both sheep and goats together as 'sheep'. Sheep grazed on the *shorab* while cattle grazed in the *goz*. This would cause enormous difficulties to any Amriya owning both cattle and sheep for it would mean dividing labour between the different grazing areas. By the time for grazing, the labour force of every family would already have been divided between rain cultivation and animal husbandry. This would make another division of the family's labour impractical for, unless one had a particularly large family or had other means of labour, such as slaves, each family would be over-extended in terms of labour. Moreover, since the majority of families owned between one and ten animals of any type of stock, it was uneconomic to divide them between two separate grazing camps.

For these reasons most of the Amriya tended to specialize in either sheep or cattle. Roughly speaking, wealthy people could be found in either or both of the two economic spheres, while relatively poor people with fewer animals would tend to specialize in sheep-rearing. Although the separation of cattle and sheep *shogara* was dictated by ecological conditions, the degree of specialization in animal rearing depended upon the number of animals owned. Fewer animals and the greater the pressure to specialize meant it was more likely to be in sheep. This did not mean, however, that sheep *shogara* was only, or even mainly, a poor man's business, nor that only people with fewer animals would specialize in either of the two spheres of economic enterprise. There were some wealthy people with many animals who still specialized in one of the two spheres of animal husbandry.

Sheep were grazed close to the *dumur* and cultivation centres and thus offered a greater opportunity for close co-ordination between livestock-rearing and agricultural production. Cattle grazing extended over a relatively wide area beginning virtually where sheep grazing ended. It was more probable therefore that people with many cattle, which needed to move greater distances and to richer grazing, would also have some slaves or several dependents and be able to maintain less continuous co-ordination between livestock rearing and cultivation.

Among the Amriya lineage sheep *shogara* was carried on in such places as Dahar al-tur and Abu Firaiwa which was not far from the rain cultivation which was combined with animal rearing during the rainy season. These places lie not more than five miles apart. Cattle grazing, on the other hand, was carried out around and to the west of Shegaig, in an area generally known as um-Dibaiba. The western limits of this area were near the Kababish boundaries where grazing conditions were more favourable to larger animals, such as cattle and camels.

DIVISION OF LABOUR IN THE EXTENDED FAMILY

The requirements of the rainy season, where labour was needed for both animal herding and agricultural production, and where diversification of economic activities was necessary, dictated the emergence of groupings and productive units wider than a single man or his elementary family. The smallest unit of economic production comprised the extended family consisting of, at least, a man and his adult sons, either married or unmarried. This extended family would usually be divided in such a way that a man and his elder son or a slave worked at the *terus* grass clearing and in daily supervision while the rest of the family, the wife or wives and their young sons, who were usually unmarried, took charge of the grazing.

This would make it possible for the man and his elder son to pay occasional visits to their families in the *shogara*. But the duration of such visits was limited by the persistent threat to cultivation from weeds and from pests such as locusts and birds. The destruction was less serious if some effort was made in time to meet it, by either physical or ritual means. The physical effort consisted in continual weeding or resowing the seeds if the plant died, by driving birds off or by tying the grain bundles. On the ritual side recourse was had to magical stones or *warga* (amulets) from the appropriate religious shaikhs whose blessings and mediation with God was believed to keep pests away.

In summary, the need for continual labour made it extremely difficult for the cultivator at the *terus* to be also leading the live-stock herding. This consequent division of labour presupposed a large source of labour, the extended family. In order, however, for this extended family to exploit the resources of cultivation and grazing most effectively, it was advantageous for it to belong to wider groupings of different orders with different functions.

HERDING PARTNERSHIPS AND THE DIKKA SETTLEMENT

There were two types of *shogara*: cattle and sheep. Extended families of various sizes turned westwards and settled in the areas appropriate to each sort of grazing. The pattern in which these families came together and settled differed greatly, however, from one type of *shogara* to another.

In the sheep *shogara*, the form of sheep-herding dictated a relatively amorphous pattern of settlement. The young offspring of sheep and goats naturally mixed together, hence the Hassaniya said 'al-ghanam yashil gana ukhwatu', that is, literally, 'sheep and goats would steal the young offspring of each other'. Consequently, not more than one or two *murah*, or herding units, would share one *zariba*, or fenced enclosure. Each herding unit would generally camp at a distance of about 100 yards from each other. Thus the larger the *murah* the more need to settle independently and the greater the distance needed to be separate from others. In the final analysis, however, everyone had to settle in a relatively limited area and the degree of separateness was often minimal.

In the cattle *shogara*, on the other hand, where no problems of this sort arose, all the families of the lineage would come together in two types of organization which I call herding partnerships and camping partnerships (see Fig. 4). I will discuss in Chapter 2 the different lineages within which these partnerships, particularly the herding one, were formed since the camping partnership comprised all herding partnerships and, thus, all members of the lineage leading the cattle *shogara*. The herding partnership consisted roughly of members of either the lineage section, called *khashm-bait*, or members of different lineage sections. The Amriya lineage consisted of about eight *khashm-baits*. Four of these co-resided in the west bank, three in the east bank, while the other led a purely nomadic existence far west of the Amriya homes.

I will discuss later the implications of this distribution. It should, however, be noted here that although the overwhelming majority did so, not all the lineage sections co-resided and led the same *shogara*; and lineage members were divided already between sheep and cattle *shogara* as well as cultivation, so that some herding

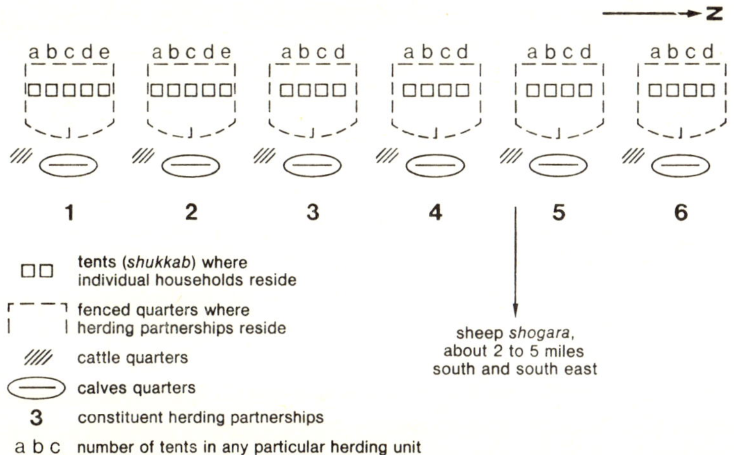

Fig. 4. Diagram of typical camping cluster: *Dikka*

partnerships consisted of members of different *khashm-baits*. However, these were usually connected by close affinal ties. The spatial distribution of the lineage and, importantly, its economic implications led members to emphasize their lineage more than their section, or *khashm-bait*, membership. This promoted lineage unity and economic interdependence and encouraged the lineage to act as a corporate group.

The herding partnership formed one *murah*, or herding unit. Its animals were all kept at one *zariba*, or fenced enclosure. The calves were kept inside the *zariba* while the rest were left outside near the fence. All these animals, belonging to four or five families, were grazed and watered together day and night. Members of the herding unit also shared one common *zariba* surrounding their dwelling tents and were consequently residentially close.

Because the demand for labour was constant, these families would tend to pool their labour resources so that a pattern emerged. Herding was generally carried out in three shifts: *dahawa* (morning session, roughly between 11 am and 2 pm), *duhriya* (afternoon session, 3–4 pm until 6–7 pm), and *sarba* (night session, any time in the early night until dawn). *Sarba* was an especially difficult job and carried on only by older people of whom there might be only one or two left in the whole herding unit. The first two shifts were taken by young boys either in alternating shifts or all together. Young boys, irrespective of which families they belonged to, also milked the cows for the unit. Young girls would bring water to the whole compound. While the different families constituting the compound cooked separately, food and especially milk was exchanged freely between all families. The herding partnership thus served the interests of all its constituent members belonging to the various extended families. This free exchange of food and milk, however, was carried on throughout the camping partnership.

The camping partnership provided the various herding partnerships with the residential integration needed for the protection of their common wealth. This was essential not only during the pre-Condominium era, when there was a great deal of raiding, for security was not absolute even under the Condominium government. There were no more organized attacks or wars, but there were still continual raids carried out mainly by individuals but also by small gangs. The thieves were from the Kawahla as well as non-Kawahla tribes. This report (1934) in one of the governmental files at Dueim, the District Headquarters, states:

Camel theft is said to be on the increase. . . . The thieves usually work in twos and threes, often as part of an organised gang, and hang around awaiting their opportunity to snap up and drive off any stray beasts.

Thus the Lahawin tribe which owned a particularly large number of camels was a natural target and the file reported that 'in the course of their annual migrations the Lahawin suffer heavily from theft. . . .

I have shown that the various families which made up the

population in cattle *shogara* were closely connected by an organizational pattern based on a division of labour and their mutual interests which were related to economic enterprise as well as common security. *Shogara* ended by the end of the rainy season. Both the herding and camping partnerships separated and redistributed themselves in various directions. Each family moved and settled at its rain farms. The animals, however, did not move from the *shogara* grazing grounds for some time because the rain crop would not yet be harvested and the animals might spoil the crops. The animals were brought for *talig*, the free eating of the uncut straw, only after the grain was harvested. Again, the herding partnership was so organized that some of its young men would stay with the joint *murah*, while the rest would join their families in the *terus*. Families took only a few animals with them for the domestic supply of milk.

DARATIYA

The movement and settlement of animals in the *terus* after harvest was called *daratiya*, stemming from *darat* – a word denoting the spell between *kharif* and winter. The animals spent this season grazing the uncut straw of the *dura* cultivation. During this time all the members of a family who had been separated by the *shogara* would come together for a brief period. But by then the river would have started to recede so the heads of families would begin to pay visits to their riverland and to sow the new crops.

The settlements of families in the *daratiya* centres were generally clusters consisting usually of members of the same lineage section but containing also many members of other lineage sections. People settled on their own *terus*, irrespective of where it was situated. This promoted lineage corporateness emphasizing and strengthening the economic relations and common interests between *khashm-baits*. Figure 9 shows a typical pattern of *daratiya* settlements based on *terus* ownership which emphasized inter-*kashm-bait* relations.

MUSHTAIA

The *daratiya* usually ended by mid-winter when the *sufra* harvest was due and families moved to the river plantations. Animals would again be left in the care of young boys until the crop was harvested. A family which had no one to herd its animals would leave them with boys of other families.

In movements from *shogara* to *daratiya* and from *daratiya* to river plantation, the brief separation of animals and families was due to two factors: firstly, families were needed for the forthcoming labour of harvest and would live for some time on the semi-mature crop by making *balila*, by boiling grain seeds, and secondly, the animals might spoil the crops. This temporary separation of animals and families offered opportunities for wider labour co-operation, because not all families would have enough members to carry on these separate spheres of economic activity. In these conditions it was in the economic interest of all families to depend on one another.

The movement and settlement of animals in the river land was called *mushtaia* (from *shita*, 'winter'). The river crop was not left uncut like the rain crop, but the straw was cut with the crop and gathered in big bundles and tied together. Some of it was given to the animals in the *mushtaia* and the rest was stored for the dry season.

Usually, if the rain cultivation was successful, and the animals had still enough fodder to be grazed in their *daratiya* centres, they would be left there to graze for most of or all the winter. Only certain categories of animals, the milch cows, the young, and the weak were taken to the river.

The *mushtaia* ended by the end of winter and people moved to settle in their permanent summer locations which were called *dumur*. If the river crop failed people would have to search for pastures throughout the summer. Usually their destination would be the former *shogara* grazing centres but they could go further if they had hope of grazing land and water for, once they were separated from the river, water supplies would again become a major problem. People of the east bank usually came in times of drought with their animals to the west bank because it had a greater capacity for grazing. Thus, it was not uncommon for the Amriya to have related *khashm bait* living on the east bank with them in addition to their annual coming together for the river cultivation of *sufra* which might continue for four months or more. This meant that *khashm-baits* living on different sides of the river might come together for a considerable part of the year. They remained separated mainly by their summer dwellings.

DUMUR

Dumur meant both the dwelling places and the movements to these settlements. People spent all the summer in these dwellings where they enjoyed leisure apart from the job of levelling *terus*. Trade flourished in the small local markets as families took some of their crops or animals to sell for cash. The Kawahla were generally unwilling to sell their animals unless extremely pressed for money. They depended usually on selling part of their crops to get market goods. However, a man could always calculate roughly the amount he needed for the next year and take the surplus to market. If later he needed cash he would have to sell part of his stored grain and depend more on milk for his subsistence. If he ran short of milk he could borrow a *maniha*, that is, a sheep, goat or cow borrowed temporarily from its owner (*maniha* means giving) until he harvested next year's crop when it would be returned to its owner. Further discussion of reciprocal exchange is to be found in Chapter 2.

The *dumur* consisted of a number of *guttiyas* (huts) made from straw and wood. A certain type of hut called *durdur* occurred, the lower part of which was made from mud. Huts were distributed in no specific order in any settlement. Residents of any one belonged to different sections of the lineage, although one or two sections tended to be better represented than the rest (see Chapter 2 for a discussion of residence).

The *dumur* phase ended with the summer and the start of the rainy season. Early showers would induce families to send their animals with young boys in search of fresh pastures scattered here and there. It was only when the *kharif* proper started that families would join the boys. Then the *shogara* was said to have begun, thus marking a new cyclical movement of animals and families.

I have said that the Hassaniya and other Kawahla moved intensively and not extensively. Like all nomadic Arabs their perpetual flux could be expressed by the proverb: *al-rahil izzal-Arab*, literally 'migration, or movement, is the pride of the Arabs'. As a Hassani's social position was related above all to the number of livestock he had, so was his need to move. A large herd would exhaust the potential of grazing centres more quickly than a small herd so that a big owner would have to move more often. A man's social position was gauged by those observing the coming and going of his animals.

This was not just a display of power but an efficient way of exploiting resources as far as animal health and breeding capacity were concerned. Once animals had been in a place for some time their health would deteriorate. Gradually the grass, water and air would be polluted with the animals' fæces, urine and fodder waste. This would directly affect the health of the herds and also create conditions which would permit the development and spread of animal disease. Such conditions were also believed to affect the breeding capability of the animals.

However, the potentialities for movement were not infinite. I have said that the desire of the tribesman to cultivate limited the movement of animals, for to go beyond that limit would jeopardize his cultivation. By going further west he might not be within convenient reach of his crops for checking weed growth, or the attacks of pests and birds, or for harvesting. The 'centrifugal' forces associated with animal pastoralism taking people away from their residential quarters near the river might have resulted in the seasonal dispersal of the various groups together with the possible lessening of exchange of labour and common interests which bound the groups together. These were counteracted, however, by the 'centripetal' forces arising from the pressures to keep close to the river and cultivation.

STRATEGIES OF LAND AND LIVESTOCK MANAGEMENT

Interest in both land and animals as a source of living was calculated as a more secure scheme than relying on only cultivation or husbandry in the uncertain environment. Riverland cultivation was not certain because of the variability of the river flood. In addition there was also the problem of pests. Rain cultivation was not certain either: rains were variable in intensity and occurrence. Clearing grass was a persistent problem. Animal husbandry, on the other hand, had its own problems – drought and animal disease.

The strategy of combining cultivation and livestock-rearing was not only economically but also politically and militarily significant. An environment characterized by raids and robbery and, before the Condominium, wars, led the Kawahla to appreciate the strategical importance and value of land. In raids or wars one might lose one's whole stock of animals overnight. This encouraged the Kawahla to stress the relative invulnerability of land. Hence they used to say *'jawad al-adu yashig alwata'*, that is, 'the enemy's horse could only move over the land'. The Hassaniya, who were originally driven out of their former habitat in the Gilif because they lost all or most of their livestock in the Abdallab raid (which took place sometime between 1589 and 1611), were particularly aware of the necessity of holding and maintaining their political viability.

In conclusion, the ecology of the Kawahla as well as the economic and political realities induced them to adopt both modes of subsistence. In such an environment it was impossible to alter the relationship between agriculture and livestock-rearing without losing security. There was always an inverse correlation between the magnitude of the relative divergence of the two modes of livelihood and the degree of security that one could achieve.

Table 3. Annual economic activities and division of labour among the Hassaniya

	(Saif) Summer (*March–June*) (*hot/dry*)	*(Kharif) Rainy Season* (*July–September*) (*warm/wet*)	*(Darat) Post-rain* Season (*October–November*)	*(Shita) Winter* (*December–February*) (*cool/dry*)
Livestock rearing	RIVER GRAZING: All animals near river grazing *fassas* and *chobbaik*	'SHOGARA' GRAZING: All animals in *shogara* centres Sheep: At Dahar al-Tur, Abu-Firaiwa . . . etc Cattle: Eid Um-Gantur	(A) 'SHOGARA' GRAZING: Continuing until the harvest of the rain crop (B) 'DARATIYA' GRAZING: All animals at *daratiya* centres	MOST ANIMALS at *daratiya* centres A FEW ANIMALS taken near river
Agricultural production	LEVELLING AND PREPARATION OF 'TERUS' FOR CULTIVATION	SOWING AND CLEARANCE OF 'TERUS'	(A) 'TERUS' HARVEST by mid-*darat* (B) STORING grain at *dumur* (C) SOWING riverland by early *darat*	(A) HARVESTING river crop, sufra about January (B) Storing grain at *dumur*
Other	MAINTENANCE of *Matamir* (Storage pits) and houses		MARKETING: Selling part of rain crop	MARKETING: (A) Selling animals (known as *kura'a*) (B) Selling part of river crop if in need of cash

2

The Genealogical and Ideological Framework: Some aspects of Lineage Corporateness and Solidarity in the Pre-Dam Period

In this chapter I present the genealogical relationships between the various tribal and intra-tribal groupings as well as the ideological mode in which these relationships are given significance. I then consider some situations in which lineage solidarity and corporate viability were reflected or promoted and utilised in the pre-dam period. Some of these, for instance the exchange and division of labour, have been outlined already. Here I give detailed examples drawn from the memories of my informants to illustrate this pattern of exchange and to demonstrate the kinship relations upon which it is based. In the discussion of endogamy and co-residence I focus on the pre-dam period, but to avoid repetition later I occasionally generalize about some aspects which have continued to the present. Where possible I have made this explicit.

GENEALOGICAL RELATIONSHIPS

The Kawahla group in the White Nile consists of five *gabilas*, which I have so far called tribes. These are: the Hassaniya, the Hissinat, the Urwab, the Muhammadiya and the Kawahla (who are said to have retained the original *shajara*, or genealogical tree). This congeries of tribes has moved and settled in the White Nile at different times from abodes in different parts of the Sudan. The Hassaniya moved and settled from Jebel al-Jilif in the northern Sudan. The other Kawahla are generally reported to have moved to this area from a previous settlement with the Beja in the eastern Sudan.

All these tribes claim common descent from an apical ancestor called Kahil (from whom the Kawahla have since taken their name). Hence they all speak of themselves as one *gabila*, or tribe. Kahil is said to have begotten thirteen children, each of whom founded a tribe. These thirteen tribes of which the Kawahla in the White Nile are only one representative, are widespread throughout the northern Sudan. The genealogical tree (Fig. 5) shows the interrelations between the various Kawahla sub-divisions.

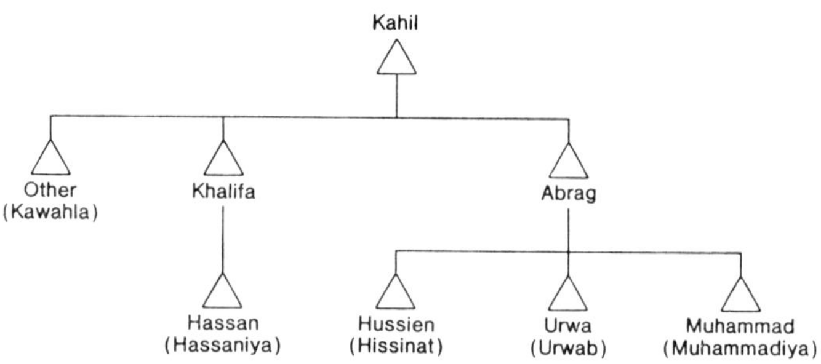

Fig. 5. Genealogical relationships between the various Kawahla tribes in the White Nile

While the genealogical tree usually presents the various founders of the Kawahla tribes as Kahil's sons, this does not necessarily mean that they were actually begotten by Kahil himself. They might have been his grandsons or great-grandsons. My native informants would sometimes admit that they did not know exactly whether the founders of these tribes were Kahil's own sons or grandsons of varying order. People would generally say to an inquirer that these tribes are '*awlad rajil wahid*' or 'sons of one man', but they mean 'descendants', and not necessarily actual sons. This point has been misunderstood by many historians and has caused much confusion about the Kawahla as well as other Sudanese tribes (see, for example, Muhammad, A. M., 1951, and MacMichael, H. A., 1912).

I shall now examine in some detail the genealogical connections between these Kawahla tribes or congeries as well as between their various sections. By the Kawahla tribes, I mean only those actually existing today in the White Nile. The Kawahla group in the White Nile, however, apart from those known or referred to as Kawahla (that is, those who have retained the original name of the group), are not themselves among the 13 tribes which have taken the names of the 13 sons of Kahil but are offshoots of some of these tribes. The Hassaniya, for example, are an offshoot of the Khalayfa and so they speak of themselves as *awlad Khalifa*. The Hissinat, Urwab and Muhammadiya are all offshoots of the Baragna, and they speak of themselves as *awlad Abrag*. Some Hassaniya claim that both they and the Hissinat are *awlad Khalifa*, while the Urwab and Muhammadiya are *awlad Abrag*. This is, no doubt, an attempt to invoke closer kinship relations with the Hissinat than with the other Kawahla tribes. But many Hassaniya agree with the other three Kawahla tribes, the Hissinat, the Urwab and the Muhammadiya, that they are opposed to the Hassaniya who are Khalayfa. We shall see the relevance of this opposition later in the discussion of tribal politics.

Now I shall examine inter-tribal genealogical relationships, giving detailed information on the Hassaniya; but I will also give some points of comparison with other Kawahla tribes, particularly the Hissinat.

Figure 6 shows the genealogical relationships between the various sections of the Hassaniya group. We can see that the Hassaniya *gabila* is divided into two main divisions, which are called Jena Muhammad and Jena Teifay, that is, the sons of Muhammad and the sons of Teifay. But the exact relationship between Muhammad and Teifay, from whom these divisions have taken their names, is not known. The Hassaniya say Muhammad and Teifay are sons of Hassan, the founder of the Hassaniya tribe from whom it has taken its name. They mean, however, that Muhammad and Teifay are the descendants of Hassan and not his actual sons. Each of these divisions is represented by a number of *furua*, literally, branches,[1] which I have called lineages. Thus Jena Muhammad has 17 branches, while Jena Teifay has nine branches. But while the Hassaniya agree on what branches comprise each division, many of the branches could not demonstrate how they are related to the founders of the divisions, Muhammad and Teifay. Thus we can call these divisions clans following Robin Fox's suggestion that their members may not be able to state their exact links to each other (see Fox 1967, p. 49).

These extra-*furua*, or extra-lineage, genealogical groupings have

---

[1] A lineage may also be referred to as *gabila* (tribe).

D

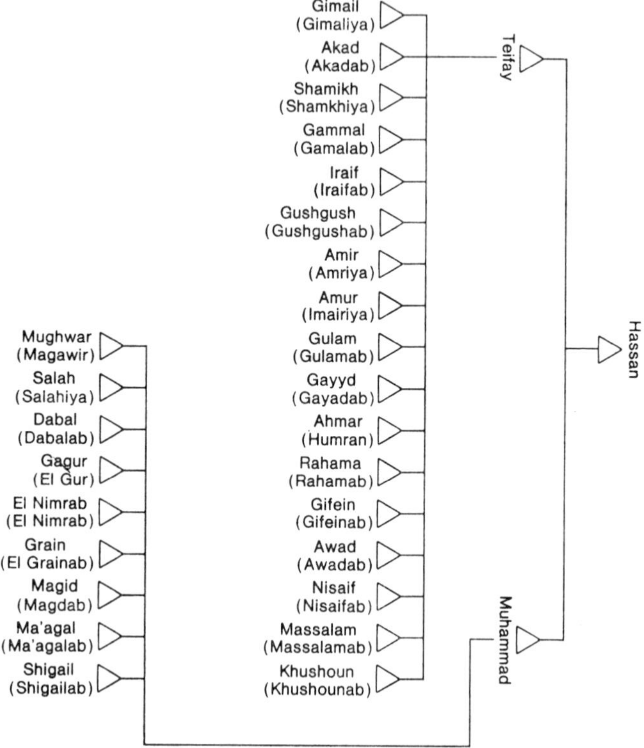

Fig. 6. Hassaniya main lineages or *furu*

not much significance among the Hassaniya, and the majority of people would only say that the Hassaniya are divided into such and such *furua*, listing all the lineages without mentioning the clans. This is because the two clans have never developed a significant economic or political identity. For the sake of simplicity, then, we can say that the Hassaniya are divided or organized into a number of lineages. These lineages are patrilineal, patrilocal and endogamous. They are of varying genealogical depth, usually between eight and ten generations. They also differ considerably in size. Some patrilineages have as few as 3,000 members while others have 10,000 or more. This variation is due not only to the factors of natural increase but also to historical factors. People have migrated to the White Nile gradually and in small numbers. Perhaps those who migrated first increased more rapidly, or some lineages migrated in relatively fewer numbers than others.

Among the Hassaniya, for instance, three lineages, the Gush-gushab, the Magawir, and the Gulamab are conspicuously larger than others. This has been one factor making for competitive political leadership between these three lineages and has also limited the competition to those lineages (see Chapter 4 on administrative politics).

Each patrilineage is divided into a number of named *khashm-baits* which can be called sub-lineages (see Fig. 7). Each sub-lineage

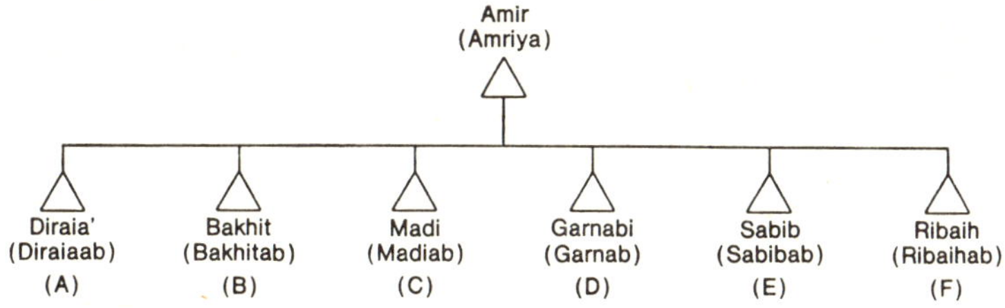

Fig. 7. Main branches or *khashm-baits* of the Amriya

consists of a number of households, or *biyut*. Sometimes a certain sub-lineage is divided into two more sub-units before finally being divided into families or households. For example, the Garnab *khashm-bait* among the Amriya lineage is further divided into Garnab Humur and Garnab Zurug, that is, 'white' Garnab and 'black' Garnab. These sub-units may also be named as above and can be thought of as *khashm-baits* in the process of formation.

PATRILINEALITY

The members of a patrilineage consider themselves as *awlad rajil wahid* or 'sons of only one man'. Here, it is very clear to see the way in which the Hassaniya use the word 'sons' for definitely not all of them would be the actual sons of one man but only the offspring of the sons of the man referred to. Thus, members of the Amriya lineage consider themselves sons of a man named Amir, from whom the lineage derives its name. They also speak of themselves as *awlad am* or paternal cousins. Although not every man would be able to trace his descent to Amir, most of them would trace their own descent to the founder of their own *khashm-bait*, or sub-lineage, and then would explain that the founders of all the *khashm-baits* comprising that lineage were sons of Amir. Some of them, however, especially those who pride themselves on possessing a special knowledge of tribal history, would show the exact genealogical connections, between the various sub-lineages.

Members of the lineage would speak of having a common *adum* which means, literally, bone. A man is supposed to inherit the bone of his father. When blood was shed in the past when the lineages were more united entities, the lineage of the offender as well as that of the victim would say that '*wagaa' fina adum*', that is, 'one of our bone has fallen'. The lineage of the offender expected the victim's lineage to retaliate. A man also inherits blood from his father. In a case of homicide the lineage of the offender would be referred to as '*ahal al-dam*', that is, 'people, or owners, of the blood'.

The Hassaniya, and the Kawahla generally, however, do not think that a man is wholly produced by his father and believe usually that a man inherits the flesh (lahama) of his mother or of his mother's brother. With the flesh, they believe, may come the physical appearance as well as personal qualities such as virtue, manliness or their opposites. In the case of the Hassaniya, however, it is extremely difficult to say whether these qualities are considered to be limited exclusively to the mother or are also potentially associated with the father, since if pressed on this point, they would usually end by saying it is no good having a good mother without having a good father or vice versa.

Difficulties in eliciting these cognitive categories relate above all to endogamy because, finally, the mother's group and the father's group are the same. Clear separations of the two, such as among the Kachin of Highland Burma, Leach (1961) are unlikely to exist in endogamous patrilineal societies. In contrast to Leach, then, I would not take these ideologies relating to 'inherited qualities and attributes' as a particular index of an oscillation between affinity and filiation but rather as ideologies associated with endogamy. They support and perpetuate the tendency to marry within the group rather than outside it or, more correctly, restrict marrying arbitrarily from unknown sources. In fact, the Hassaniya do not mind marrying or giving daughters to 'strangers' if they know them well through continual residence among them and are familiar with their qualities and attributes. It is the aspect of ritual purity which makes the Kawahla afraid of marrying strangers for they believe that purity is inherited exclusively from one's mother. This is the only aspect which the father cannot affect. The Hassaniya believe that there are *baatia* (people) especially among the non-Hassaniya who live as ghosts after death. They believe that a son or daughter of a female *baatia* would be a ghost but the offspring of a *baati* (male ghost) would not. The importance of these concepts relating to descent and inherited qualities concerns their explanatory power with regard to endogamy and marriage. This is only one of the factors involved in endogamy, but it helps to explain as well as to perpetuate it, so that it may be a cause as well as an effect.

Now let us turn again to the concept of *awlad 'am*, which I have mentioned above. I have said that all members of the patrilineage consider themselves as *awlad 'am*, or cousins. But the term, *awlad 'am*, although at one level it reflects unity, reflects equally collateral segmentation and kinship distance. Thus, people of the same sub-lineage (*khashm-bait*) may be nearer or closer *awlad 'am* to one another than people of different *khashm-baits*. Within a sub-lineage extended families conceive of themselves as being closer *awlad 'am* than other families in the same group. The closest *awlad 'am* of all are first cousins who may belong to the same extended family.

The situation here is similar to that described by Talal Asad (1970, p. 105) for the Kababish. He states that:

It is possible to distinguish between two conceptual models of agnatic kinship . . . on the one hand they view *awlad 'am* as a homogenous category of kin – those who have the same origin, the same clan name and therefore the same identity as oneself . . . on the other hand, they see *awlad 'am* as differentiated bodies of kin, for with the succession of generations a series of agnatic lines extending downwards from the male members of a given family produces an increasing distance between descendants!

It was the circumstances of the pre-dam period, however, which made one model or level of agnatic kinship more dominant, namely, the norm of solidarity based on the notion of common origin *vis-à-vis* the norm of separate interests based on the notion of individuated households. These circumstances are expressed in the pattern of ecological and economic organization discussed above. There I emphasized the basis of this solidarity before discussing the way in which it was undermined in the post-dam period.

ENDOGAMY AND MARRIAGE

Like most other Arabs, Kawahla patrilineages were endogamous, preferential marriage being with *bit al'am*, a patrilateral parallel cousin. The first patrilateral parallel cousin, or father's brother's daughter, was ranked most highly of all, and her marriage was referred to as '*zuwaj al'iz*', or 'marriage of honour'.

But *bit al'am*, like *wad'am*, a category which I have discussed above, denoted any girl of the patrilineage. I also noted that when Arabs referred to sons and daughters, as for example in the phrase *banat al'am*, 'uncle's daughters', or *awlad al'am*, 'our uncle's sons', they did not necessarily mean actual sons or daughters but descendants. Because the founders of the various sub-lineages were brothers, all their offspring were related as cousins, *awlad'am* and *banat'am*.

Most non-Arab scholars have misunderstood their Arab informants or have taken them literally when they told them 'we marry our uncle's daughters'. Hence, when these scholars did not find that people actually married their fathers' brother's daughters, but all cousins of varying order, including both patrilateral and matrilateral parallel as well as cross-cousins, they did not conceive this inconsistency to be a matter of definition which implied a wider meaning to *bit al'am*.[2]

My Kawahla informants would readily describe any lineage girl as *bit'am*, but could, if pressed, specify the exact relationship. Although they would call first cousin marriage a 'marriage of honour', they generally did not make any real distinction between the first cousin or FBD and other categories of cousins, especially FFBSD/FFBDD FBSD/FBDD. Thus we should not take the FBD marriage alone to be preferential but rather that marriage with all these categories as well as with other lineage mates.

Looking at the pattern of marriages among the Amriya lineage in Table 4, the following conclusions can be reached:

(a) the FBD marriage forms a major category of its own in the last generation enumerated above;

---

[2] See, for instance, Rosenfeld, Henry (n.d.).

Table 4. Distribution of marriages conducted by males within five generations among the Garnab (Zurug) section of the Amriya Hassaniya[2]

| Generation | *Khashm–Bait* (sub-lineage) marriages | | | | *Lineage* | | *Tribe* | | *Other Kawahla* | | *Other* | | *Total* | |
	FBD mrgs no.	%	*Other* mrgs no.	%	mrgs no.	%	mrgs no.	%	mrgs no.	%	mrgs no.	%	mrgs no.	%
5	—	—	—	—	—	—	—	—	—	—	1	100	1	100
4	—	—	—	—	—	—	2	66.6	1	33.3	—	—	3	100
3	—	—	2	12	10	59	1	6	1	6	3	17	17	100
2	—	—	10	28	5	20	3	12	—	—	10	40	28	—
1	8	18.5	16	37	6	14.5	2	—	—	—	11	25	43	—

(b) the overwhelming majority of marriages of both males and females were made inside the patrilineage. Marriages conducted outside the lineage were mainly with non-Hassaniya as well as non-Kawahla;

(c) more females were always 'taken in' than females 'given out'. Most of the females 'given out' were given to closely related affines;

(d) in the earlier generations, most convincingly in generations two and three, endogamous marriages were roughly equally distributed between those within the sub-lineage and those outside it but within the lineage; in the next generations there was a gradual trend in favour of marriages within the sub-lineage.

I have already discussed briefly the Kawahla beliefs and values related to descent and inherited qualities and argued that some of these values were intimately connected with endogamy. As such they should be seen as ideologies to restrict wider intermarriage rather than to eliminate it altogether, for whatever their impact, they remained still ideologies and not actual or empirical categories of social behaviour. In any particular situation there might exist other values or considerations which would make a man marry 'outside'. The following discussion examines briefly the considerations inducing a marriage within the group together with those which explain marriages which were made outside it. This will involve the discussion of a wider context and comprising different Kawahla customs and values relating to marriage together with its social and political consequences.

Although Kawahla lineages ultimately were patrilocal, marriage was usually followed by an initial period of uxorilocal residence. At first a newly married couple were supposed to live together for 40 days and confined to their marriage hut. This confinement took place within the bride's compound and the husband was not allowed to go out, work or even smell the open air outside. Until the man had begotten two or three children he would not be allowed to take his wife to his own father's compound. However, after the 40 days' confinement ended he was allowed to go and work with his father's family. He would be connected mainly with his father's family, although many economic activities would involve him closely with his in-laws (see Chapter 3 on extra-family relations). At the end of the confinement period a man would build a hut for his wife near the father's compound. When he moved to his father's compound he collected the materials from which he had built this hut and took it to his father's compound where he rebuilt his permanent house. Among the Kawahla, then, the hut never, as Reid has reported, belonged to the wife (see Reid 1930).

Until a man had begotten two or three children he was governed in his relations with his wife by a number of prohibitions and separations. A wife was not supposed to look at her husband and was strictly commanded to put on a veil, called *tarha*, whenever she approached him. She was not allowed to speak to him except in the most formal and limited manner. She was also not allowed to eat with him. This last prohibition covered the whole of her life since it would soon merge into the overall social separation keeping apart the dining areas of men and women.

Most of these Kawahla customs and prohibitions regarding a new couple's relationship should be seen as emphasizing the fact that the wife remained a stranger to her husband until he actually begot two or more children from her, or that the wife was not actually his until he was connected to her by children.[3] The Kawahla woman enjoyed generally a separate economic identity and concomitant independence from her husband which is unparalleled in other Arab communities. On her movement from her father's compound to that of her husband she received gifts from both her father and father-in-law. This was the first and probably the last time in her life that she could acquire a basic source of capital, for a woman generally did not inherit from either her husband or her father. Although the Kawahla are Muslims, they do not apply the Islamic law of inheritance,

---

[3] The Kawahla woman is never assimilated into her husband's close group or comes under their authority, as say, a Chinese woman who came under the complete jurisdiction of her husband's lineage and was lost to her father's group for ever. The Kawahla woman, in the strict sense, remained the property of her father's immediate group: the man mainly had rights over children. If the husband died, the woman would go to her father where she remained, and it was the right of her father or immediate group to arrange any remarriage. This was not like the Chinese case, where the husband's group retained an ever-existing and unchallenged right to arrange a remarriage for her, mostly within their own group. Only if a woman left her husband voluntarily or divorced him on her own initiative (a thing which was generally very rare), did it remain the right of her husband to seek compensation from any forthcoming prospective husband to his ex-wife. Without the consent of the husband and his compensation, marriage would not be possible in such a case.

according to which inheritance should be divided among all inheriting males and females in a proportion of two to one.

Nevertheless, the prestation she was offered on her movement (*rahula*) to her husband's compound, was generally substantial enough to provide her with wealth. The presentation of gifts to the wife at that stage was known as *shurat*, or 'promising'. Thus, the moment she left her father's compound her father would stand up and declare publicly: 'I promise to give you such and such a number of animals and/or such an amount of land'. Animals were the most common sort of prestation on this occasion. When she reached her father-in-law's compound, he was supposed to lead the reception during which he announced the gifts he was promising his daughter-in-law. The newly arrived wife was not supposed to dismount from her donkey or camel before this declaration was publicly made. This series of gifts both emphasized and contributed to her developing independent status. The husband was given similar gifts by his father, receiving animals or land.

Nevertheless, the Kawahla woman was never quite independent like the Fur woman (Barth 1968) whose economic independence from her father was absolute, because the Kawahla woman was prevented by social values from engaging in economic activities, such as manual labour in both cultivation and animal husbandry. Unless she was a relatively old woman, she could not engage directly in any such labour. These were jobs to be undertaken by men. Even the milking of animals which is reserved to women among some other pastoralists was here left to men. Women would milk only small animals when a few of them were left for the household supply and the men were absent. This did not mean, however, that women were not economically productive, for there were a number of other activities which were undertaken by them. I shall discuss these activities later which include the making of food such as *samin* (clarified butter) for household consumption. Women also spun cotton from which clothes were made by local experts who were usually strangers.

The capital of the new spouse, in animals and/or land, was kept together and included in the *murah* (herding unit) of the extended family in which they moved. The husband as an individual or as a member of the extended family, was in charge of management and utilization of the combined capital of the newly formed nuclear family. But although kept together under the direct supervision of the husband, both the wife's and husband's wealth were separately recognized. On divorce, for instance, she would claim her animals back and take them to her father's group. In the case of the death of her husband she might also take her animals and go to her father's group. If she died without children, however, her wealth went to her husband, and this would help him to get a new wife.

From these Kawahla regulations regarding marriage it is clear that the begetting of children was essential to a man's independence and prospects of wealth. He could not take his wife from her father's home without two or three children. He could not get his semi-independent capital without the offering from his father on the occasion of his wife's movement into her new home. Marriage itself would not give him authority over anyone, for the wife remained semi-independent and attached to her father or to his immediate group. Only by getting children would he assume absolute authority and control over others. For the wife, on the other hand, her production of children qualified her to move and settle with her in-laws and to accumulate means of wealth for the first time in her life. But why was the production of children so important for the Kawahla to the extent of its being a constant condition of entry to economic independence or economic identity?

The Hassaniya woman, specifically, was stereotyped as '*um arbia*', 'mother of four children', for only then would she move to her husband's group. Being prolific, the Hassaniya were referred to by other tribes as '*awlad al-bit al-mankhura*', or 'sons of the penetrated girl'. The capacity of their women to produce children was thought to be so strong that they could conceive without being actually sexually approached!

Children, especially males, were required by the Kawahla patrilineage to increase the group and make it economically more viable and politically secure. This relates to their past when the hostile environment characterized by raids and wars made the need for adult men a condition of survival (see Chapter 4). The Hassaniya marriage institutions, like their political behaviour, were geared to their military and political goal of the 'survival of the fittest'.

In a context where the patrilineage had to stand alone against other lineages and where its relations with these lineages, especially the neighbouring ones, would be characterized by innate competition and conflict, the lineage would be most reluctant to give its women to other lineages. Lineages, in a sense, were engaged in a constant 'zero-sum game', one in which a rise by one was a defeat over all others and where such lineages would try to get women from outsiders and 'strangers' to increase their own membership and manpower against other lineages. This would explain in part lineage endogamy and the fact that most of the women 'taken in' were from absolute strangers and not from Hassaniya or Kawahla lineages.

The pattern of the Kawahla rules regarding marriage also suggests other reasons for both endogamy and the high percentage among the limited number of out-lineage marriages or marriages to 'strangers'. We have seen that Kawahla marriage regulations made it difficult to marry someone from other Kawahla lineages because he had to undergo long and conditional uxorilocal residence. This would make the situation less advantageous to him, at least economically, and also disadvantageous for his group or patrilineage because it would result at any particular time in the dispersal of its members. But strangers did not have similar regulations regarding marriage so that it would be easier for a Kahli (from Kawahla) to get a wife from strangers rather than from other Kawahla. The fact that most of the women 'taken in' were only taken in as second wives would also contribute to this for some of the conditions that would generally compel a man to remarry would also make him more anxious to have his wife with him rather than endure her long absence with her own lineage.

CO-RESIDENCE

As I have said, the patrilineage was a patrilocal unit. Although some of its members were dispersed, most of them shared a common residence in the lineage's traditional homeland. The degree of dispersal was more conspicuous among non-Hassaniya Kawahla. Among the Hassaniya, the relatively slight dispersal is also a relatively recent one. Among the Amriya, for example, the dispersal started mainly after the establishment of the Gezira Scheme and the migration of some of the Amriya to that area as casual labourers for cotton-picking. In the late 1920s some of these people were able to get *hawashas* (farms) and settled permanently there with their families. However, most of the Amriya lived together in the lineage homeland. Only one sub-lineage, Bakhitab, was relatively separated from the parent lineage, leading a purely nomadic life to the west of the traditional Amriya area. There were other sub-lineages living on the east bank but, as I have said, these sections would join the parent lineage during a great part of the year (see Chapter 1).

I discussed also in Chapter 1 the way in which the co-existence of the lineage members gave them the opportunity for economic co-operation and thereby laid the basis of possible corporate unity and integration. I shall now examine briefly the pattern of residence of the Amriya lineage and see the relation of this to other social and economic factors.

Although the early part of marriage started with a limited period of uxorilocal residence, the ultimate aim for a man was to move with his wife and children and settle with his father or his father's extended family. Here he built a house for his own family consisting of either a straw hut (*guttiya*) or half-straw-mud hut (*durdur*). The house was simple in structure, and could be made with the help of close relatives for whom he made a feast on completion. He would slaughter one or more animals as both a reward for the work and a *karama*, or sacrifice, on the occasion of the erection of the new house.

The house was furnished with a few simple things: a large double bed called a *sarir*, made from date-palm branches, together with some cooking pots and utensils. The double bed usually occupied most of the hut space and dominated the room. It was an imported item bought from local markets at Ashigaig and Dueim. All the family, the man, his wife and unmarried sons and daughters also slept on it. The cooking articles were either locally made or imported from regional markets.

The movement of a wife into her in-laws' compound might sometimes be over a very small distance. Where her own family lived in the same *dumur* the journey might be as small as from one house to the neighbouring one. Another factor which made the movement of the wife not so significant to her in terms of contacts and relations with her own family was that different families would usually come together in the *shogara* centre, and most probably she would share one herding unit with her own family. In both *daratiya* and *mushtaia* she might also be with her family. The pattern of the Amriya settlement represented in Figure 8 suggests the following conclusions: a lineage consisted

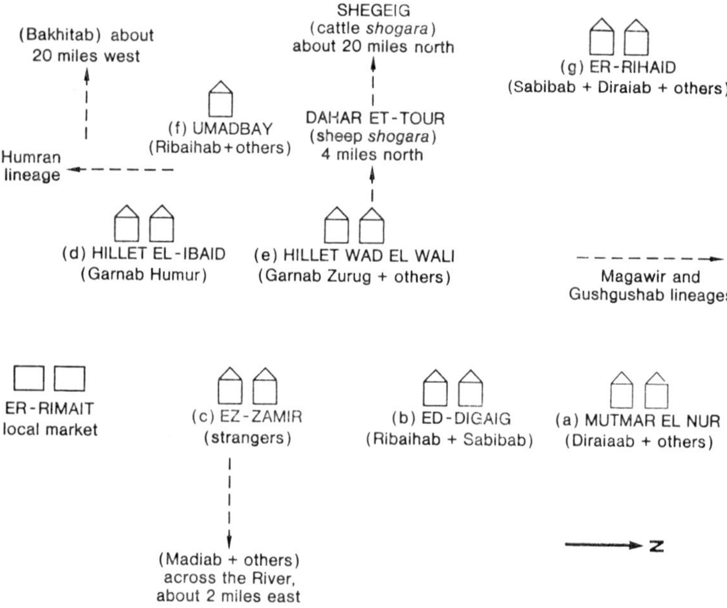

Fig. 8. Residential settlements of the Amriya lineage in the pre-dam period

usually of a number of relatively small settlements not far from each other. Each settlement consisted of a number of huts occupied by people of different *khashm-baits*, or lineage sections; although one or more sub-lineages were usually better represented in any particular settlement. These settlements were permanent and were called *dumur*. They were usually built between the river and the rainland. Most of them, though not all, were built on the type of land known as *shorab*. Few of the settlements were built on the small *gozes* which lay within the *terus*. The *gozes* were essential to the *terus* irrigation for they forced the gathered rain-water downhill to the lower-lying *terus*.

Settlements in the various *dumur* were not based exclusively on sub-lineage loyalties, for although we find a concentration of one or more sub-lineages in any specific settlement, inter-sublineage residence seemed to be equally prevalent. The general pattern, therefore, was rather that of a cluster. The emergence of this cluster pattern of residence and the concomitant inter-sub-lineage co-existence, was due in part to several social and ecological factors.

First, I have already discussed the uxorilocal aspect of the early years of marriage. This would no doubt account for the fact that some non-sub-lineage members would be living with a particular sub-lineage at any time. Secondly, and most important, was the economic and ecological factor related to *terus* distribution. A man would generally prefer to reside near his *terus* so that he could perform the economic activities related to rainland cultivation while he was still living in his *dumur*. The constant supervision and labour needed by the rainland cultivation required the cultivator to be near his plantation. Take, for example, the case of the Ribaihab sub-lineage of the Amriya. The fact that the sub-lineage was divided into two parts, one section in the Digaig *dumur*, the other in the Umadbay *dumur*, was due to the fact that the *terus* belonging to the members of this sub-lineage lay in different areas, one being near Umadbay, the other facing the Digaig *dumur* from the west.

Another ecological factor helped to account for the distribution of sub-lineage members. As I have said, the sites for permanent settlements were mainly on the *shorab* and *goz* land. Due to their irregular ecological occurrence, potential residence sites were limited in size. The most important consequence of this was that a site would become 'saturated' with residents so that a new site would become the nucleus for a new settlement. This tendency was apparent during the course of my fieldwork when some settlements of recent date were formed mainly because of this saturation of population.

LINEAGE LAND AND RESOURCES

As I have noted, land was distributed between various tribal sections which I call lineages from the arrival of these tribes in the area. Each lineage of the Hassaniya and Hissinat (see Fig. 1) held a plot comprising both river and rainland. Each lineage also had access to certain grazing centres which generally lay to the west of the cultivation strips. So each lineage, with some qualification, had equal access to natural resources and was more or less self-sufficient. This did not mean however that each lineage had a share exactly equivalent to that of the others, for the land a lineage owned was relative to the size of its population. The Aramab lineage of the Hissinat tribe held the largest share of land owned by a single lineage.

There was no general principle of rank which allowed one lineage more land as by right. Nimir, chief of the Gushgushab lineage did assume certain privileges and took additional land before the advent of the Condominium government, but this seems to have been an exception.

Land ownership was not concentrated in the hands of one group. Members of the Gushgushab lineage, for instance, who assumed political leadership for a considerable time, were not landlords to other members of the tribe. I will discuss in Chapter 3 the ways in which land was a source of economic and political power; but it was power diffused among the wealthy big men, the ummar, throughout the tribe.

Although tribal lands were owned in definite blocks, it was not unusual to find individuals owning land in the middle of an area belonging primarily to another lineage or tribe (see, for example, Fig. 9, showing certain blocks of land among the Amriya lineage). On the other hand, although land is identified with lineages, and people speak of or refer to certain blocks of land as 'Amriya land', 'Salahiya land', and so on, land holdings are also identified with individuals. Thus, the individual's rights to land included selling, renting and mortgaging. Although the actual registration of land in the names of individual owners took place under the Con-dominium government only in the 1920s, these considerable rights of individuals to land, as many writers have observed before, appeared to have been an indigenous growth and not introduced arbitrarily by administrative measures. However, *goz* land has a more corporate character, where each tribe and lineage knows roughly where its block of *goz* lies and where individuals can only attain rights of use, known locally as *hikir*, derived from their initial clearance of land from bush and trees, and subsequent cultivation.

The recognition of such clear individual rights to land made it feasible for people to adapt easily to the highly individualistic system of land tenure introduced by the government in the post-dam period, to settle *hawasha* (farm) rights in the newly intro-duced schemes according to which *hawashas* are assigned to certain individuals and registered under their names excluding

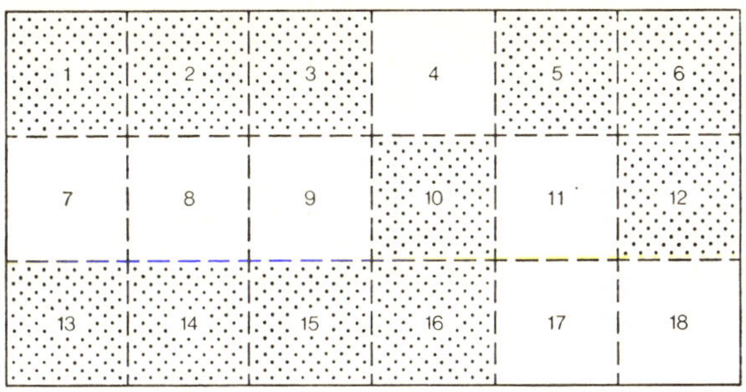

Terus and river land belonging to members of
Ribaihab *Khasm-Bait* of the Amriya lineage

Terus and river land belonging to non-Ribaihab:

4 Hamad ad-daggash (Sabibab/Amriya)

7 & 8 Daughters of Imam Shuroumi (Sabibab/Amriya)

9 Tahir Kawaig (Nimrab lineage non-Amriya Hassaniya)

11 Khalifa Wad El Haj Musa (Aramab lineage of the Hissinat)

17 Muhammad El Hassan El Igail (Sabibab/Amriya)

18 Ali Musa El Igail (Sabibab/Amriya)

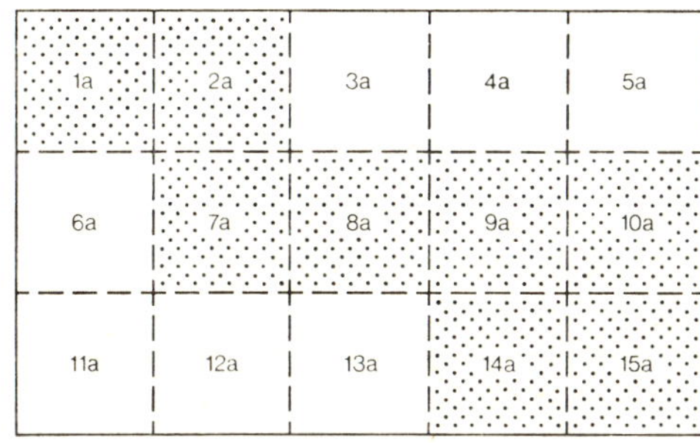

Terus and river land belonging to members of
Ribaihab *Khasm-Bait* of the Amriya lineage

Terus and river land belonging to non-Ribaihab:

3a Et-Tayib Gibreil (Garnab/Amriya)

4a Ahmad Gabbashi (stranger)

5a Esh-Shaikh Ali Kurtumun (Garnab/Amriya)

6a Ali Kurtumun, father of 5a (Garnab/Amriya)

11a Mahdi Haj Abdel Bagi (Sabibab/Amriya)

12a Muhammad Ali Idris (Sabibab/Amriya)

13a Abbas Ibrahim Tabga (Madiab/Amriya)

Fig. 9. Random blocks of *Terus* and riverland showing lineage and *khashm-bait*
identification with land

E

others who traditionally shared with the newly entitled owner of the *hawasha* the rights to the land for which the *hawasha* is given as a compensation. Traditionally, as we have seen, the general rule among the Kawahla was that inheritance should be assumed by all the sons of a deceased owner, though females were generally excluded. These measures, however, have undermined the relative identification of lineages with land and other resources like pastures, and have had sociological significance in the post-dam period.

RECIPROCITY, EXCHANGE, AND THE CASE OF FAMINE

Between members of the patrilineage there existed a complex system of essentially generalized reciprocity and exchange.

These tenets of reciprocity were firstly highly developed in the sphere of labour. I have already shown how some agricultural activities were carried out by *nafir*, the collective type of work assistance given by kinsmen or lineage-mates, the most significant form of which was *terus* levelling which was, technically speaking, a group and not an individual activity. The *nafir* was usually accompanied by the offering of food and drink on behalf of the host for whom the work had been done. But the offering should not be seen basically as a counter-payment for the services of those who helped with their work, for what was most important about the *nafir* was the sort of deferred payment represented by the obligation of the summoner to give help to others when his turn came.

Again I have also discussed briefly the arrangements of various families comprising a lineage in the sphere of livestock herding. These arrangements resulted in a division of labour to meet the different and mutual interests of various families comprising a herding partnership. Now I shall consider more closely some cases where different families met together in herding partnerships to handle the herding more efficiently. I shall also examine the general kinship relations upon which such organizational forms were based.

COMPOSITION OF EXTENDED FAMILIES AND HERDING PARTNERSHIPS

Both the extended families and herding partnerships could be seen as mutual aid groups, working together to handle their economic activities in a way that seemed to them most satisfactory. There were certain ecological and economic constraints which made most people deploy their resources and human power in this traditional fashion. Kinship had offered people a convenient means of recruitment and an ideology to further their goal of economic viability. Here are some examples of extended families and herding partnerships, whose composition, structure, and mutual aid character are examined:

EXAMPLES OF HERDING PARTNERSHIPS

Herding partnership 1 (see diagram of typical camping partnership, Fig. 4).

The herding partnership 1 consisted of five residential huts, occupied by units of three extended families. The members of these units and the kinship and genealogical connections between them are illustrated by Figure 10.

The three families belonged to the Ribaihab *khashm-bait*. As the diagram shows, the three families are Jena-Kambal (that is Kambal's offspring) represented by (i).

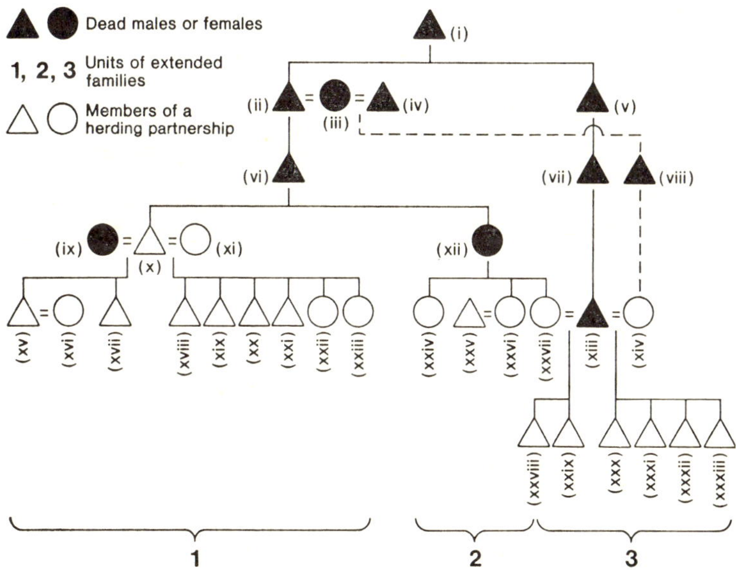

Fig. 10. Genealogical relationships between partners in a herding unit among the Amriya lineage of the Hassaniya

The composition of the three families engaged in the herding partnership is as follows:

UNIT 1 (see Fig. 10)

No. of persons in figure	Name	Relationship to head of unit
x	Yusuf Fadlallah	Head*
xi	Sharifia	Second wife
xv	Hammad	Elder son
xvi	Um Haggain	Daughter-in-law (xv's wife)
xvii	Fadlallah	Son*
xviii	Mirghani	Son
xix	Hassan	Son
xx	Hamid	Son
xxi	Muhammad	Son
xxii	Rabha	Daughter
xxiii	Fatma	Daughter
xxiv	Taiba Ibrahim	Sister's daughter

UNIT 2

xxv	Gamaa' Khair Es-Seid	Head
xxvi	Amna Ibrahim	Wife
	Other member of unit	Father, Mother Brother and wife, Brother and wife*

UNIT 3

xxx	Muhammad Ali Awad El Karim	Head
xxxi	Muhammad En Nur	Brother
xxxii	Es-Sadig	Brother
xxviii	Shaikh Ed Dein	Half-sibling
xxix	Ibrahim	Half-sibling
xiv	Fatma Ibrahim	Mother
xxvii	Nafisa bit Taha	Step-mother
xxxiii	Gar En Nabi	Brother
	Muhammad and wife	Elder brother and wife*

* indicating that he or she was not participating in the herding of cattle but engaging in cultivation and/or sheep *shogara* to the south and east.

DIVISION OF LABOUR IN THE THREE UNITS AND THE HERDING PARTNERSHIP

Unit 1

(a) Yusuf Fadlallah (x) and his elder son Hammad (xv) managed the rain cultivation. Taiba (xxiv) who was the ZD of Yusuf, remained at the Degeig *dumur* to do the domestic work for them. She was 45 years old and unmarried.

(b) Yusuf's son Fadlallah (xvii) grazed sheep around Abu-Firaiwa area. He was helped by a hired shepherd from the Jumua'iya tribe.

(c) The rest of the group, comprising the extended family, grazed and looked after cattle at the *dikka*. These were: Mirghani (xviii), Hassan (xix), Hamid (xx), Muhammad (xxi) and the females Rabha (xxii, unmarried), Fatma (xxiii, unmarried), Sharifia (xi) and Um Haggain (xvi).

Unit 2

(a) Gamaa' (xxv) and wife were responsible for cattle herding at the *dikka*.

(b) His father, Khair Es-Seid, and mother cultivated the rain land.

(c) His brothers Ibrahim and Ahmad and their wives looked after the sheep grazing. But they also used to help their father in the cultivation of the *terus* from time to time – so also Gamaa' (xxv).

Unit 3

(a) Muhammad and wife managed the rain cultivation.
(b) The rest of the group grazed cattle at the *dikka*.
(c) The unit had no sheep, only cattle.

In the herding partnership made up by these three families, the herding of animals was organized in the following way:

(i) The *dahawa* (the morning session) was usually organized by *awlad* Awad El Karim of unit 3.

(ii) The *duhriya* (the noon or afternoon session) was usually organized by *awtad* Yusuf of unit 1.

(iii) The *sarba* (night session) was invariably the responsibility of Gamaa' of unit 2.

We have to note that Gamaa' (xxv) was the only elderly man

in the herding unit and so it was only he who could conduct the *sarba* or the night session. The night grazing required an experienced man because animals could easily disperse very quickly and because they could be attacked easily by thieves.

The pattern of allocating morning and afternoon sessions to particular personnel was not always closely adhered to, though it generally formed the basic division of labour in the herding partnership.

With reference to Figure 4, this herding partnership consisted of five residential huts. Two huts were occupied by unit 1, one by the young men, their mother and sister, the other by their brother's wife, Um Haggain (xvi). Two huts were occupied by unit 3, one by the young men and their mother Fatma (xiv), the other by Nafisa bit Taha (xxvii) and her sons. The fifth hut was occupied by Gamaa' and wife of unit 2.

The huts were of two kinds: (a) *shukkab*, or straw hut which was the common type of dwelling; (b) *sha'ar* (literally wool) or huts made from the animals' wool. This was usually the residence of the well-to-do.

HERDING PARTNERSHIP 2

(a) Abdel Magid and Khamis Ali Toura (brothers) together with their wives. Each occupied a separate hut.

(b) Toura Sulaiman and his wife – occupying one hut. Abdel Magid and Khamis Ali Toura were first paternal cousins to Toura Sulaiman.

(c) Awad El Karim Ali and wife – occupying one hut.

(d) Bakhit Awad Alla of the Garnab (Zurug section) *khashm-bait*. He was a lineage mate of (a), and (c). His mother, however, belonged to the Ribaihab *khashm-bait* and was considered a close paternal aunt of (a), (b) and (c).

THE ORGANIZATION OF LABOUR

(a) The father of Khamis and Abdel Magid was dead, and only their mother was alive at the time. Abdel Magid and Khamis looked after the rain cultivation by themselves, while they left their cattle to be grazed by the rest of the group. Their wives too were left with the group in the *dikka*. Abdel Magid had sheep also and he used to hire a shepherd (an ex-slave) to look after them. His mother helped the shepherd at the sheep grazing centre.

(b) Toura and wife looked after the cattle grazing. His father, step-mother and half-sibling (small children) were responsible for rain cultivation; his own mother was dead. He had no sheep.

(c) Awad El Karim and wife managed the cattle herding. He had no sheep. His father was dead. His brother, Ed Dali and mother were responsible for the rain cultivation.

(d) Both Bakhit's parents were dead. He had no full siblings, only half-siblings. He had no sheep. He performed the rain cultivation by himself and left his wife with the herding group which grazed his cattle. His half-siblings also carried out rain cultivation.

Thus (a) and (d) depended exclusively on the other members of the herding partnership in the grazing of their cattle. The organization of labour in this partnership followed a similar pattern to that outlined in the partnership discussed previously.

HERDING PARTNERSHIP 3

This was composed of the following:

(a) Ali Musa of the Sabibab sub-lineage of the Amriya who attended to the cattle-grazing while leaving the rain cultivation to his mother and the attached female ex-slaves (including the mother of (b) below). He had no sheep.

(b) Nursal Saeid, an ex-slave (formerly Ali Musa's slave) who carried out the cattle herding while leaving the rain cultivation for his mother. He had no sheep.

(c) Ali Bugra of the Ribaihab *khashm-bait* of the Amriya who belonged to a different sub-lineage from Ali Musa but was a lineage mate. He was also married to (a) Ali Musa's sister. He had no sheep. He did the cattle grazing while leaving the cultivation for his young sons and an ex-slave.

(d) Muhammed El Hassan of the Sabibab sub-lineage of the Amriya. He was a FBS or first paternal cousin of (a) Ali Musa. He had no sheep. His brother, El Igail, owned some sheep and looked after a distant sheep *shogara*. Their mother, helped by a female ex-slave, used to cultivate their rainland.

What pattern of reciprocity prevailed in the subsistence sector of activity among members of the patrilineage? I have mentioned that cooked food, milk and most of its by-products such as butter and *rob* (diluted and residual milk from which *samin* has been extracted) were exchanged freely between members of the patrilineage. *Samin*, however, was not usually exchanged but instead was taken to local markets and sold. Grain for both consumption and agricultural purposes could be borrowed from kinsmen to be returned from the yield of the subsequent crop. This practice was particularly prevalent in good years when some or most families could afford to lend to the needy whose supplies of grain had run short. In the more difficult years, however, people would depend mainly on buying their grain from local markets or from wealthy traders from their own or neighbouring lineages. I will discuss later how people could afford to do this.

There existed also a reciprocal exchange of animals on various occasions. At marriage, for example, when the bridegroom was supposed to '*yamla al-matmurea farit*' (literally, 'fill the *matmura*, or storage pit, with faeces of slaughtered animals') for his mother-in-law, the groom did not depend only upon his limited stock but was presented with animals by his kinsmen and was supposed also to go and take any animals he wanted from various relatives without actually asking their permission. This was based on the tacit consent that '*albahayim bahayim alkul*', 'our animals are communally shared', and before long you would be giving to those from whom you took animals.

The exchange of animals was especially important during a famine. Although famine could be caused by diseases or drought, especially when it continued for several years consecutively, most of the famines were caused by crop failure due to the variability of rainfall or river flood. In the absence of rain in any particular year both cultivation and animals would suffer. Faced with such fluctuating physical resources people developed a system by which animals were quickly redistributed in time of famine. The redistribution was, however, temporary and geared to the end of the famine. Strictly speaking this was borrowing, and exchanges of animals were called *manayih* (offerings, sing. *maniha*). *Maniha* was given by those who owned much to those who owned little or nothing. The borrower was supposed to live on the animal's milk, and return it to its original owner by the end of the difficult year. The borrower should return not only the animal or animals but also any offspring they produced during the course of the loan. If a borrowed animal died, he was supposed to present some witnesses to its death and/or show the skin of the dead animal to the owner as a proof of its unfortunate death.

Although the owner ran a risk in distributing his animals to others, in that he deprived himself or his family of access to their milk, such a loan was not entirely unfavourable to him. Since his animals would be grazed by others this would enable him to avoid the consequences of overgrazing and overstocking. A man who enjoyed the borrowing would be anxious to seek pastures and good grazing conditions for his *maniha* since his own living depended on their existence. Also the right of the creditor to the offspring of his animals gave him the chance to collect more animals than he originally offered. It was true that they might have increased by reproduction with their original owner anyway. But the intensive care one could give to a relatively small number of animals would be more favourable for the animals' health and breeding capabilities. In a sense then, the relationship between the borrower and the creditor was a reciprocal one and based on mutual interest and trust.

FEUD, HOMICIDE AND LINEAGE CORPORATENESS

The patrilineage, consisting of male agnates tracing their common descent to the founder of the lineage, formed a corporate group responsible for the protection and defence of the whole lineage membership. They formed one vengeance group *vis-à-vis* other patrilineages or tribes. For the time being I will concentrate on the shedding of blood to emphasize the role of the patrilineage as a vengeance group, both in seeking vengeance and as the target of possible vengeance.

First, let me examine briefly what usually happened if a homicide was committed beginning with the offender's lineage. As I have shown earlier, the localities of patrilineages were relatively close and contiguous. The main threat to lineage contiguity occurred at the time of *shogara*, animal herding, when people became dispersed. In the sheep *shogara*, people especially would settle in twos or alone. In case of homicide all the lineage members would come together in one *zariba* or fenced enclosure, the cattle and sheep-herders as well as the cultivators. A state of emergency and full alert was then declared. A curfew was also enforced from dusk to dawn and no one except affines or cognates was allowed to carry out the *sarba* (the night session of grazing). During the day people could go about their activities freely, although they had to move in groups, the main threat of possible raiding by the victim's lineage occurring at night. Agnates were warned that if a man broke the curfew regulations at night he had to bear the responsibility of his own action and there would be no group action in his favour.

The emergency regulations subsequent to homicide had several functions. Firstly, the coming together of the lineage in one *zariba* made it more capable of defending itself. Secondly, while agnates were warned not to go out of the *zariba* by night, they in fact could still go by disguising themselves under the umbrella of non-agnatic connections, especially if they were not very well known to people outside the lineage. The victim's lineage was supposed to attack at night when a group from it (known as *talia'a*, or attacking regiment) would raid the offender's lineage enclosure. Thus if they did happen to spot someone outside the *zariba* they would probably dismiss him on the assumption that he might not be a real agnate, but only related to the lineage through marriage.

These aspects of post-homicide behaviour concerned the measures that were taken by the patrilineage to protect itself and to act as a united group. But this was only one context in which the patrilineage was supposed to act. The other concerned the resolution of conflict. After a homicide took place the government, represented by the police stationed at Ed-dueim and El-Geteina, would be informed of it by the Omda or Deputy Nazir (see Chapter 8 on administrative politics). The police would take away the offender and keep him in prison pending trial. From the time he committed homicide until he was taken by the police it remained the responsibility of his lineage to protect him. The responsibility or protection, mainly by hiding, fell on the lineage in the case of both agnates and cognates. Vengeance was another matter. While the government was to deal mainly with the actual offender, it remained for the lineages involved to solve their subsequent conflict.

The most common and effective resolution of conflict was through arbitration. The lineage elders, ummar, and the lineage shaikh, if it happened to have one, would call for other notables from other lineages, together with other religious shaikhs, to go to the victim's lineage, to seek their counterparts. The arbitrating team would usually refuse to dismount from their donkeys or camels unless *afu* (pardon) was readily granted by the victim's lineage. If the answer was in the affirmative the arbitrating team headed by the shaikhs would dismount and accept the hospitality of their hosts. After food was served the two sides of the conflict would agree on the amount of *diya* (blood money) to be paid. However, *diya* was not always paid for, sometimes, especially when the lineage was headed by a shaikh, he might grant complete pardon without actual payment of *diya*.

If *diya* was accepted and paid it would be distributed roughly in the following way: a quarter to the arbitrating shaikhs, a quarter to the victim's lineage leaders and shaikh and the rest among the whole lineage. Most of the last, however, was sent to those most affected by the death, namely, the victim's extended family.

The actual collection of blood-money among the Hassaniya was somewhat unique in character. For *diya* was usually collected from the whole tribe or even other tribes as well, each man subscribing a *girish* or piastre, which was roughly equal to the new British penny. Thus *diya* among the Hassaniya was generally referred to as '*girish al-Hassaniya*', 'Hassaniya piastre'. After the tribal collection was made, the offender's lineage, especially its notables, would make a special contribution. The rest was paid by the immediate relatives of the offender who might be members of his extended family.

The power of the arbitrating team depended mainly on the religious standing of the shaikhs heading the team. These shaikhs enjoyed enormous respect and power among the Kawahla. Their authority was supernaturally sanctioned. If a shaikh's arbitration was refused he was supposed to '*yanfud al-farwa*', 'shake off the *farwa*', the animal's skin on which the shaikh usually said his prayers. This was interpreted as a very dangerous sign of curse on the victim's lineage rendering ineffective any retaliatory measures they might make. Thus the shaikh's power was supposed to inhibit movements of their *talia'a*, or attacking regiment, by causing them to imagine various sorts of illusions, for example, that they were inhibited from attacking by a concrete wall or the like.

The measures outlined above give a general picture of what usually followed a homicide case. These measures, however, were usually loosely formulated so that the regulations regarding homicide, particularly the aspect of vengeance were never clearly developed among the White Nile Arabs. From my information it was clear that vengeance was rare and the payment of *diya* was not very common. What usually happened, especially after the intervention of the government and the consequent trial of the offender, was that after a certain time the situation would return to normal and the homicide would become an event to be remembered rather than acted upon. This was due particularly to the role of the shaikhs who were enormously powerful, for in either the acceptance or the non-acceptance of his arbitration, the shaikh remained the cardinal element in restoring things to normality. Where his arbitration was not accepted, he would still be the one responsible for the abstention of the victim's lineage from actual revenge. No one would say 'look they haven't sought revenge'. The attitude would rather be 'look how Shaikh X has inhibited their intrigues and plots to revenge'! This religious factor, coupled with the *zariba* arrangements that a lineage would make to defend its members, were the main factors in resolving homicide cases and certain subsequent hostilities. The assumption by the lineage of a common responsibility to defend its members shows that its role as a vengeance group was more preventive than operational and that homicide was regulated, strictly speaking, by the threat to use force rather than the actual use of force. This was not due mainly to the presence of the colonial government or its intervention, for while, logically, the government could affect the extent to which actual force would be used, it could not affect the mere threat to use force.

So far I have managed to show the various aspects in the pre-dam period in which lineage solidarity is reflected and/or promoted. I have mainly considered non-differentiated relationships, that is, relationships between fellow lineage members as equals. In the next chapter I discuss relationships between non-equals, between the privileged category of ummar and common people. In these relationships a new dimension enters in which lineage solidarity and viability were given expression in the pre-dam period.

HOMICIDE CASES

Case 1

  Case: Homicide: Amriya *v*. Hissinat/Aramab
  Time: Towards the end of the Turko-Egyptian regime (1821–1885) – in winter, during the harvest of the river-crop, *sufra*

Abuel Hassan of the Aramab was the officially recognized Shaikh-Khat (paramount chief) over the Kawahla and other ethnic groups in the White Nile. Es-sayid of the Aramab, a first paternal cousin of Abuel Hassan, was his *khafir* guard. He came with a group of government soldiers and some Hissinat elders for the purpose of collecting cultivation tribute for the government. A quarrel arose between him and a certain man from the Ribaihab/Amria, named Ali Fadlallah, who then stabbed Es-sayid to death.

Ali Wad Gisayir and Ali Wad Gabbashi from the Sabibab/ Amriya went at night because they feared the Hissinat to *Dumur* Abuel Hassan where both Abuel Hassan the paramount chief and El Haj Musa, a well-known shaikh belonging to the Aramab lived. It was said that it was the custom of Abuel Hassan to pay El Haj Musa a morning visit every day to take his *baraka*, religious blessings, before he went out to perform his daily labours. The Amriya representatives went to Haj Musa and asked for his pardon (*afu*). In the morning, when Abuel Hassan, the chief, came to visit El Haj Musa, the latter introduced the Amriya men to him saying, 'Shake hands with my sons from the Amriya'. Abuel Hassan exclaimed, 'Is this not Ali Wad Gisayir whose paternal cousin has killed mine?' El Haj Musa replied, 'Yes, he is – but I have given him my pardon, so for God's sake, you should give yours too. If you don't, whoever refused to smear his face with milk, I will smear his with blood instead', meaning he would kill him. Abuel Hassan said 'I give them my pardon, now they can leave during the day rather than during the night, for no Hissinawi will smear your face with anything' (meaning, 'no one can harm you').

There was a wealthy trader from the Amriya living on the east bank, by the name of Ali Wad Mannallak. He belonged to the Madiab sub-lineage of the Amriya. Abuel Hassan went to him and said, 'Your father's brother's son has killed mine.' Ali Wad Mannallah replied 'Yes, I know. If you want *diya* (blood money), I will pay it for you; if you want my head I am also ready for that.' Abuel Hassan told him that he wanted *diya*. Wad Mannalah paid him what was worth £S 100 and sent a letter to the Amriya telling them about the *diya* settlement and said, 'The Amriya are now free of obligations for the Hissinat'.

The Amriya, on the west bank, collected blood-money from the whole lineage and sent it to Wad Mannallah. But he refused to accept it and the money was re-divided among the lineage. The *diya* was collected in cattle, sheep and goats, which were then sold at the market for approximately two pounds per head for cattle and 25 piastres per head for sheep or goats. The collection was made from all the sub-lineages of the Amriya, everyone paying according to his ability. It was not made from the offender's group alone, which in fact paid no more than the others.

After the *diya* settlement a certain religious notable from the Aramab Hissinat, by the name of Abdellah Muhammad El Nur El Ansari, married the daughter of Ali Fadlallah, the offender, and begot a son, named Muhammad. Muhammad became a respectable religious leader among the Amriya and married one of their women.

This case is very interesting because it illustrates the high degree of lineage corporateness. The offender belonged to the Ribaihab section, the two men who went to see El Haj Musa belonged to the Sabibab section, the men who actually paid the *diya* belonged to the Madiab section, and the attempt to repay Wad Mannallah was made by the whole lineage.

Case 2

Case: Homicide: Gushsughab *v*. Iraifab (neighbouring lineages)

Time: About 1926, at the time of Shaikh Idris Habbani, the first nazir

The incident took place at El Hesai market where the offender, Ali Yusuf, of the Gushgushab lineage, and Homoudi, of Iraifab lineage, were doing their shopping. Homoudi trod on Ali's feet, presumably unintentionally, but Ali was very angry and said to Homoudi, 'We will meet soon.' Homoudi asked, 'When is that going to be?', and Ali replied 'Tonight!'

People said that there was previous friction between the two men but no details were given.

Homoudi went to a *mareesa* (local beer house) for a drink. Ali Yusuf followed him there and the two fought each other. Ali killed Homoudi.

Court: The case was tried by a government court under the presidency of the district commissioner. The nazir was a member of the court. The Iraifab told the court, 'Either you execute him or we shall take revenge by ourselves.' The court decided on seven years' imprisonment.

Case 3

Case: Homicide: Gushgushab *v*. Iraifab

Time: About 1928

This murder took place just two years after the previous homicide between the two lineages. The victim was the brother of Homoudi, the one killed in the previous case.

Abdellah Muhammad Keiwat of the Nimrab/Gushgushab was tending his animals at El Ikhailid, near Wad Nimir village. Kalmon, Homoudi's brother, left the Hesai market on his way home. When he spotted Abdellah, he confronted him and said, 'Be ready, I am here for you', i.e. ready to fight. He attacked Abdellah with a knife, but Abdellah was faster and killed Kalmon with a stick. The Shamkhiya and Imairiya lineages neighbouring the Iraifab were in the vicinity of the killing. They informed the Iraifab of what had happened but they did not interfere.

Abdellah was imprisoned for some time, but he was not tried, for *diya* was arranged between the two parties. £S 150 were paid. They said this was a *diya* for a man and a half, because the Gushgushab inflicted two deaths then on the Iraifab, and a *sulh* was made.

It is interesting to note that the *diya* in this case was collected from among all the Hassaniya.[4] It is said that the Gushgushab refused to offer *diya* themselves because they said it was a case of self-defence. To avoid *fitna* (intrigue or feud), the Hassaniya *agawid* (arbitrators or elders) collected the *diya* from all the Hassaniya and asked the government to close the case and free the offender. The government agreed but the offender died in prison before he was freed. After the *sulh* the two lineages were pacified and some intermarriage took place.

---

[4] People say that no one paid more than a piastre. This is why people say *Girah El-Hassaniya yahil el-diya*, i.e. the Hassaniya's piastre resolves the *diya* conflict. Today when people ask for a subscription for anything, they say Pay us the Hassaniya piastre.

3

The Traditional Sources of Social Stratification and Power: the Ummar Leadership

Unlike most of the egalitarian lineages described in early anthropological writings, for example, the Nuer (Evans-Pritchard 1940), the Kawahla lineages were highly differentiated internally. The pattern of lineage differentiation approximated to the Chinese model (Freedman 1966) in which the mass of people were rice-growing peasants while a few were rich traders, scholars and officials. In the Kawahla context, we find that the majority of people were carrying on a subsistence life based both on cultivation and animal husbandry, while a few were wealthy men or traders known as *ummar gabila*. We also find a group of men drawn into this category mainly because of their position as religious shaikhs.[1]

THE PATTERN OF STRATIFICATION AND ITS VARIABILITY

The pattern of stratification among the Hassaniya and other Kawahla can be conceived of as consisting of two distinct social strata. The upper stratum consisted of those they used to call *ummar gabila* (well-to-do tribal elders) – people distinguished from others by their wealth and concomitant social power. They are those I call 'big men'. The lower stratum consisted of ordinary people with fairly limited resources who were carrying on mainly subsistence activities. These latter formed the majority at any time and I shall refer to them as 'commoners'. Within the upper stratum, however, there was a further important distinction between the ordinary ummar, whom people generally referred to as *kubarna* (*kubar* means both 'elderly' and 'big' and it is an apt reflection of their position), and a special category formed by

---

[1] The title *Ummar Gabila* can either include or exclude religious Shaikhs.

people who were religious shaikhs referred to as *fugarana* (from *fagir*, the singular of *fugara*, a title for religious leaders of various orders). The last category was also sometimes known as *awlad al farash* literally, sons of the mattress, that is, those whom you should welcome as guests by offering them respectable beds nicely made up with mattresses and coverings. This special gesture was possible because they would be mainly the guests of their own kind of people, other big men.

In the past, and before the Condominium, the term *awlad al farash* was used also to refer to the chiefs of the Gushgushab lineage. At the start of the Condominium the phrase was extended to instituted chiefs who were appointed by the government. But while *awlad al farash* comprised both the religious shaikhs and tribal chiefs, particularly before the Condominium, shaikhs were also distinguished as *ahal al-Kitab*, 'people of the book' (Quran), in contrast to the tribal chiefs, the *ahal al-farasa*, or 'people of the sword'. This distinction reflected the fact that tribal chiefs led their tribes in war against other tribes, while shaikhs abstained from actual engagement in fighting, limiting their role to blessing those they supported. During the period of the Mahdiya (1881–99), this distinction was blurred because both tribal chiefs and shaikhs joined the Mahdist rebellion and fought side by side with the Mahdi. Not all the shaikhs fought, however, and those who actually did so were affected by the Mahdiyya and the emergence of religious and political dualism.[2]

In the following discussion I limit my concern to the pattern of stratification which existed at most lineage levels, and between the commoners and the big men, including the shaikhs. The pattern outlined is a very general one. The Kawahla lineages varied considerably in degrees of stratification. Some lineages, such as the Humran, approximated to an egalitarian model with no developed big men shaikhs. It is said of them that '*maandahum kabir wa la fagir*', 'they haven't got a big man or a religious shaikh'. They are accordingly considered difficult to communicate with. At the other extreme, lineages such as the Shamkhiya, were generally known to possess only one big man. Between these

---

[2] Under such circumstances the emergence of religious and political dualism is very common. This usually accompanies the rise of charismatic leaders, e.g. Abdallah el-Hassan in Somalia and El-Sanusi in Cyrenaica (see Lewis 1965, and Evans-Pritchard 1949).

F

extremes lay the majority of Hassaniya and other Kawahla lineages having varying degrees of stratification but mainly with one or more ummar and one or more shaikhs. The position of the ummar and shaikhs also differed from one lineage to another depending on their wealth or religious standing and above all on their number in any particular lineage.

Most of the Kawahla lineages recognized an allegiance to a particular shaikh whom they would generally consider to be the lineage shaikh. Sometimes he would be a fellow lineage member, and sometimes a stranger to the lineage. Most of the lineages, however, acquired their shaikhs from among their lineage members. Some of them, particularly in the case of the Hassaniya, had drawn their shaikhs from outside the tribe. Most of the Hassaniya lineages who had outsiders as shaikhs recruited these shaikhs from either the Hissinat or from among complete strangers like the Ja'aliyin. Thus the shaikh of the Amriya at the time was a man from the Hissinat.

In some cases there were more than one lineage recognizing allegiance to one common shaikh, thus, for example, the Rahamab, the Magdab, and the Imairiya, recognized Shaikh Birair of Ja'aliyin stock as their shaikh. The common religious leadership of the Hissinat lineages was represented by the Gubush family of the Aramab lineage of the Hissinat.

In a few cases a lineage might have more than one shaikh, for example, the Shamkhiya were divided between a Kababish religious leader and Magawir (Hassaniya) shaikh; but most lineages had one common religious leader whom their members would generally follow.

Shaikhs were essentially holy men venerated for their well-known piety and miraculous power. Most of them were heads of religious *tariqas*, orders, mainly Sammaniya and Qadriya. Religious orders had spread in the White Nile area since the days of the Funj Kingdom of Sennar and the Turkish régime prior to the Mahdist revolt in the Sudan, towards the end of the last century.

The Hissinat, especially the Gubush of the Aramab lineage, were among the first men to acquire the teachings and knowledge of these *tariqas* and to spread them to others, particularly the Hassaniya. Before Turkish rule the Hissinat Gubush had the monopoly of these religious *tariqas*, but from that time on people from other tribes acquired the teachings of the *tariqas* either through the Gubush or directly from whoever brought them from outside. Most of those who were religious heads of their own lineages among the Hassaniya, for example, had acquired their religious standing in the latter way.

Among the Kawahla, however, religious *tariqas* had never developed a tangible organizational pattern of the sort reported elsewhere for example, among the Sanusiya in Cyrenaica or even in the Somali context (Evans-Pritchard 1949 and Lewis 1965). I am excluding here the Ansar Brotherhood which developed a highly organized pattern during the last century and was revived in one form or another from the 1930s onwards. It will be dealt with separately in Chapter 8.

The overwhelming majority of people in the White Nile area were content to put their faith in a particular religious leader irrespective of his *tariqa*. The *tariqa* was something concerning the shaikh, and remained his own business – for it was the unknown source of his miraculous power. People should not enquire about the source – they should be content to receive what they got. This did not mean that religious men were reluctant to profess their teachings or knowledge. It was just that people were not interested in these things. Those who were educated by the shaikhs were people interested in becoming shaikhs themselves. In the Kawahla context, therefore, real and tangible membership of a *tariqa* separated the leaders from those whom they led.

What, then, were the connections between the shaikhs and their followers? The shaikh was responsible for the well-being and security of his lineage and all those who accepted his religious leadership. To them he acted as an intermediary before God and acquired the knowledge and miraculous power (*baraka*) to qualify him to deal with most of the contingencies and insecurities of life. By his miraculous power he could bring rain and protect crops. He was also responsible for the health and well-being of people and animals. He gave people magical stones to be thrown in the fields, or *warga* (charms) to be tied to the growing plants so that birds and pests were kept away. If he succeeded, God had accepted his mediation; if he failed 'it was God's wish' and the shaikh should not be blamed. To protect or treat human or animal diseases he provided *highbat* or *wargas* (charms) or *mihaya* (holy water) over which some verses of the Quran were read, and which were later swallowed by the patient.

None of these religious practices prevented people in any way from applying the usual technical measures to protect crops and animals. They illustrate the additional protective functions of the Islamic religion in an uncertain environment.

In addition to what has been said about the spiritual leadership of the religious shaikh, there remained another important role always reserved to him which was that of *agwad* (arbitrator). Religious men were thought of as men of modesty, honesty, and peace and their judgment was believed to be always guided by what was right and just, irrespective of the interest of any person or group. Their role as arbitrator was not limited to their own lineage for they could be used also by other lineages. People at that time were reluctant to go to government and tribal courts and most of their conflicts, individual or tribal, were referred to shaikhs for arbitration. In a hostile environment with conflicting lineages or tribal interests the role of the religious shaikh as mediator was highly valued and appreciated, especially in the pre-Condominium era when wars, raiding and counter-raiding were normal facts of life.

We must, however, distinguish between two categories of religious shaikhs; those who were strangers to a lineage and those leading their own lineage. For while the former depended mainly on his spiritual power, the latter had the additional power of kinship status. In both cases, however, the shaikh did not conform exactly to the mediatory patterns which have been reported elsewhere by anthropologists, namely, those where the arbitrator was supposed to come to terms with the conflicting interests of the parties to a dispute so that his final judgment, which was by no means his own, was nothing but a reflection of the conflicting interests, and what he would say might be in other words what the parties to a conflict had already said themselves. Among the Hassaniya and the other Kawahla the men of God used always to have a standard form of judgment called *afu*, which meant literally, 'excuse' or 'pardon'. In the case of homicide, for example, *afu* would mean accepting the *diya* or blood money payment. Where the shaikh was leading his own lineage, it might mean that the two parties to a conflict had agreed to open a new page in their diplomatic relations and that *diya* might well not be paid.

This factor of complete *afu* by lineage shaikhs was a major factor in making *diya* payment uncommon.

In all his mediatory activities the shaikh was backed by supernatural power. He was sanctioned, as has been pointed out, by a very strong curse known as '*nafd al-farwa*', or 'shaking aside the *farwa*', a sort of a mat or carpet made of animal skin and used for praying. It symbolized all his supernatural powers and religious capital. With the *farwa* being shaken the powers would be enraged and would attack those who challenged and humiliated them. This was believed to have fatal effects.

The role of the shaikh as arbitrator both within and without his lineage was very important. I have already suggested that although governmental and tribal courts existed, people were generally inclined to solve their problems by their traditional means of arbitration rather than by taking them to courts. Members of the same lineage would rarely resort to courts and any conflict inside the lineage would be solved by the intervention of the shaikh and the big men of the lineage. These two categories were not rulers nor had they any official authority or power. They were essentially arbitrators depending for their effectiveness on both their lineage affiliations and on their religious standing and/or their economic position.

There were rarely any serious feuds inside a lineage, for, as we have seen, the economic and social bonds between members of the lineage militated against threats to their unity. Where such occurred, members of the patrilineage would generally try to put pressure on the offender to move to another part of Dar Hassaniya away from the lineage homeland.

Between different lineages, however, serious disputes did arise and the role of the shaikhs was crucial, for people respected the shaikhs and feared their spiritual powers. In addition, some religious shaikhs headed a number of lineages of the same tribe or of different tribes. As such they would emerge as the only main link between different lineages. The Gubush of the Hissinat especially, and the Ja'ali stemming from the J'aliyin tribe, shaikh Birair, and his sons, had a wider inter-lineage and inter-tribal network of religious followers. Among the Hassaniya shaikhs, a certain Shaikh El Khanger had achieved a conspicuously wide religious leadership extending over non-Hassaniya as well. So the role of the shaikh as an inter-lineage, inter-tribal mediator was prominent, especially in such a hostile environment characterized by raids, robberies, homicides and the persistent conflict of interest between lineages and tribes in the region.

In cases of homicide the government had to a great extent preserved the traditional arrangements for resolving conflict. While the government insisted upon judging the case, it allowed the arbitration through shaikhs and big men to proceed. Whether the accused was judged guilty or not guilty, a tribal settlement which could include *diya* was also endorsed by the government. Where the offender was proved guilty, government policy was to save the offender's life and to imprison him. Only when the offender committed homicide more than once would the government refuse to accept a tribal settlement and insist upon hanging the offender. Where the accused was found not guilty, for example in cases of self-defence, the government still endorsed tribal settlements, including *diya*, because it felt that it must judge according to the law, while the lineages and tribes dealt with the *causes* of conflict. An official report pointed out that tribal settlement could succeed in cases where government courts could not.

The government so much appreciated the role of shaikhs as arbitrators that it kept a special file listing their names and lineages. It also gave some of these shaikhs occasional payments (*mukafa*) in return for their acknowledged services as arbitrators: these payments were too nominal and infrequent to have any real significance. In a sense they reflected the government's attempt to bureaucratize traditional institutions by absorbing them into the administrative structure (see Chapter 4).

The role of the religious shaikh as arbitrator, spiritual guardian and leader of his lineage was closely linked with his position in the community. This role, in turn, gave him special access to resources, and hence to improve his position as a big man in the lineage or region. How did his spiritual leadership enhance the wealth and resources upon which his position as big man depended?

In return for the services which the religious shaikh rendered his lineage or lineages, he received a continuous flow of gifts and payments. After every successful harvest, for which the shaikh's rain service or magical stones were believed to be responsible, the cultivator was expected to take one-twelfth of his crop (one *kaila* in every *ardeb*, to his religious shaikh. When a man or any one of his close relatives was sick, they would be taken to the shaikh for treatment. Those concerned were supposed to make an initial payment called *biad*, and then leave a deferred payment called *hadiya* (present) till the patient was cured. The fee might not be paid at once, but deferred until the client could afford it, in periods of plenty and economic prosperity. When there was epidemic animal disease, a man would come to the religious shaikh to promise him a gift if his animals were unharmed or cured. If a man lost some of his property because of theft, he could come to the shaikh promising to pay him so much if he would find his lost property. Or, if a man was to appear before a court, especially in cases of homicide, his relatives might approach a religious shaikh, usually the lineage shaikh, and promise him a gift should his intervention enable their relative to win the case. Finally, a shaikh or a number of shaikhs who were arbitrators in a dispute, especially homicide, would be given a quarter of the *diya* (Reid 1930), a payment which was central to the distinctive qualities of the religious shaikh and to his role as arbitrator. The *diya* was £100 or, traditionally, 100 camels or cattle.

This continuous flow of gifts and payments underwrote the position of the shaikh as a big man. Like many other ummar he was able to establish himself as an owner of both a large capital of livestock and grain stores. The social category of *ummar gabila*, including the shaikhs, was distinguished from others by two factors: the ownership of large herds of animals, sometimes numbering several hundred, and the possession of big storage pits (*matamir*) in which the threshed grain was deposited. Among the Amriya lineage, for example, there was one shaikh, Muhammed Wadal Haj Musa, who came from the Aramab lineage of the Hissinat. There were also at least five *ummar gabila*, two of whom became wealthy traders. The development of the amir into a wealthy trader involved changes of degree rather than kind. It meant simply that the amir's wealth became sufficient for him to acquire huge storage pits of grain and a larger surplus with which to undertake grain marketing and storage. This type of big man is especially interesting because his emergence is rooted in the uncertainty of the environment and in the delicate balance between livestock rearing and crop cultivation.

The decisive factor promoting the *ummar gabila* in their various orders lay in the ownership of large heards of livestock as capital.

Most people among the Kawahla owned animals but only in small numbers. In times of famine or hardship these either perished quickly or were insufficient to meet the required level of subsistence especially when, due to a crop failure, the demand for animal's milk for subsistence was high. As a result, people who had no animals, or those whose stock were few or had perished, would be compelled to attach themselves to those who had a surplus and these were most frequently the ummar.

Big men did not arise out of an *a priori* cleavage in the ownership of land. For there was much evidence that land was never a scarce commodity among the Kawahla (Reid 1930). As I have shown earlier, land had been divided among the various lineages since the time of the Hassaniya chiefs, Keiwat and Shelai. Although these chiefs took the especially fertile land and a relatively bigger share for themselves and for their lineage, nevertheless, as Petherick (1869) reported, there was always ample uncultivated land among the Kawahla, though this was more likely to be rainland than riverland. The lack of special pressure on land was shown also by the relatively high percentage of land owned by strangers for example, non-Kawahla, which had been given freely to them by the Kawahla either for payment or as gifts, especially to those who were affinally connected to the original owners of the land. I have shown also that the Hassaniya in particular were not great enthusiasts for *goz* cultivation. This is another indicator of the relative relaxation of pressures on other categories of land as well.

The position of the big man did not derive exclusively from his management of many livestock, but depended also on his ability to develop another resource, the *matamir*. Either by barter or by selling some of his livestock, an amir could exchange some of his livestock for a number of slaves which were a form of both capital and labour. Slavery as a legal institution was banned in the late 1920s, around 1928. However, where their lords could afford to support them, slaves preferred to stay with them. They continued to supply an economic function, only now their bond to their masters was voluntary rather than obligatory.

Slaves allowed the amir to secure a big yield every year, for, even if there was poor rainfall, by having a source of labour under his command the amir could sow a large area and so compensate for the relatively low productivity of the land. Slaves thus offset deficiencies in the productivity of land in a particular year; extensively, by sowing a large area; intensively by resowing a crop if it was destroyed by pests or an unexpected early drought.

As I have shown, it was not the ability to summon a *nafir* for the levelling of *terus* which set its limit but the ability of a man to carry out the later activities, that is sowing, grass-clearing and harvest. The number of dependants which a man could draw on, his slaves or members of his extended family, was a more critical factor in that it controlled the labour required for extensive or intensive cultivation.

The amir could also use his livestock in the contraction of more marriages to acquire a large following of dependants. I have already discussed the institutional arrangements regarding marriage, and shown that if a man was the head of an extended family his wealth was being constantly drained by the continual outflow of gifts accompanying the marriages of both his daughters and sons. These costs related the number of marriages to the assumed relative size of a man's wealth. The majority of people among the Kawahla married one, two or at best three women; the big men and especially the shaikhs, were able to contract a much larger number of marriages. One shaikh, Al-Sammani, of Ja'aliyin stock, married more than 22 women. Many members of the Gushgushab ruling lineage had more than ten women; one of them more than twenty. Among the Amriya, two ummar had married more than seven women, and one had begotten a very large number of children.

Agricultural production among the Kawahla involved four main phases of crop cultivation: the preparation of the land, sowing the seeds, hoeing and weeding, and lastly, harvesting. Big men, with seeds and a guaranteed source of labour at their command (slaves and dependants), would be able to finish the first three activities earlier than the commoners, and would be in a good position to benefit from the relative idleness of the latter during the harvesting, particularly since commoners' fields would not yet be ready for the same sort of labour.

In addition to the slaves and his immediate dependants, an amir was entitled to summon a *nafir* (work-party) like anybody else. He was not only entitled to that help which was an institutionalized right but also had a claim to service from those whom he fed and would feed in times of future hardship. He might be more able then to benefit from work-parties than anybody else, because he could afford to feed many people during the feasts accompanying them, especially at times of hardship when grain was scarce.

The big man was thus more likely to manipulate or withstand effectively, the environmental uncertainties of the region, particularly the fluctuating rainfall. I have shown earlier that there were many risks involved in rain cultivation and these risks, endemic to crop cultivation among the White Nile Arabs, were more likely to be withstood if one had animals or grain stores to rely on. I have also suggested that an amir's wealth could enable him to enter the risky business of grain-marketing.

The general pattern of grain-marketing depended on manipulating the fluctuating annual production, for people had come to realize the possibility of famine or general food shortage. Why then did they not take the initiative of buying the crop at a low price when there was a surplus in good years, and accumulate it for the difficult years when the price would be very high? Only the ummar with resources could afford to do this. It was made profitable by the institution of *shail*, or borrowing. According to *shail*, a man could come and borrow a certain amount of grain from the big man. The total cost of the borrowed grain was calculated according to the current market price. When the debtor returned the crop he had to return *the amount whose total cost would be equivalent to the total cost of the originally borrowed grain.* The general ebb and flow of borrowing and settling of accounts accompanied the general pattern of variable economic production, so that people generally borrowed at times of hardship and settled their accounts at time of plenty. Since the price was higher when borrowed, the amir was able to receive back a larger amount of grain than he initially lent.

In these market-transactions the big man was not confined to his lineage members but had also a wider network of trans-lineage and trans-tribal commercial relations. He would have become bankrupt if he had depended mainly on his own lineage members because, owing to the wider reciprocity and exchanges carried out inside the lineage, most of his kin would be receiving cooked food from him. The grain trade extended throughout the region and outside it to such towns as Khartoum and Omdurman.

The most important point was that the big man's transactions outside his lineage were exclusively commercial. The reciprocal exchange reflected in the *shail* institution was, in Sahlins' terms, negative reciprocity, or a tendency to get something for nothing with impunity (Sahlins, p. 165). It was essentially a relation between political equals and offered no opportunities of dominance or the assumption of authority. Therefore trans-lineage, trans-tribal relations were mainly commercial, voluntary and non-alliance oriented.

However, between the *amir gabila* and his fellow lineage members a general pattern of both interactional and transactional[3] reciprocity existed which governed overall lineage relations more clearly: in terms of Sahlins' refinement of Polanyi's scheme (see Sahlins 1965, pp. 151–2) this involved both 'generalized' and 'balanced' reciprocity. Food might be freely exchanged throughout the entire lineage and the big man's guest house (or men's house) would be the lodging place for the needy and the poor. In times of famine and hardship the amir shared the responsibility with other lineage mates to help the needy 'withstand the difficult year' (*yemrogo min al-sana*). Thus his animals would be distributed as manayih among those who happened to have fewer animals or none.

In most of these reciprocal relations one could find traces of both 'generalized' and 'balanced' reciprocity. Thus, for example, tenets of the *quid pro quo* which was characteristic of 'balanced' reciprocity could be seen in the fact that by feeding a commoner, the amir could have him working in his fields at that time or later, or by giving him some animals to live on, the amir would expect him to rear the animals and seek good pastures and water holes and to return them in a healthy state together with any offspring the animals had had. Like all other lineage members, the big man also benefited from belonging to herding partnerships in which he could exchange labour opportunities, and camping partnerships in which common security was provided. The fact that he had more animals than others perhaps made him more conscious of a debt to the communal defence of the lineage, especially in a hostile situation. The amir, who had more animals than others, was the most likely target for security-disrupting factors.

However, the obligation to reciprocate was not always so clear and the amir was expected to offer instant and occasional help to

---

[3] See Bailey 1969, pp. 36–7, for this distinction.

his poorer lineage mates without any explicit or direct material return – a characteristic of generalized reciprocity. Thus, he was expected to offer occasional gifts, for example, some *kailas* of *dura* or some animals to the very poor or to suddenly bankrupted lineage mates. If there was any expectation to reciprocate it was vaguely on the understanding that he would do something about it when an opportunity arose. It was a pattern, to put it in Morton Fried's words, 'of those who can, give and continue to give . . . those who need, take and continue to take' (Fried 1967).

It was clear that the notable attained a special position in his lineage, that he was the focal point in this pattern of reciprocal relationships and the social functionary on whom the solidarity of his group was based. The centrality of his position in the social structure was underwritten by the environmental hazards which made an attachment to an amir a built-in method of insurance against such contingencies as crop failure or animal fatality.

The following account, written by an educated Amriya informant, gives a vivid impression of the rise of a typical Amriya big man – Muhammad Ali Idris (*c.* 1860–1950).[4]

Muhammad Ali was a man of wisdom and vision. He was an able, mighty man; a man of accepted word among the Amriya. He was the only leader of this group. He was 95 when he died. It is now 20 years since his death. Muhammad Ali owned a lot of money. They say he managed to own this money during the Mahdiya, especially during the Khalifa Abdullahi's reign – for he was adviser to the Khalifa in Omdurman. People say that after the battle of Omdurman, Muhammad Ali came to this land with a lot of gold. He bought quantities of grain and built storage pits for it. During famine, he used to distribute grain or hand it out to all the groups even to non-Amriya. As a matter of fact, many groups such as the Iraifab, Ja'aliyin, Gur, Ahamda, Humran, Shamkhia, Gushgushab, Nimrab and others used to come and borrow grain from Muhammad Ali.

He was a father, a guardian and a leader of this group, the Amriya. In his reign, the Amriya were very strong in that they were respected and feared by other tribes. Any intruder or trespasser on Amriya land was beaten up by our gang (*isaba*). What Muhammad Ali liked most were the bodyguards. He used to give them a free hand in many respects. He owned many slaves, males and females – today there are three of them.

---

[4] This case is given to illustrate the position and role of one of the big men and is fairly typical of most.

Muhammad Ali also owned some boats for crossing the river, always ready for public use. But anyone from our group who used other boats than Muhammad Ali's was fined by him. If any one of us needed money for an urgent matter, Muhammad Ali was the man who was always ready to give that money.

But Muhammad Ali loved two things: the collection of money and the storage of grain. He used to build sheds in the local markets and collect fees from the users. His slaves and gangsters would punish anyone who refused to pay. Moreover, no one could build a shed in the market without the approval of Muhammad Ali (a token of payment had to be made). It did happen once that some shed owners refused to pay and Muhammad Ali called on his gangsters and his kin who demolished most of the sheds. They were stopped by Muhammad Ali himself only when the shed owners agreed to pay on the spot.

There is also an interesting thing about Muhammad Ali. It is said that when there was a death in any other group he used to summon most of the Amriya and say '*Muhammad Ali fi el furash*', that is 'here is Muhammad Ali going to the mourning place, collect what you can pay and bring it to me here'. When the group's money was brought for him, he used to add a lump sum of money from his own pocket. At the mourning place, he used to give the money to the people concerned and say 'Here is the Amriya contribution'. This was always the case, whether in mourning, marriage, etc. See how we were united and how we acted as one man at that time. What a big difference is life today!

Nevertheless, the security of the amir himself was mainly relative, for environmental insecurity affected him as well. In terms of the protection of property, the fact that he had more wealth than others would tend to make him dependent on collective defence. Thus the powerful Amriya amir, Muhammad Ali Idris, is quoted as saying '*in ma akalna sa'aligna sa'alig al-gair bi takulna*', literally, 'if we didn't feed our *sa'alig* (commoners, jobless, workless), those of others would eat us'.

These factors were very important in understanding the real position of the big man, for he emerged as a special sort of political leader. His position was endorsed with an enormous show of respect for his person and for his word. He emerged as a lineage spokesman in communications with other lineages. A lineage without an amir was referred to as '*ma' indaha kabir*', for example, 'it has no wealthy elder', and thought of as an odd case to communicate with. For as I have shown, the ummar were generally approached in any matter concerning their lineages. In Rousseau's sense, they appeared as representing the 'will of all' of their lineages and had a vital interest to preserve that will. Inside the lineage, they acted as strong arbitrators and their judgment was profoundly respected and usually accepted.

The ummar were also given the consent of the lineage to act on its behalf in any matters involving other lineages. The degree to which an amir would assume this authority depended on his social and economic power and the number of other ummar like him. His ability to mobilize the lineage in general political action depended on his capacity to convince the lineage that the action to be taken was in the common lineage interest.

The most significant role of the ummar was to act as spokesmen or representatives for their lineages in the tribal council (meglis) of elders which was summoned wherever there were inter-lineage issues requiring discussion and settlement. The council, usually referred to as *nas shura*, 'people of consent', or *agawid*, 'arbitrators', was a longstanding and important organ of Kawahla political life in the region. Even during the era of Keiwat, the strongest and most respected leader, the tribal land was distributed by him and the elders of the various lineages. A report in the administrative files[5] at Dueim entitled, 'Sidelights on Hassaniya-Hissinat History and Tribal Organization', comments on this:

In contrast to the more powerful Kababish the Hassaniya chief has nearly always had permanent *agawid*. . . . At the present time there are well-known *agawid* for each section and in addition certain acknowledged holy men who deal with difficult points of Sharia law.

In the next chapter it will be shown that despite the continuing attempts of the colonial administration to centralize the administrative machinery, the role of the big men and the council remained virtually unchanged during the entire pre-dam period. After an important council meeting at Geteina in 1927 to select a paramount chief (nazir), the district commissioner reported,[6]

during the recent meglis at Geteina the fact that we had fairly complete information as to the *agawid* or *nas shura* of the tribes concerned proved of great assistance. I refer of course to *nas shura* exclusive

---

[5] Administrative Files, Dueim (66.D.2.12, 20 October 1927).
[6] Administrative Files, Dueim (66.F.2.12, 20 October 1927).

of omdas [see Chapter 6]. I think a list of *nas shura* should be kept in every file and there should be in the file the special heading for 'personalities'. Sometimes *nas shura* are more influential than the omdas or shaikhs (see Chapter 4).

In the next chapter a detailed consideration of inter-lineage politics will be made in connection with administrative and political developments during the early part of the Condominium. The main aim in this discussion will be to show the pattern of politics that prevailed together with the role of the ummar and the meglis in inter-lineage and inter-tribal politics before the dam was built.

4

Tribal History and Politics in the Pre-Dam Period

In this chapter a brief account of the early political history of the Hassaniya and other Kawahla will be presented with emphasis upon the main features of the Hassaniya polity and political leadership in the pre-Condominium era. Against this background, I proceed to discuss the administrative and political developments which occurred during the early part of colonial rule, that is, in the pre-dam period. These developments affected the legal structure of the tribal polity rather than the basic features of that polity. Real changes in the political structure became evident only in the latter period of colonial rule, during the 1930s and afterwards, that is, after the dam had been built.

EARLY HISTORY AND POLITICS OF THE HASSANIYA
AND OTHER KAWAHLA IN THE WHITE NILE[1]

The Northern Sudan is today the homeland of a great number of tribes claiming Arab origin and descent. They are thought to have migrated from Arabia to the Sudan through several routes of which the most important and widely used were those through the Red Sea in the east, and through Egypt in the north. The Arab population of the Sudan is commonly classified into three groups: the Ja'alyin, the Juhayna and the Kawahla. This division is based on their alleged common descent and origin in Arabia.

The history of the Arabs in the Sudan dates as far back as the pre-Islamic period, but the history of the Kawahla tribes and the Hassaniya in particular is a relatively recent one. Muhammad Awad Muhhamad (1951) suggests that the Kawahla must have moved to the Sudan during the eleventh century A.D. or thereabouts. He considers that all the Kawahla migrated to the Sudan

---

[1] For more information on the history of the Kawahla and the Hassaniya see MacMichael 1912, 1922, Muhammad 1951, Yusuf F. Hassan 1967, Petherick 1861, 1889, and Reid 1930.

through the Red Sea, and that they settled with the Beja for some time and then moved to the White Nile and to other parts of the Sudan. Some of the Kawahla tribes, particularly the Hissinat, accept this view. The Hassaniya, however, do not and say that they migrated to the Sudan through Egypt and before moving to the White Nile settled first in Jebel al-Jilif, a well-known place in the Bayuda Desert, west of the White Nile near Shendi. The movement of the Hassaniya to the White Nile seems to have been caused by a conflict with the Abdallab rulers of the northern part of the Funj Kingdom. The Hassaniya maintain that a certain Abdallab chief, called Agib al-Manguluk (1589–1611),[2] virtually crushed them by a surprise attack because they refused to pay him tribute. Accordingly, it may be calculated that the Hassaniya move to the White Nile took place at the beginning of the seventeenth century. They chose to move to the White Nile possibly because some of their 'cousin' tribes were already there. The other Kawahla moved into the White Nile region in about the sixteenth century. They dwelt to the south of Jebel Awliya as far down as Abu Hugar on the east bank of the White Nile.

When the Hassaniya came to the White Nile they found that the land to the south of their 'cousins' was inhabited by a multitude of tribes, such as the Massalimiya, the Kurtan, the Khanafra, the Dueih and others. The Hassaniya were said to have been diplomatic in their relations with these 'host' tribes and managed to rent land from them. They seem to have been a submissive, poor and disorganized people who did not seem to be related to one another. As they grew in power, however, through their increasing numbers and further immigration from the north, they rebelled against their host tribes by refusing to pay tribute and by claiming ownership of the land. This rebellion was led by their first heroic and charismatic leader, Keiwat, whose emergence had the function of unifying these formerly disorganized groups of kin – the Hassaniya and the Kawahla in general. In response, the host tribes united under a leader, Feteihat, who was said to have belonged to the Massalimiya tribe. They sought help from the Kunjara cousins, the Massaba'at, who were rulers in Kordofan on behalf of the Kunjara, the Sultans who established the Funj

---

[2] For information on this Abdallab chief see Shibaika 1964, pp. 48–9.

G

Sultanate in 1596. Different stories are told today of the way in which Keiwat managed to win the support of the Massaba'at against the disappointed host tribes and defeat them. This, together with the role of the Hassaniya leader, Keiwat, is reported by Reid (1930) who describes various stories telling of the qualities and attributes ascribed to the Hassaniya leader Keiwat: his bravery, alertness and outstanding diplomacy. This incident was such that today a Hassanit tribesman, confronted with difficulty or a problem in his day-to-day life, will be heard to say '*ya gbarat Keiwat alai feteihat*', meaning literally, 'Oh, Keiwat's determined victory over Feteihat'.

After this victory, Keiwat made his first approach on behalf of his people to the Funj Sultan, presumably to Badi Abu Digin.[3] He is said to have taken 20 mares to the Sultan as a present and as recognition of his power. He also promised to pay the Sultan tribute from time to time. In return the Sultan endorsed Keiwat's chieftainship and gave him a *wasiqa* (certificate) entitling him in person and on behalf of his people to the ownership of a clearly demarcated area of land. The boundaries of this land appear to have been Abu Hugar and Wadi Afu in the north, and Goz Marfa'eib just to the north of Tura's al-Khadra. Hence, this demarcated land came to be known as Bahr Keiwat, that is, Keiwat's river. Keiwat and the ummar of the various lineages were said to have distributed this land in tribal blocks between the various lineages, according to the size of their membership and, hence, their ability to cultivate. Each lineage was given a block of land running east to west and including both river and rainland for cultivation and livestock herding.

Keiwat was supposed to have paid an occasional tribute on agricultural land which was known as *sharia*, amounting to one-tenth of the crop, but it seems that this tribute was collected only from strangers, non-Hassaniya. The *sharia* tribute on agricultural land was claimed to be separate from the tribute collected and paid to the Funj Sultans from time to time. This latter was collected in animals and presented to the Sultan in Sennar by Keiwat. There was no indication, however, that this tribute to the Sultan was paid in a regular form, nor was there any developed or clearly set procedure for its collection. It was mainly an *ad hoc* matter.

---

[3] This diplomatic move is also reported by Reid 1930.

EXTERNAL RELATIONS DURING KEIWAT'S ERA

Keiwat was not only a 'statesman', but also an enactor of 'foreign policy'. His role as a political leader and his responsibility to defend his people's security dictated a move at the regional level. Being surrounded by hostile tribes which he was able to drive to the south and south-west, he was anxious to secure his frontiers on all other sides by building up good relations with his neighbours.

Starting with the other Kawahla tribes neighbouring on the north, or specifically the Hissinat, he was able to build an impressive Kawahla bloc. Its political leadership has since then become highly interconnected. The bloc was based on the ideology of common descent, of being '*awlad'am*', that is, 'cousins'. Most importantly, it was based on a loosely structured reciprocal or transactional pattern of political and religious leadership.

The other Kawahla were far less organized militarily than the Hassaniya. To begin with, they were relatively dispersed. Secondly, they lacked the strong political leadership of the Hassaniya. They had no *fursan* (horsemen) comparable to the Hassaniya team headed by their competent leader, Keiwat. The Hissinat, the second most powerful group after the Hassaniya, were led by a religious group belonging to the Kashashib section of the Aramab lineage. They were shaikhs, holy men, known as *fugara*. Like the Somali shaikhs, or saints, of North Africa, their power was mainly spiritual, derived from their piety, miraculous power and their mediation before God as saints of Islam. The role of religious shaikhs has been discussed in detail above in Chapter 3. As we saw, they were not rulers so much as arbitrators depending to a great extent on religious sanctions and their lineage status. Among the Hissinat themselves, however, they had very considerable powers.

A pattern of transactional religious and military leadership developed between the religious heads of the Hissinat and Keiwat, the leader of the Hassaniya. Because of the values attached to their religious standing as arbitrators and men of peace, the religious men disengaged themselves from fighting in the tribal conflicts and disputes which were frequent. In military defence they depended heavily upon the *faza'a*, help given to their tribe by Keiwat and his *fursan*. One context in which this aid was given will be examined presently. But *faza'a*, as the Kawahla use the term, did not mean only physical aid but could mean also spiritual aid. This was given by the Hissinat religious leaders to Keiwat in return for his military aid. It is said that they gave him the *fatha*, the religious blessings which were extremely important for military victory, for fighting morale, and for activating Keiwat's *gubara*, that is, his predetermined success. This was the essence of Keiwat's diplomatic policy and the source of his political acumen among the Kawahla. The reciprocal political and religious leadership that he established between the Hassaniya and the Hissinat continued until the middle of this century, around the 1940s and 1950s, when the socio-economic conditions created by the institution of the dam and the accompanying administrative policy led the Hissinat religious shaikhs to rebel against the political leadership of the Hassaniya (see Chapter 8).

With the neighbouring Kababish to the west, Keiwat reached an agreement regarding their common boundaries. This remained for some time a source of occasional conflict between the Hassaniya and the Kababish. It was expressed in Keiwat's famous judgment: 'west of the shadow of this hill thy Dar, and east of it my Dar' (Reid 1930), the reference being to the hill known as Jebel al-Tain which thereafter became the traditional boundary of Dar Hassaniya. Keiwat was worried also about the rising power of the Jumu'iya tribe which was adjacent to his cousin Kawahla tribes to the north. He accordingly implemented a mutual defence treaty. This was based on their combined oath, '*yarbutna habil wa yagtaana saif*', that is, literally, 'we shall be tied together by one rope, to be cut together by one sword'. Unfortunately, however, Keiwat soon broke his oath when he recognized that it was difficult for him to manoeuvre easily within this network of bilateral agreements. Presently, a conflict arose between the Hissinat and the Jumu'iya. Keiwat at first played the role of peacemaker, but the Jumu'iya refused to listen to him. In this critical situation, Keiwat did not seek a solution but allied his forces with the Hissinat. In this decision he was influenced not only by the fact that the Hissinat were his 'cousins', but also by the fact that since the Jumu'iya would not accept his authority, he might be the next victim for Jumu'iya invasion. His decision, to stand with the Hissinat, was based not only on his moral commitment to his cousins, the Hissinat, therefore, but also on pragmatic calculations of possible Jumu'iya strategy.

Many informants told me that this conflict between the Jumu'iya and the Hassaniya was the source of the famous proverb '*la taman al-Hassani wainkan garib buldani*', that is, 'you should not trust the Hassani even if he be a stranger to your land'. Sometimes this proverb is completed with a corollary '*in taman al-Hassani taman al-marfaeib ali gana al-dani*', 'if you trust the Hassani you are trusting the hyena with the lamb'.

From these events it is evident that Hassaniya political history was never a narrow, isolated or inward-looking one. The political leadership of the Kawahla tribes had been closely related since their early settlement in the White Nile, and the Hassaniya leader was not only a leader in his own tribe but also an initiator of foreign policy.

THE HASSANIYA LEADERSHIP AFTER KEIWAT

The era of Keiwat is likely to have been somewhere between 1610 and 1710. Many informants told me that Keiwat's son, Khogali, assumed the Hassaniya leadership after his father, but there is no information about Khogali and so it is doubtful that he assumed leadership. Khogali's elder son, Shelai, however, was a prominent leader and stands on an equal footing with Keiwat in Hassaniya political history. Shelai was reported to be the Hassaniya leader up to the advent of the Turkish régime in the Sudan in 1821. Some writers have even mentioned him as the chief for some time during the Turko-Egyptian régime (Reid 1930).

Shelai was known as *abu-al-Afia*, that is, father of Afia, his daughter. He was represented in Hassaniya traditions as an unbeatable warrior. Many stories are told today of how he alone fought various people. Shelai's prominence in Hassaniya political history was due mainly to the fact that he consolidated Hassaniya supremacy in the White Nile and made possible their permanent occupation of their present habitat.

In Shelai's time the multitude of tribes, which had been driven away by Keiwat to the south and the south-west of Hassaniya land, reorganized themselves and formed a powerful army. Shelai tried to gain political concessions from them but they refused and made it clear that there was no alternative but for Shelai and his tribe to move out of the White Nile. The matter became even more complex and critical for Shelai when a branch of the Hissinat tribe joined the threatening enemy. The details of this, however, are not clear. People say that they were members of the Shatawiya lineage of the Hissinat who had moved and settled in Dar Baggara to the south of Dar Hassaniya since early times. This pattern of Hissinat dispersal has been mentioned. They came in conflict with the Jimiya tribe living there, as a result of which they were driven out. Under a leader called Asha wad Biaishim, they moved towards their collateral cousins in the north. On the way, however, the Hassaniya's enemy welcomed them warmly and offered them refuge and a means of livelihood. In return, the Shatawiya were put on oath by their hosts ('*yarbutna habil wa yagtaana saif*', 'to be tied together with one rope'), presumably before the hosts declared openly their intentions of hostility towards the Hassaniya. Shelai tried hard to get the Shatawiya excluded from the conflict which ensued, by asking the Hissinat religious leaders to mediate with their Shatawiya cousins under their leader, Asha. The most prominent Hissinat religious leader at that time was Muhammed al-Aghbash. Al-Asha refused his arbitration and said to Muhammed al-Aghbash, 'if this finger [referring to his own finger] could be separated into two parts, I would then separate from these people' (meaning the Hassaniya's enemy). The alliance between Asha and the Hassaniya enemy was known as *um-Imais*, a word connoting brutality. They abused the Hassaniya with the taunt '*nihna um-Imais al-mabnindar nakutl alzul nasido humar*', literally meaning, 'we are *um-Imais*, the unwanted; we would kill a person and pay a donkey for him as *diya*'.

Finally, Shelai fought these tribes near Tura'a al-Khadra in a fierce battle known as *um-Imais*. The Hassaniya, owing to Shelai's military leadership and Muhammed al-Aghbash's spiritual backing, were able to inflict a complete defeat on their enemy. For a long time after this battle the Hassaniya used to filter the water of Tura'a al-Khadra, a well-known stream or water course to the north of Dueim, before being able to drink it.

The battle showed that Kawahla kinship obligations which demanded that cousins help each other against external threats, were not always fulfilled. Asha stood with *um-Imais* against the Hassaniya, and Muhammed al-Aghbash stood with Shelai against Asha. Muhammed al-Aghbash was asked his reasons for giving Shelai the *fatha*, spiritual blessing, in preference to his cousin, Asha. He replied, '*mab nafut rufag umshaba*', that is, 'we shall not separate from um-Shaba's companions'. Um-Shaba' was the place

where the battle between the Jumu'iya and the Hissinat was said
to have taken place, and Muhammed al-Aghbash was referring
here to Keiwat's aid.

After this battle, of *um-Imais*, the amount of Hassaniya land was
increased. More Hassaniya came from the north to settle in a
pattern roughly similar to their present distribution. The movements of the Hassaniya in small numbers to the White Nile, however, together with the wide gaps between movements have
increasingly produced a more loosely structured relation of kinship between the various sections (*furua*) of the tribes. This is
illustrated by the *um-Imais* battle.

Shelai produced a title deed from the Funj Sultans showing the
redefined boundaries of the Hassaniya land. The southern limit
was Khor abu-Gasaba to the south of Ed-dueim town. The
eastern limit was *had al-la'outa min al-kitra*, which is a term given
to two kinds of trees. The limit was the natural division which
occurred between them. The northern and western boundaries
remained as they had been. The whole strip of land thus comprised came to be known as Dar Shelai. The deed from the Funj
Sultans, who were mainly titular heads at that time, entitled
Shelai to the personal ownership of the Hassaniya land. This was,
however, a general procedure during the Funj Sultanate. Shelai
was said also to have managed to collect tribute from strangers in
his land.

THE TURKISH GOVERNMENT AND THE KAWAHLA CONFEDERATION (1821–85)

The Turkish Government found that Bushara, Shelai's son, was a
leading figure among the Hassaniya. Among the Hissinat and
other Kawahla there emerged some other forceful characters who
received authority from their tribes to collect tribute for the Funj
Sultans. Unlike the Hassaniya chiefs, however, they had no right
to any separate personal tribute based on agricultural land. They
were primarily mediators between their tribes and the Funj rulers.
Among the Hissinat the religious shaikhs chose these personnel
from cousins who were not religious in vocation. As they were
tax collectors, and tax collection was generally an ad-hoc matter,
they had no official status. Among the Hissinat, for example, this
tax collection was delegated by the religious shaikhs to one,
Muhammed, nicknamed *karafiu*, a type of bitter local beer

which he used to drink to excess. The Turkish Government, however, was interested primarily in establishing an effective system of taxation. They recognized the standing of these delegates among the Urwab and the Hissinat and gave them the official title of Agha. They were made responsible for tax collection and were paid for their services with part of what they collected.

At the start, Turkish policy was to create larger administrative units known as *Khutut*, literally, lines, each *khat* (the singular of *khutut*) being headed by *shaikh-khat*. The *khat* consisted usually of an agglomerate of tribes brought together under the chief of the dominant tribe.

A *khat* among the Kawahla comprised all its tribes, together with strangers in the Kawahla Dar. The office of the *shaikh-khat* was given to Bashara, the Hassaniya chief. The Aghas of the different tribes under him were asked to pay him tribute. Together with the *shaikh-khat* office, the Turks established some elements of bureaucratic structure. Certain clerical functionaries were appointed and trained to deal with matters such as records, files and payment of taxes. They worked under the chief to whom the taxes were really paid. The Turkish Government instituted a Sharia court, applying the principles of Islamic jurisprudence to aspects of family law. Since, however, people were and still are inclined to deal with these aspects of life in traditional terms rather than by taking them to court, the effects of such innovations have been slight.

The main innovation occurred in the structure of authority. The tribes were brought together within a formal framework and the Hassaniya as well as the non-Hassaniya were subjected to the authority of the instituted paramount chief. He became, as a result, the focus of intrigues and plots by competing chiefs and notables of other tribes and tribal sections.

As I have mentioned, both Keiwat and Shelai used to collect tribute from strangers in their Dar. Under the Turko-Egyptian Government, however, taxation became a severe imposition and no one could pay both the government and the chief. Bushara, like many other tribal chiefs in the other parts of Sudan, responded by collecting an amount higher than that fixed by the government. The extra payment went into his own pocket as a substitute for a separate tribute. The competing leaders found in this a means of ensnaring the Hassaniya chief. They exerted pressure upon the clerical officials, presumably by bribing them since it was well known that these government officials were corrupt (see Petherick 1861, 1889, and MacMichael 1912), and devised a court case against Bushara accusing him of 'eating' the government money by collecting taxes twice. Bushara was found guilty, fined heavily and imprisoned in Khartoum, where he died.

After this purge, the office of *shaikh-khat* among the Kawahla fell to the highest bidder. It was assumed to have been taken by Wad Gar-al-Nabi of the Urwab tribe. But Wad Gar-al-Nabi was not able to exert his authority over the Hassaniya. He sent a team headed by a close relative to collect taxes from the Hassaniya which was attacked by members of the Gushgushab lineage. Wad Gar-al-Nabi's relative was killed. In reprisal the government took many Gushgushab to Khartoum and imprisoned them. Soon another competitor and challenger to the Urwab chief appeared in the shape of Abu al-Hassan of the Hissinat tribe. He accused the Wad Gar-al-Nabi of intentionally provoking the Hassaniya by making plots (*fitna*) and thus causing the government trouble. The government appointed Abu al-Hassan as *shaikh-khat*. But Abu al-Hassan encountered the same fate when a relative of his, heading a team to collect taxes from the Hassaniya, was killed by the Amriya lineage who were close neighbours of the Gushgushab. This case, however, was settled by *afu*, or pardon, soon after the intervention of the Hissinat religious shaikhs.

Meanwhile Bushara's elder son, Nimir, was pursuing a court case in Khartoum, claiming ownership of the Hassaniya Dar. He said, 'whatever happens to the chieftainship, I want my Dar'. Clerical officials in Khartoum may have been bribed by the non-Hassaniya chief to hide Nimir's *wasiqa*, certificate, claiming the land ownership. It does seem that Nimir bribed the chief of the officials, Abdel Gadir Basha, by registering in his personal name a wide strip of the Hassaniya land, some part of which is still owned by his descendants.

So Nimir was made chief of the Hassaniya, and the office of *shaikh-khat* was abolished. Nimir registered a wide strip of very fertile river land in his name and called it *Kursi-Nimir*, 'Nimir's chair'. He managed to collect the traditional tribute from the strangers and the non-resident Hassaniya. However, again Nimir was accused by the clerical officials of collecting taxes twice. The court fined him heavily and took away his chieftainship. The chieftainship appears to have been occupied for some time by Wad Magboul of the Hassaniya Magawir lineage. This was close to the end of the Turkish rule in Sudan and the rise of the Mahdiya, however, so that there is no account available of his role.

In contrast to the Funj Sultanate, the Turkish Government had tried hard to bring the White Nile under its control. It established a garrison in the south of the Hassaniya land near Dueim town, and had a patrol of soldiers known as *bas-busug* constantly employed to safeguard peace. This was a primary factor in the establishment of a degree of stability which had not previously existed. The White Nile was the bridge to the western and southern Sudan and it was vital to the government for administrative, military and trade purposes.

THE MAHDIYA ERA (1885–98)

When the Mahdist Rebellion broke out, Nimir's three sons, Abdel Gadir, Muhammad and Nasser, were among the first prominent tribal figures to give it support. Nasser, in particular, declared his support when the Mahdi's movement was still in an embryonic form on Aba Island. Nasser's mother was a former slave, by the name of Bit al-Barrum. She was living in Aba Island with her father's people when the Mahdi declared his opposition towards Turkish rule. When the Mahdi fled to Gadir after having defeated the Turkish soldiers in Aba Island in his first engagement, Abdel Gadir joined him there and swore allegiance to him (*bia'*). In the Mahdi's battles against the government which followed, Nimir's three sons were among the Mahdi's prominent horsemen (*fursan*). When the Mahdi moved with his troops from El-Obied to Omdurman, all the Hassaniya as well as other Kawahla joined them. Abdel Gadir was made *Amir-Amura*, Chief Amir of all the Kawahla troops. Under him were many Amirs, two from the Hassaniya, three from the Hissinat and one from each of the Urwab and the Mohammadiya.

Soon after the death of the Mahdi and the establishment of his rule in Omdurman, Abdel Gadir died of smallpox. His next senior brother, Muhammad, assumed the office of *Amir-Amura*. He was sent by the Khalifa, Abduallahi, the Mahdi's successor, to Galabat, where a battle with the Ethiopians took place. Muhammad died during the course of that battle and Nasser, the next eldest brother became Amir-Amura.

However, Nasser was said to have involved himself in a conflict with Khalifa Abduallahi. Nasser was a very strong character, and an extremely courageous and able knight. His extraordinary bravery and combat power were believed to have been no less than that of the early chiefs honoured by the Hassaniya, Keiwat and Shelai. Some said that Nasser was even greater than his great-grandfather, Shelai, for while Shelai was a man to whom you could speak and look at, it was impossible to look Nasser in the face when addressing him.

Nasser paid for his heroic personality. Some people, being jealous of Nasser's power, told the Khalifa that Nasser was planning to separate and that he had privately rejected the Khalifa's authority. These intriguers were not named but many hints lead me to believe that it was Wad Habbani, a powerful man from the collateral branch of the Gushgushab chiefly lineage. Wad Habbani was a prime confidant of Nasser and installed as his deputy (*wakil*). Shaikh Yusuf-Habbani, the Hassaniya Nazir during the course of my fieldwork, told me that his father Idris Wad Habbani, Nasser's deputy, said that Nasser used to tell him privately and jokingly that the Turks were coming back and that he was in contact with them, but he would not say whether his father used to report this to the Khalifa.

The Khalifa imprisoned Nasser for some time. A certain Kawahla notable, named Wad al-Kirail, the Urwab Amir, mediated and asked the Khalifa to let Nasser free, saying: 'whatever you think of Nasser he is still the legitimate chief of his people' (Reid 1930, p. 156).

It was not long after Nasser had been set free by the Khalifa that he was killed by a random Hawawir raid upon Hassaniya cattle. The Hawawir were living with the Kababish tribe neighbouring the Hassaniya to the west. The place in which Nasser was killed was known as Id Umgumtur, a cattle-grazing centre to the north of Wad Nimir village. The nearest village to where he was killed was Sangir, hence the Hassaniya's rhyme:

> *Halag tair alai Sangir*
> *Kitil Nasser Abu al-Igail*
>
> Birds are flying over Sangir
> For Nasser, Igail's father, has been killed.

Before Nasser was killed by the Hawawir, a rhyme was recited by his female slaves:

> *Ya ahal Naima haraito*
> *Nasser ga laibaito*
>
> You cowards at Naima
> Nasser has come back to his home.[4]

This is another reason which led me to believe that accusations regarding the circumstances of Nasser's imprisonment were well directed at Wad Habbani, the man later to become the Hassaniya Nazir under the Condominium government.

Nasser's death occurred just before the Anglo-Egyptian re-occupation of the Sudan. His youngest and last brother, Ibrahim, was wounded with him in the Hawawir raid. When Lord Kitchener, the Condominium General came south on the steamer touring the White Nile, Ibrahim was taken to him on a bed, still suffering from his wounds. However, when the time came for the new government to decide the chieftainship they appointed Wad Habbani and not Ibrahim as the paramount chief or Nazir. The government felt public sentiment was against Ibrahim and against the Nimrab section of the Gushgushab lineage which had assumed Hassaniya political leadership for a considerable time before the Condominium. As I have mentioned, Nasser was tough and severe, and their experience with him made the Hassaniya generally uneasy with the Nimrab branch of the Gushgushab. Nasser was reported to have said, '*Al-Hassaniya hangoog yalin bi aldag*', meaning literally 'the Hassaniya are like the *hangoog* [a sort of handy clearing tool made from a stiff plant which was hit and pressed hard to become manageable], only manageable with hard pressing and work'. Nasser was referring to the growing opposition of the various Hassaniya big men, which culminated in his imprisonment. He constantly disregarded the elders as '*nas shura*', or 'people of consent', but as we shall see in discussing the Hassaniya politics in the Condominium era, it was impossible to disregard *nas shura* in any decisions involving the whole tribe. They were categories of people who used to have great influence over their lineages. It was only during the last two decades or so that they lost a deal of their power and only at this stage did their

---

[4] Wad Habbani was living at Naima village.

role become curtailed by the increasing powers of the instituted administrative chiefs.

ADMINISTRATIVE DEVELOPMENT AND TRIBAL POLITICS DURING THE EARLY PART OF CONDOMINIUM RULE (1900–37)

The new colonial government took as its first task the establishment of law and order, starting in 1905 with the institution of White Nile Province. This had its headquarters at Dueim and sub-district headquarters (*merkaz*), at Dueim, Kawa and Geteina. The administrative head of the province was the governor at Dueim. Helping him were assistant-governors and three commissioners (*maamir*) at the headquarters of the sub-districts. This was the period prior to the policy of devolution known today as *ayam al-maamir*, pre-local government.

TRIBAL ADMINISTRATION AND THE INSTITUTION OF 'SHAIKHSHIPS'

The government saw that its task of establishing law and order could not be accomplished without the assistance of the tribal authorities. It was decided to institute shaikhships (from shaikh, generally elder, but here the term designates the office created) at the level of the tribal sections (*furua*), which have been spoken of as lineages. The main task of the shaikh was to collect taxes, mainly animal-tax, from his kin-group and forward it to the *merkaz*. The means of collection were rudimentary: the shaikh was asked to collect a certain amount fixed by the district commissioner, *mamur* (singular of *maamir*), according to his personal estimation of the wealth of that particular lineage. This amount was paid into a pool by the whole lineage, each man according to the number of his animals and his ability to pay. Usually it was paid on the spot by the lineage big men, including the shaikh himself, and later the other members of the lineage contributed. Strictly speaking, the office was not an innovation amongst the Hassaniya, for they used to pay their taxes or tribute in this way before the Condominium. Nor did it introduce any notion of competition in the lineage for people saw it as *wagib*, a duty on behalf of the lineage, rather than *sulta*, an expression of authority. Usually it was given to the wealthy man in the lineage who could have readily settled the lineage account with the government at any time. This made tax collection relatively convenient both for the people and the government. Most lineages had one shaikh, but some had two or more. Those which had more than one shaikh were those with the greater wealth in animals, both cattle and sheep. We have discussed earlier how ecological conditions separated the pastures and husbandry of cattle and sheep and kept them apart for most of the year. Thus, it was convenient to have one shaikh to collect sheep-tax and another to collect cattle tax. Probably this procedure started after the pre-Condominium period, especially during the Mahdiya when animal-tax was mostly collected in kind rather than in cash. Some big men used to rear one category of animals only, for instance, cattle, so it was convenient for them to pay in cattle. Moreover, people who specialized in cattle could better appraise the taxable wealth of their cattle-rearing fellows.

THE ESTABLISHMENT OF OMODIYAS, NAZIRATES AND THE RISE OF COMPETITION

A second step in creating formal positions of authority, this time at the tribal level, came when the government decided to establish Omodiyas[5] (larger administrative units than Shaikhships). All the tribes in the region were designated as constituting separate Omodiyas and the office of omda was given to whoever appeared to have traditional authority. The omodiya boundaries and tribal boundaries became the same (see Map 2). This matter was settled without much trouble with most of the tribes in the White Nile, except the Hassaniya. Among the Hassaniya there emerged four strong competitors for the office. Firstly, there was Shaikh Ibrahim Nimir, the last son of chief Nimir, of the Turko-Egyptian era, whose three brothers were chief amirs, princes or military leaders, over the Kawahla during the Mahdiya. He saw himself as the legitimate inheritor of his brothers' position.

Secondly, there was Shaikh Idris Adam Habbani who saw his claim to the office based on two factors: that he was the deputy or *wakil* of the late chief Amir Nasser, and that the people did not want Ibrahim Nimir or any one of his family to be a chief. Since

---

[5] Omda is a title given to certain tribal heads since the Turko-Egyptian era (1821–85), usually to heads of tribes of moderate sizes; the administrative units under *Omdas* are spoken of as *omodiyat* to be written here as *omodiyas* or *omodiya-ships*.

both Shaikh Idris and Ibrahim Nimir belonged to the same section of Awlad Khogali of the Gushgushab lineage, he saw himself as the legitimate inheritor of the office.

The third competitor was Shaikh Ali Massalem of the Magawir lineage. His claim rested on his view that tribal leadership was not limited to the Gushgushab lineage in the past and that his father Massalem Wad Magboul was the last chief during the Turko-Egyptian régime. He also claimed that the Hassaniya consisted of two divisions, Gena Muhammad and Gena Teifay, and both the two former competitors were from Gena Teifay and not Gena Muhammad. So, if the government was to recognize one of them as omda, he should be omda only over Gena Teifay, while he himself should be omda over Gena Muhammad. However, Ali Massalem failed to get the approval and backing of the Dabalab lineage as their spokesman for the part of Gena Muhammad. The Dabalab big man abused Ali Massalem, saying mockingly 'it is only now that you come to see us!' The fourth competitor was Shaikh Wad Rugba of the Gulamab lineage. He claimed that his lineage was the strongest lineage among the Hassaniya and that the office should be given to the largest lineage in terms of population.

From the course of this dispute, we can see that each of the four competitors sought justification for his claim on different grounds. Only one exclusively emphasized the inherited legitimacy of the office, the other three claims ranging between modification of the inherited claim to the absolute insignificance of inheritance. In a sense, the government might have seen the emergence of so many competitors as something not to regret but to be thankful for, for the government believed that the Hassaniya tribe was too large to be administered by only one omda. It thus resolved the conflict by giving each of the four claimants the title of omda.

However, two of them were limited to their own lineages, Shaikh Ali Massalam and Shaikh Wad Rugba, while Shaikh Ibrahim Nimir was recognized as omda on the west bank and Shaikh Idris Habbani on the east bank of the river. There is no doubt that the government knew of the failure of Ali Massalem and Wad Rugba to get the support of other lineages. Finally, around 1915, the government decided to institute a unified tribal administration known as the nazirship or nazirate, from nazir, the office, which literally means 'overseer' or 'paramount chief'. Until that time, native administration was not yet formulated as a policy and the government was concerned primarily with taxation rather than with real tribal administration. The government was impressed by the personality of Shaikh Idris Habbani and wished to appoint him nazir, but, considering the difficulties it had encountered in the institution of omodiyaships, sought first the support for its decision from the tribal council of elders. This council was not a formally constituted body with fixed authority or composition. It comprised the ummar and shaikhs of the various lineages, particularly those from lineages with large populations and considerable wealth.

THE ALAGA MEGLIS (TRIBAL COUNCIL)

In the installation of omodiyaships the governmental authorities did not seek the direct consent of this meglis, because, as I have said, they were basically in favour of instituting four omdas, but the office of Nazir could be given to only one man. So in Alaga, a village about 40 miles to the north of Dueim, the government summoned the various tribal leaders from all the Kawahla lineages. Alaga is the centre of the Magawir lineage and the place where Shaikh Alia Massalam lived, a main competitor to Wad Habbani. The government might have thought it a good idea to hold the meglis at his home village – a boastful gesture which would keep him silent?

I have no detailed information of what occurred in that meglis, but it is probable that it was typical of Geteina councils in all respects (see p. 103), and that the government told the tribal gathering that the office of nazir was to deal primarily with taxation and that it would be an experimental rather than a settled policy. The governor suggested that Wad Habbani be given this office because he had proved himself to be very capable in dealing with taxation. He said that he was not in favour of giving the office to Ibrahim Nimir, the right inheritor of the office, and that in any case Wad Habbani should be seen as the rightful heir. The government suggestion was finally approved by the meglis and Wad Habbani became the Nazir of the Hassaniya as well as of the Kawahla in general. He was appointed to the council primarily on the bureaucratic principle of personal merit although as we shall see in another case, the government continued to emphasize the traditional principle and Wad Habbani's inherited right to the office. The government's argument was that Hassaniya political leadership represented a continuous legacy vested in a certain section of the Gushgushab lineage alone, so that, in terms of that legacy Shaikh Ibrahim Nimir had the best right to be a chief. But since Ibrahim Nimir, in the government's view at least, was not capable of being a nazir (see the report on Geteina Meglis, p. 103) the selection of Wad Habbani would resolve the dilemma of keeping the office inside the Gushgashab lineage and also of providing them with a capable person. For them, then, the selection of Wad Habbani was based on a traditional and bureaucratic decision. The bureaucratic basis of the government selection was more apparent in its appointment to the office after the institution of omdas, for this promoted one of the omdas to nazirship rather than creating a new appointment of nazir. After the promotion of Wad Habbani as nazir, his old omodiya was taken by one of his sons, and was later divided into two omodiyas under two of his sons.

THE TURA'S MEGLIS AND CONSOLIDATION OF WAD HABBANI'S POSITION

About 1920 a conflict arose between Wad Habbani and Ibrahim Nimir regarding the position of some Hassaniya on the west bank whom Ibrahim Nimir had previously agreed to leave under a Ja'aliyin omda called Wad Magawah. Wad Magawah was an influential man, a possible competitor to Wad Habbani as Nazir should the government include other tribes in the region in one nazirate instead of limiting the office to the Kawahla. Shaikh Ibrahim Nimir, who had lost his case with the government, made a deal with Wad Magawah of the Ja'aliyin to have these Hassaniya left under his authority so that he would have more people and a larger territorial unit to administer. Thus he could become a potential competitor to Wad Habbani. Wad Habbani filed a law suit against Ibrahim Nimir and Wad Magawah. He accused Ibrahim Nimir of getting money from Wad Magawah to oppose his authority, and argued furthermore that the majority of the people under Wad Magawah were Hassaniya and their omda should be Hassani.

To solve this problem the government summoned a tribal meglis, consisting of the big men of the Hassaniya concerned, the parties to the conflict, and some religious shaikhs. The council decided that the majority of the people under Wad Magawah were Hassaniya and should be given their own omodiya.

The separated Hassaniya were organized by the government into the omodiyas given to the two leading lineages, the Magdab and the Imairiya. Wad Magawah was made omda over only the Tura's village and later, when he died, the office was reduced to a shaikhship. The government accepted that Shaikh Ibrahim Nazir was intriguing against Wad Habbani and penalised him by taking his omodiyaship and reducing him to shaikh of his own section of the Gushgushab lineage. The omda position was given to Haj Muhammad (Debeig) one of the Wad Habbani's sons. Wad Habbani was thus a nazir, while three of his sons were omdas.

The office of nazir was still mainly concerned with collecting taxes. The shaikhs collected taxes and passed them to the omdas, who passed them to the nazir. All of them received a share (*makafa*), a percentage of what was collected. While Wad Habbani was made nazir over all the Hassaniya, his supervision over taxation was actually limited to the Geteina district and to a small part of the Dueim district. The Hassaniya in the other parts of the Dueim and Kawa districts were not organized into omodiyas nor were they accessible to his authority. A governmental file reports 'but, as many of them [the Hassaniya] belonged to Kawa and Dueim district and the general administration was bureaucratic, it seems likely that the effective control was largely confined to the omodiyas near him in Geteina'.

About 1925 the Urwab and Muhammadiya quarrelled with the nazir over the remuneration from tax collection and were allowed to separate themselves from the nazirate. The British administrators did not seem to take this separation seriously, dismissed it as a petty quarrel and blamed it on the machinations of the Egyptian Mamur. The British administrators believed that all the Kawahla had been under the Hassaniya chief throughout their history. This was not true – the Hassaniya chief was made superordinate to all the Kawahla only during the Turkish régime (1820–1885) and then only in a formal and nominal sense.

In 1927, Shaikh Idris Wad Habbani died, leaving the office of nazir vacant. The government organized a council, and managed to get its backing in the selection of Wad Habbani's elder son, Abdel Gadir, as nazir in his father's place. The following record of this meeting is instructive:

Note on the Hassaniya, Hissinat and Kawahla Meglis at Geteina on
15.10.1927
Present
   (a) (1) Mr J. A. Reid, A/Governor, White Nile Province
       (2) Mr J. W. Robertson, A/District Commissioner, Geteina
       (3) Muhammad El-Fadl Ibrahim, Mamur Geteina
   (b) 'Outside Agawid'
       (1) Shaikh Adam Hassan El-Khalifa, of the Hararin Hawawir
       (2) Shaikh Sulaiman Esheiger of the Bol Muhammad Gimma'
       (3) Shaikh Ibrahim Hassan of the Ga'afra
       (4) Shaikh Khidir Musa of the Magdiya
   (c) All the omdas and many of the Shaikhs and 'ummar' of the
       Hassaniya, Hissinat, Kawahla and Awamra tribes.
Proceedings at Meglis
After preliminary interviews with the outside *agawid* a full meeting
of the tribes concerned was held. *Special attention was paid to the desir-
ability of the hereditary councillors (nas shura) being present and many of
them were named and asked to attend.* [My italics.]

The acting governor gave a short sketch of the genealogy and
history of the people, laying special emphasis on their inter-
relationships and common historical tradition. The mantle of the
old ruling house should rightly belong to the Awlad Nimir and
their descendants but when the old branch became withered, the
young branch should bear the weight of the fruit. Nimir's son,
Ibrahim, was still alive but all admitted that he could not sustain
the authority of a ruling chief. Similarly Abdel Gadir Wad
Nimir's son, El-Asama, was available but he was unsuitable for
reasons well known to the tribe. There remained the sons of the
late Nazir Idris Habbani. It was true this was the cadet branch of
the family, but the late Nazir had served the government loyally
and well and it seemed fitting that his eldest son Abdel Gadir
should be given the opportunity of proving his fitness for the
Nazirship.

The proposal of Abdel Gadir's name as nazir was received with
acclamation. There was not a single dissent and it was agreed that
he should be recommended as Nazir of all the Hassaniya and
Hissinat in the White Nile and Kawahla and Awamra of the
Northern District.

The proceedings terminated with the *fatha*. The time occupied
was less than twenty minutes.

THE ESTABLISHMENT OF THE ADMINISTRATION

Although the institutionalization of formal positions of authority at the tribal and tribal-section levels began from the turn of the century, the colonial policy of indirect rule became fully mature only in 1930 when it was agreed upon and referred to throughout the Sudan as 'the Native Administration'. In White Nile Province, this policy was expressed in the institutionalization of the Hassaniya Nazirate over all the province and people. Native Administration endorsed the principle of placing smaller tribes with larger ones so that larger administrative units were created and the largest tribe in that unit formed the backbone of its administration.

We have to note that until 1929 there were three districts in the province: Geteina, Dueim and Kawa. In 1929, however, the Kawa district was abolished and merged with Dueim. In 1930 it was decided to put the two districts, Geteina and Dueim, into one administrative unit which was referred to as the Hassaniya Nazirate – with a hierarchical system of administrative, financial and judicial functions. Naima village, where the nazir lived, was established as the headquarters of the Nazirate, and with the transfer of power to it, Geteina district became redundant. It was abolished in 1932.

FORMAL ADMINISTRATIVE ORGANIZATION

The Nazirate is headed by the nazir who is the supreme administrative and judicial head. Under him are three *wakil* nazirs, or deputy nazirs (referred to as *wukala* or generally *nuzzar*). The administrative unit under each *wakil* is referred to as *wakala*, deputyship. The wakilships coincide with the old district divisions of Dueim and Geteina, there being two wakilships in the former Geteina district and one in Dueim district. In fact there were originally two wakilships in Dueim district, but one was abolished in the mid-1930s when the deputy nazir at the time was sacked by the government for misbehaviour as a result of a well-planned intrigue by the Habbania family. This leader was the Ja'afra omda at Dueim, Shaikh Ali Ibrahim Hassan, who was chosen at the time by the government and the tribes concerned as the representative of the non-Hassaniya or, more correctly, non-Kawahla. The original man chosen for this office was his father, Omda Ibrahim

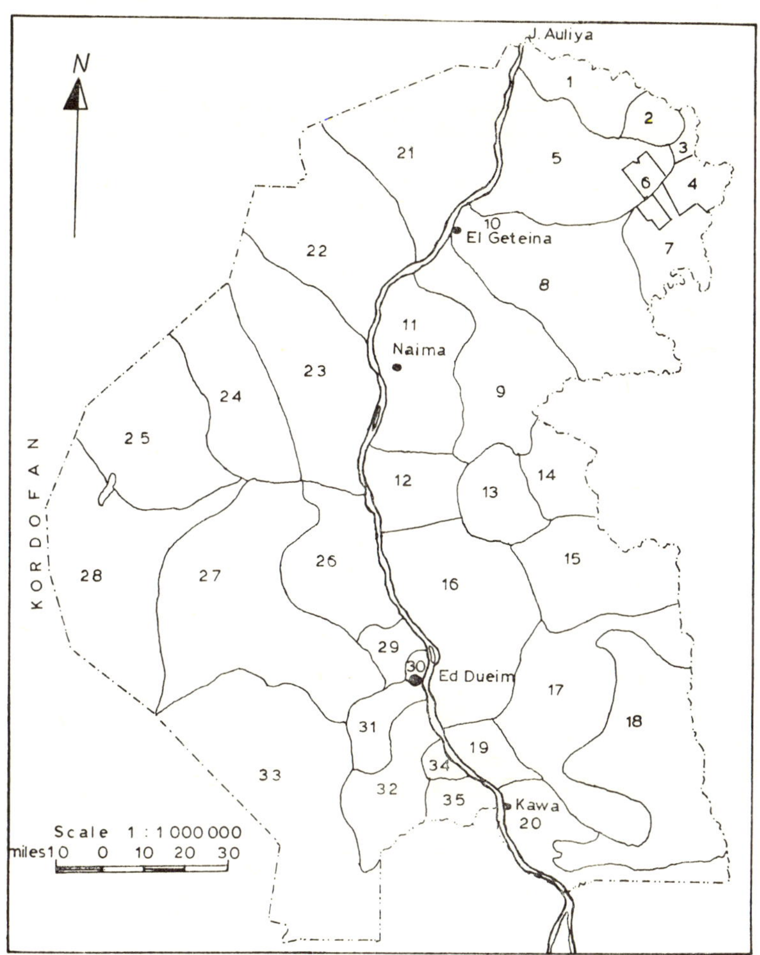

Map 2. Blue Nile Province, Dueim District, Omodiya boundaries

Source: Dueim Survey Office DSO/CAD/38/59 of 25.3.59 Nos 1–33 refer to the different Omodiyas for administrative convenience and have no significance.

Table 5. Tribal and administrative composition of the Hassaniya Nazirate[1]

No.	Deputy, 'wakil'	No.	Name of Omda	Tribe	No. of shaikhs	No. of herd tax-payers	Note
2	Haj Omer Mohd[2]	1	Naim Abdalla Kereil	Mohammadiya	28	1434	
	Idris Habbani	2	Mohd Magboul Gar El Nabi	Eruab	16	871	
	(nephew of Nazir)	3	Mohd Idris Kinein	Nusseinat	22	1448	
		4	Mohd Ali Shatir	Husseinat	27	1822	
		5	Koko Abu El Hassan	Husseinat	11	534	
		6	Abdel Latif El Ami	Awamra	17	971	
		7	Mohd Dud Bashir	Agaliyin	6	434	
		8	Suleiman Musaad	Bustab	3	206	Very small Omodiya
		9	Ahmed Fadlalla	Geteina (Ja'aliyin)	—	193	Very small Omodiya
		10	El Sadig Fadlu	Geteina (Dangla)	—	235	Very small Omodiya
3	Idris Abdel[3] Gader Idris	11	Mohamed Abdel Gader (son of Nazir)	Hassaniya	29	1905	
	Habbani (Nazir's eldest son)	12	El Haj Mohed Idris (brother of Nazir)	Hassaniya	19	1858	
		13	Mohd Tom Musa Rigba	Hassaniya	17	1452	
		14	Ali Mussalam	Hassaniya	17	1362	
		15	Yunis Abdel Salam	Awlad Rif	2	120	Insignificant
		16	Mohd Geili	Danagla	2	129	Insignificant
3	Yonsif Habbani (Nazir's half-brother)	17	Mohd El Heila	Hassaniya	22	1925	
		18	Ali Mohd Zein	Hassaniya	19	2616	
		19	El Zein Omar	Hassaniya	13	805	
		20	Ahmed M El Zein	Hassaniya	16	1306	
		21	Ahmed M-Abu Sheiba	Husseinat			

22	Bella Muhammadani	Husseinat	13	508
23	Musa Jadalla	Kawahla	10	730
24	Ismail Mohd	Ehuweihat	15	731
25	Mohd Zein	Lahawiyin	3	72
26	Ali Ibrahim Hassan	Dueim Town (mostly Canfera)	—	1535[4] Before was deputy over Omodias 26–39
27	Gaafer Mohd	Um Gerr West (Gaafera)	16	327
28	Abdel Hadi Osman	Um Gerr East (Gaafera)	3	186
29	Mohd Duweih	Kawa Town (mixed)	13	967
30	Lbrahim Mohd	Messellemiya	12	546
31	Mohd Famal el Din	Messellemiya	14	319
32	Mudawi Gismalla	Messellemiya	11	794
33	Ahmed I El Niteifa	Arakiyin	37	1184
34	Mohd Nur Huda	Towal	12	484
35	Khidir Musa	Magdiya	7	350
36	Mohd Fadlalla	Kurtan	18	593
37	Muzemmil Yusef	Dueih	13	559
38	Jazuli Omar	Shaigiya	5	174
39	Mohd Abdallah	Shanabla	24	633

[1] Ref. administrative files at Dueim (ND/66/K.4–20/7/34). Apart from changes in the numbers of shaikhs and tax-payers, the structure remained virtually unchanged in 1969/70. There were definitely changes in personnel, but mostly hereditary and insignificant.

[2] Died in about 1942, office taken by brother Idris Mohamed Idris till 1949 when Idris was transferred to no. 2 *wakil*ship while his brother Khogali Mohamed Idris took this office till 1969/70.

[3] Made *Nazir* in 1939, office given to Idris Mohamed Idris Habbani, cousin – Idris was transferred to *wakil*ship no. 1 in 1942 (see Chapter 6 for causes of transference) when Haj Cmer, *wakil* no. 1, died. His brother Khogali was appointed to this *wakil*ship. But in 1949, Idris and Khogali were made to exchange their *wakil*ships (see Chapter 6).

[4] Town tax-payers.

Hassan, who died in 1930 after which his son, Ali, took the office. The Habbaniya succeeded in plotting against him and the government took the office of deputy from him and left him as omda in Dueim town only. The whole wakilship previously under him merged to form one wakilship under Shaikh Yusuf Habbani, the brother of the current nazir and the last Hassaniya nazir before the abolition of the Nazirate.

The tribal and administrative units comprising the Dar are shown in Map 2 and Table 5.

1. *The Nazir*

The nazir was the administrative and the executive head of the hierarchical organization. The administrative machinery under him, apart from deputies, omdas and shaiks, constituted a large salaried staff of clerks, *muhafzin* (messengers) *ghufara* (guards) all residing in Naima, the capital or centre of the Nazirate, and in Wad Nimir and Dueim the headquarters of the two wakilships. Today, the nazir has considerable power over his staff, including the appointment and dismissal of both the clerical and tribal functionaries.

In the past, prior to the last two decades, the power of the nazir over this staff was nominal. Clerks were usually appointed and dismissed by the government. The tribal functionaries, omdas and shaikhs, were elected or chosen by the support of their people. Indeed, most of them sat in the tribal council which used to have an important role in the selection of the nazir himself. Today the nazir has effective control over them and their relation is one of superior to inferior.

The nazir is the executive of the Native Administration Budget which has been in existence since 1933. The budget consists of revenues from herd tax, land tax and fines at native courts. Animal or herd tax is levied annually on individual owners of animals at rates ranging from between 80 piastres for a camel to about 15 piastres for a goat. Land tax is levied annually on tenant farmers in cotton schemes and amounts to about 10 piastres for an individual plot. The scheme extracts this money from the account of the farmers and transfers it to the Native Administration Budget. Fines from native courts consist of fines made in the nazir's deputies' and Omdas' courts. In the case of omdas the fines are handed over to the deputy nazir who then enters the money in the local treasury at his office. From these revenues the nazir pays the salaries and services of the staff under him. The surplus is paid to the central government as a contribution. The accounts kept are simple, kept in plain foolscap notebooks, and consist of treasury funds, revenue and expenditure.

Routine payments are made by the Native Administration accountant himself against signature on his payment. There are three accountants, one attached to the nazir and two to the deputies. Non-routine payments, for example, against services, are made only on a signed order by the nazir or the deputies. The nazir, deputies and omdas are all salaried, while shaikhs get a 10 per cent share (*mukafaa*). The Nazirate also has expenditure for rewarding court members and *fakis* or *khalwas*, that is Quranic teachers, and for various services, such as repairs or building, the expenses of tribal gatherings, the council, the feeding of prisoners, and so on; but these items are relatively limited in scope and range.

The nazir is not only the financial and executive head, he has also the greatest judicial powers. The constitution of the Native Court Ordinance of 1932 has the Native Administration linked by a single Native Court with panels in various places, and with powers delegated to omdas (ND/66/K.4 – 20/7/34; Administrative files). The nazir, according to the constitution, is the president of the court, and all powers held are held from him. The maximum authority of the nazir's court is to order three years' imprisonment, a fine of £S 50 and/or 25 lashes.

2. *The deputies wakil-nazirs (or wukala nuzzar)*

Under the nazir are three deputies directly responsible for the administration of the wakilships. They have administrative powers relatively similar to the nazir, but they are all, at least formally, under his close supervision and control. Each deputy presides over a panel which has power to impose six months imprisonment, a fine of £S 50 and 25 lashes.

During the last two decades there has been considerable decentralization of power from the nazir to his deputies. Although the nazir's authority remains supreme, the deputies are the administrators in their wakilships. This decentralization has been possible because the nazir and his deputies come from the same family, the Habbaniya, and act as a corporate group in tribal administration and politics. Their corporate character and sense of equality in spite of the hierarchical nature of the formal administration, is comparable to the position of Awlad Fadlallah among the Kabbabish (Asad 1970). Detailed consideration of the socioeconomic and political role of the Habbaniya in Dar Hassaniya today is given in Chapter 8.

3. Omdas

The omda has limited administrative and judicial powers which rarely include imprisonment. Most have only power to impose a maximum fine of £S 25. Those with power to imprison are either members of the ruling family or favoured by it. In both cases the limit of their judicial power is six months imprisonment and a fine of £S 25. The degree of an omda's administrative power is also a function of his relationship with the nazir and/or his deputies. Omdas with the most power are those three of the nine Hassaniya omdas from the Habbaniya family. Apart from the collection of taxes from shaikhs, the omda is expected to undertake administrative duties such as the settlement of cultivation rights over government land, rights known as *hikir*, right of use, and public security within his unit.

4. Shaikhs

The main function of the shaikh is the collection of taxes and to act as the channel between the government and his superiors and the people in his shaikhship. In the past, shaikhs used to have considerable power over their lineages, with which they were inevitably closely identified.

To what extent did these fiscal and judicial measures bring the lineage under the control of the instituted chiefs to the disadvantage of the traditional authority of the ummar and shaikhs? To what

Table 6. Native administration revenue in 1934

(1) Animal Tax	£S 10,637
(2) Cultivation Tax	3,757
(3) *Sufra* Tax	785
(4) Land Tax	125
(5) Rent of Markets and Ferries	406
(6) Fines of Native Courts	100

Source: Administrative Files, Dueim: N.D./K.4, 20/7/34.

extent did these measures affect the federal units, the lineages, themselves?

The traditional socio-political organizations, based on the corporate identity of the lineage and the power of their big men to control both their external and internal affairs, had adapted to these external forces. The administrative machinery, particularly regarding taxation and courts, was actually built upon the existing lineage structure.

The officials at levels above shaikhs were supposed to pass the tax collected over to the government and to have nothing to do with the assessment of individual wealth within the lineages. Herd-tax was based on a rough estimate or census made by the government, usually by the District Commissioner. It was supposed to be revised from time to time, but this was rarely done. A major check was made in 1952 only after a great loss of animals due to reservoir conditions and the spread of animal diseases before veterinary services effectively controlled them. In the absence of an effective check on animal health in the region, the taxation system has always depended on changing the rates, not the actual number of animals.

In the pre-dam period the estimation was made for the whole lineage rather than for individuals. The estimation of lineage wealth was converted to money according to fixed rates and the shaikh of the lineage was asked to collect that sum of money from his lineage members.

The shaikh had to submit a list showing how he distributed the payment. The list would take the form of a proper herd-tax listing, carrying names of people and the number of animals owned. But the list was for the record and would not tell how many animals were actually owned by individuals; the list showed how the money was collected, not how animals were assessed.

Taxation was thought of as a lineage account with the government rather than as an individual matter. The lineage members saw taxation as a thing for their wealthy leaders to settle rather than something to be personally worried about. Complaints were never raised against the shaikh by lineage members at the time. But later, in the post-dam period, this became a common cause of friction, a justification for fission and the formation of smaller shaikhships. Thus the Amriya lineage had three shaikhs between 1900 and 1940, but a total of eight by 1969/70, that is, a zero increase for 40 years and about 160 per cent increase in less than 30 years.

The ummar used to hold the lineage together in its wider field of socio-economic co-operation. Taxation gave that institution another dimension of horizontal solidarity rather than undermine it in favour of an encroaching outside power. The newly imposed chiefs and the government took this as both *de facto* as well as *de jure* by recognizing the lineage as a tax-paying group and the delegation of individual assessment and collection to the shaikh of the lineage. Taxation, then, had not given the chiefs a means of access to the individual Hassani, and the Hassaniya were still in general limited, in their interaction and leadership, to their shaikhs and ummar.

The provision of judicial powers to the instituted chiefs started as early as the 1920s at the time of Shaikh Idris Habbani, the first nazir. He was given 'the book of authority', *sulta*, to keep a record of tried cases and given the power to fine to the limit of £S 25. When he died in 1927, the book of authority, which had been with him for about three years, was returned empty to the government. The government's comment on this was that he ruled by diplomacy and tact rather than by authoritative power (see report on Geteina Meglis, p. 103).

There were two factors relating to the insignificance of courts and to authoritative power in this period. Firstly, the corporate structure of the lineage was incompatible with the type of disputes that could be taken to courts. If disputes arose, they were considered as petty quarrels and settled within the lineage rather than taken to someone outside. They formed part of the internal lineage political process.

Secondly, inter-lineage disputes still remained the domain of the shaikhs and big men, acting as arbitrators between the two parties. It is interesting to note that where cases were taken to the new courts, the court became a tribal council, in which the ummar and the shaikhs of the lineage concerned were present together with some from other lineages, and the newly instituted judges would act as arbitrators rather than as judges trying to find the guilty and punish him according to the rule of law. The principle on which the court acted, like most tribal councils was *sulh* (pardon agreed by the two partners to the dispute). The following cases are an illustration of this point.

Case 1

> *Time*: 1935 (summer)
>
> *Case*: Armed fighting between the Amriya lineage and the Gushgushab lineage
>
> *Cause of conflict*: The Amriya cattle invaded the Gushgushab rain cultivation. The Gushgushab retaliated by dispersing the cattle. As a result of this, about 30 men of the Amriya and more than that number from the Gushgushab fought. No one was killed but many were injured. The incident was started by a personal duel between Gas-al Nabi of the Amriya and Boshara of the Gushgushab. A certain Amriya notable called Wad Karmalla tried to calm the situation by arbitrating. The Gushgushab broke his prayer beads as an insult. The fighting then involved members of the two lineages.
>
> *Court*: The court was headed by Nazir Abdel Gadir Habbani. Present with him were:
> (1) District Commissioner.
> (2) Agawid (i.e. arbitrators)
>   (a) Fekki Wad Iwaida of the Gushgushab lineage
>   (b) Fekki Shaikh Ahmed of the Gushgushab lineage
>   (c) Khalifa Musa of the Amriya lineage
>   (d) Fekki El Ansari Abdallah of the Amriya lineage
>   (e) Tom Asad: Gulamab Lineage
>   (f) Wad-El-Asam: Ja'aliyan Omda
>   (g) A certain Ja'afra Omda from Garrasa.
> (3) Court Members:
>   (a) Omda Haj Muhammad: From the Gushgushab lineage
>   (b) Abdel Rahman Rajab: Administrative Shaikh, Amriya lineage
>   (c) Sulaiman El-Haj: Administrative Shaikh, Amriya lineage
>   (d) Amin El Tom: Administrative Shaikh, Humron lineage
>   (e) Tahir El-Khalifa: A Salahiya lineage notable.
>
> *Summons*: The hearing of the case ended by *sulh* and *fatha* (Quranic blessing) each party agreeing to open a new page in their relations.

Case 2

> *Case*: Tribal meglis and conflict over the appointment of Haj Omer Habbani as Deputy Nazir on the east bank, responsible for the administration in the Abu-Guta Scheme.

Time: 1935

The appointment of Haj Omer as deputy nazir was announced by the government. The Hissinat, Urwab, and Muhammadiya objected to the appointment. They claimed that they formed the majority in this settlement and the deputy nazir should be from among their members. The governor summoned a council, consisting of all omdas, shaikhs, religious shaikhs and ummar in the area concerned, as well as the agricultural inspectors in Abdel Magid Scheme.

The governor pointed out that the appointment of deputy nazir was not a new appointment but a reallocation of certain powers of the nazir which were taken from him and given to another member of his family. The governor told the gathering that the deputy was not going to interfere in the internal affairs of the other Kawahla and would co-operate with the omdas, shaikhs and ummar, or *a'yan* (notables) of these tribes. He then appealed to the council to accept the appointment and give Haj Omer the chance to prove himself to be friendly.

I was told that Wad Magboul, omda of the Urwab, and a notable of this tribe, was very critical of the government policy in this matter and is said to have asked the governor at the beginning of the meeting, 'Should we say that we are here for consultation or for the camel's penis?' ('*nagoul fi shura walla zib gamal*'). The implication here is that someone is going to make a deal one does not accept, and this position will be similar to the camel which is said to have rejected the penis given to it by nature, or God, because he is so big and the penis is so small.

The Hissinat religious shaikhs intervened and asked their people to accept the appointment and emphasized the importance of adhering to a policy of non-interference on the part of Haj Omer.

5

The Dam: The Changing Ecology, Technology and Economy

The White Nile flows from Lake Victoria in Uganda and enters the Sudan to join the Blue Nile at Khartoum, after which they form together the river Nile. The Nile passes northwards through the Sudan and Egypt before it flows into the Mediterranean. The Nile waters have thus been the concern of the people in all these countries and agreements between their governments have been made concerning the regulation of water use.[1]

After the First World War the Egyptian government approached the Anglo-Egyptian government in the Sudan concerning the possibility of building a dam on the White Nile at Jebel Awliya, about 40 miles south of Khartoum, to store water in the rainy season to be used for irrigation in Egypt in the summer.

The Sudan government hesitated for a while, bearing in mind the possible impact of the proposed dam upon the area south of it, the expected opposition of the people, the problem of submergence of agricultural land, and the provision of alternative means of livelihood for the people affected by the dam.

Under persistent pressure from Egypt, however, an agreement was reached with the Sudan government in the late 1920s. The dam was to be built pending popular approval and compensation of £S $2\frac{1}{2}$ million was to be paid by the Egyptian government. This sum of money was to be used for two purposes: (a) the compensation for land, property and other losses to the people concerned; (b) the provision for dispossessed Arabs of a new means of livelihood. There was special pressure on the Sudan government to accept the project during this period of world

---

[1] The most important of these agreements is that made on the eve of Jebel Awliya Dam in the late 1920s.

economic depression. The Sudan government felt that the money to be used for compensation would help alleviate national financial problems, if part payment to the people was deferred.

THE DAM CAMPAIGN

The government, with regional headquarters at Dueim, saw as its first task the need to convince people to accept the dam project by assuring them of fair compensation for their land and a rosy future, with the promise of social and economic securities that their environment had hitherto lacked. The middleman between the government and the people was the nazir, Shaikh Abdel Gadir Habbani. There is no doubt that he was put in a difficult and embarrassing situation, since he had to please the two sides, the government and the people. Like most middlemen,[2] he misrepresented the two sides to each other. The government, although decided on the issue, wanted the consent of the people. The nazir, using any means, had to extract that consent.

The reaction of the tribesmen varied: the Hassaniya were sceptical of the compensation and the promised future. But the nazir kept assuring them that the government would keep its word. The nazir used to spend days with the big men and the prominent religious shaikhs of the Hassaniya trying to explain to them what the government wanted to do while emphasizing his claim that the Hassaniya would be the most privileged tribe if they supported the government plan. Some men from the Amriya lineage told me that the nazir, Shaikh Abdel-Gadir, used to visit Shaikh Muhammad Ali Idris, the most notable amir of the Amriya lineage, and stay with him as a guest for two days or more. The main aim of these visits was to discuss the dam issue. Shaikh Muhammad Ali would then give a summary of these discussions to his lineage.

The Hassaniya later gave their approval when the Geteina villages, whom the Hassaniya called *gallaba* ('northerners', 'strangers'), led the militant opposition to the dam. The issue was manipulated by the nazir and some big men since there was disagreement as to who should have the right to make such decisions and who was the rightful owner of the Dar – the Hassaniya or the strangers.

---

[2] See the concept of the middleman as represented by Bailey 1969, pp. 167–76.

Among the Kawahla, the Hissinat, the Urwab and the Muhammadiya led a fierce opposition to the dam. They were the people nearest to the proposed dam and they were told that they would be moved from their riverain settlements and settled in the interior, around a place known as Abdel Magid. The people and their leaders, omdas, shaikhs, and ummar, all rejected the idea. The nazir depended mainly on resorting to the Hissinat religious shaikhs to mediate and convince their people to accept the project. He told them that the government was going to build the scheme anyway, and if they did not support the government before it was too late, they would not be treated well by it. Hence the most significant message came from the religious shaikhs to their people. This was, 'The holy men of the Jebel, the awliya, have ordered us to move'. Many of the holy men buried near there have been buried since the Funj and Turko-Egyptian periods. The mountain around which they are buried is referred to as Jebel Awliya, or the mountain of the guardians.[3] This was a mythical directive which the people found difficult to ignore.

The nazir then gave his consent to the government for the project, assuring it that all the people involved had agreed to the plan. But when the Governor General of the Sudan visited the region on the eve of building the dam, he was met by petitions and demonstrations in Geteina,[4] mostly from the *gallaba*, 'strangers', but there were also a few Kawahla and Hissinat with them. As a result of this incident, the governor became very

---

[3] Many of these awliya have tombs. Today, these tombs form a beautiful scene around Jebel Awliya bridge.

[4] The Geteina population are mainly Danagla and Shaigiya. The Kawahla refer to these people as 'strangers'. But they were among the first in the White Nile to be enthusiastic for education and before the Dam, education was wholely limited to Geteina and Dueim. Since then the Geteina sons have become scattered all over the Sudan in government appointments of various kinds. They were more aware than others of the possible effect of the Dam on their village, and in fact the impact of the Dam on the village has been very great and can be shown by this extract from a letter sent by the Civil Secretary to the Governor, Blue Nile in 1946: 'Several visitors from the village of Geteina have called on me recently (you will remember I have spent eight years in Dueim and Geteina at various times and I have many friends there) and have emphasized very strongly to me the poverty-stricken nature of the village now. Their old livelihood as the market and entrepot of a large riverain area has been killed by the Dam, and the trade which used to come into the place, is now non-existent, or transferred to Abu-Guta Feteisa areas.' (Reference: Administrative files, Dueim CS/SCR/2./R.4 – Civil Secretary's office, Khartoum 4 Dec. 1946.)

I

concerned as he had been assured by his local officials that he would find complete public approval. In his view, they were to be blamed for what happened, but the local officials put the responsibility on the nazir, accusing him of concealing popular opposition. He replied that the opposers were a small minority, they were strangers and not the real people concerned in the Dar. He also claimed that the Kawahla who had joined them were too few to be taken seriously and that they had been intimidated by the 'stranger' minority. The nazir suggested that the Governor of the province should tour the Hassaniya and Hissinat area and see the truth of his story. Preparations for the tour were made. The main campaign of the nazir among the Hassaniya was to manipulate the Geteina incident, emphasizing that they should show their strength as real owners of the Dar and not let the strangers take the initiative; that if they did not show their real support for the project, the strangers would succeed and would be the ones with whom the government would communicate from that time on. The conflict between the Hassaniya and the 'strangers' became the model in which the opposition and support for the government project revealed itself. Touring the Hassaniya and Hissinat area, the government found unanimous approval and decided to implement the scheme.

THE DAM AND ITS MAIN EFFECTS

Calculations, surveys, and reports about the dam, covering various aspects such as land, property, crops, and the people to be affected, had been in progress since 1925. However, it was only in the mid and late 1940s that the full impact of the dam was felt and earlier reports and calculations were reconsidered in the light of the new facts. Table 7 summarizes the effects of the dam and the policy of the colonial administration to counteract these.

The division of the area into two parts, north and south of Hareidana, is an extremely significant division. It marks two different ecological settings and two main groups of people affected. The main groups living north of Hareidana are the Hissinat and other Kawahla. There are also some Hassaniya groups like the Gemeiliya, the Magawir and the Gamalab. South of Hareidana live the bulk of the Hassaniya tribe. It has already been pointed out that in the northern part of the White Nile, the Kordofan desert comes so close to the river that there is no room

Table 7. Some calculated effects of Jebel Awliya Dam

	Population	Feddans of land	Ardebs dura	Measures proposed
(a) North of Hareidana	37,000 mainly Hissinat	*Riverland* Native: 175,000 feddans Government: 48,000 feddans Total 223,000 feddans	24,000	(a) Alternative livelihood to be found by canalizing 60,000 feddans in the Abdel Magid area
(b) South of Hareidana	120,000 mainly Hassaniya	*Rainland* Native: 20,000 feddans Government: 90,000 feddans Total 110,000 feddans	36,000	(b) Alternative livelihood to be found by: (i) Basin cultivation (ii) Low lift cultivation (iii) Increased pump schemes (iv) In interim period by manipulation of reservoir levels
Totals	157,000	333,000	60,000	

Source: Administrative files, Dueim-Jebel Awliya Compensation Committee. These calculations were made before the dam was built.

for the clay *terus* land, traditionally utilized for rain cultivation. Hence most people living in this part of the region have had their rainland on the east bank. The result of this was that the east and west banks of the river emerged as inter-dependent economic units. Even though some of the lineages were divided between the two banks of the river, they attained a high degree of social and political solidarity because of that economic integration.

In contrast to the north of Hareidana, the south has plenty of clay land on the west bank. The existence of these two geographical and ecological zones has resulted in the dam affecting the two groups of people in different ways. The people south of Hareidana have lost their riverland but not the rainland and so have had schemes built for them at home. The people north of Hareidana could not have schemes built for them near their traditional homes around the river, but only far away in the interior to the east. This is why the people of this area have been settled in Abdel Magid Scheme, about 30 miles east of the White Nile, and the measures proposed for the post-dam policy have been different for the two zones (see Table 7).

THE POST-DAM ECOLOGICAL SETTING

With reference to the pre-dam ecological setting (discussed in Chapter 1) the post-dam ecological setting can be summed up in the following:

(a) The loss of the river land due to its submergence by the high dam water. People were compensated for the loss of this land on the basis of a fixed rate – two pounds per *feddan* divided into two equal instalments, one paid to them in 1939, the other in 1952.

(b) Most of the clay *terus* land traditionally used for rain cultivation, is today utilized for building schemes. In the case of the government-owned schemes, the land has been expropriated from its original owners and compensation paid at the rate of one pound per *feddan*. In the case of private schemes, the land was not expropriated. The number of government-owned schemes and large private schemes, their sizes and distribution is shown on Map 3. The small pump schemes are innumerable.

(c) The *shorab* land traditionally used as *dumur* has been evacuated. The high reservoir level has brought these homes very close to the river and the swamps which are created by the receding river when the dam is opened each summer. The residential settlements have been rebuilt on the small *gozes* which interrupt the layout of the *terus* land and on the western *shorab* traditionally used for sheep and goat grazing.

I shall now examine in detail the effects of this new setting on the semi-nomadic life of the White Nile Arabs.

THE EFFECTS ON GRAZING

In the discussion of the ecological and economic setting in the pre-dam period, I have shown that animal husbandry was a mainly local occupation. I have argued that animal husbandry, as part of a semi-nomadic life, was dictated by the necessity of diversifying economic activities in order to meet more effectively, and with

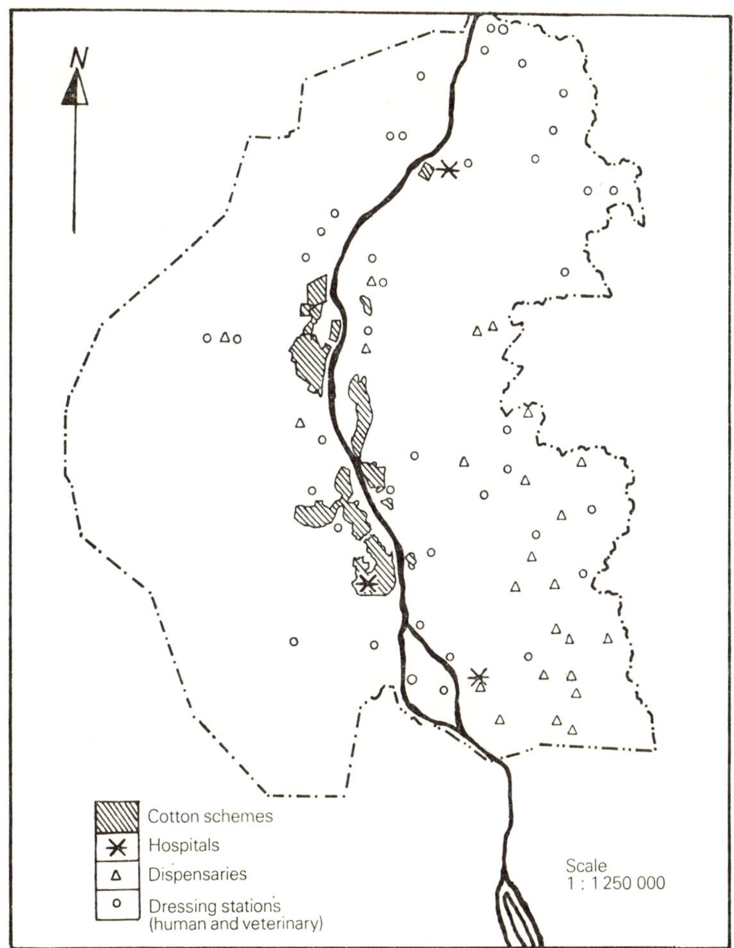

Map 3. Cotton schemes and health and veterinary centres in the Northern White Nile Region

greater viability, the unpredictability of the environment and natural resources, especially in connection with subsistence cultivation. In the post-dam period, however, through considerable advancement of farm technology in the schemes and the technological control of the Nile waters by the dam, agricultural production has become highly secure and dependable. On the other hand, animal husbandry has been greatly undermined and has finally lost its significance as a main occupation. It has become a secondary economic activity in which large-scale investment, characteristic of the earlier big men, has become economically and politically unpromising. At this point, it is necessary to discuss the factors that have shared in undermining the role of animal rearing, factors either directly or indirectly related to the dam and its effects.

It has been shown in Chapter 1 that the *dumur*, or permanent settlements were built on the eastern *shorab* land near the river. After the dam was built the ultimate reservoir level brought these settlements very close to the river. When the dam is opened every summer the receding river fills the area with swamps and the *khairan* (pools, or water courses) which furnish a breeding ground for insects, mosquitoes and flies. The sanitary conditions around the river have been highly affected by these reservoir factors.[5] As a result of this, the traditional *dumur* centres have been moved from near the river and rebuilt in two places: (a) on the small *gozes* interrupting the layout of the *terus* land; (b) on the western *shorab* strips to the west traditionally used for the pasturing of sheep and goats. Sufi, Wad Nimir and Shatawi are examples of villages built on (a); El-Hasien, Alaga are examples of villages built on (b). Since these places of resettlement are on traditional grazing grounds, they have taken up much of the area and have thus limited the grazing opportunities, especially in the case of large-scale grazing needed by big herding units.

---

[5] The deteriorating sanitary conditions have obliged the government to introduce health services on a wide scale. Since the early forties many dispensaries, hospitals, and veterinary units have been established throughout the region. Other social services have developed as well. The most significant of these is education. Before the Dam there were only two schools in the northern White Nile, one at Dueim, the other at Geteina. There was also a sub-grade school at Naima.

The development of these social services, as will be shown later, has most of all affected the social position of the shaikhs. The schools have undermined the significance of Quranic schools; the veterinary units and dispensaries have undermined the traditional services the religious shaikhs used to render in these spheres before the Dam.

Secondly, the swamps created by the dam reservoir encouraged the growth of certain grasses which harboured a disease caused by the liver-fluke known locally as *abu-kabda*. In 1948 the District Commissioner reported to the Governor of the Blue Nile, 'there have been big losses in animals lately as a result of the liver fluke from the reservoir grasses'.

We have to remember that until the mid-1940s veterinary services did not enter White Nile on any significant scale. Thus G. Hawkesworth, District Commissioner at Dueim wrote to the Governor, Blue Nile Province on 9/10/1943:[6] 'It is . . . unfortunate that during recent years a Senior Veterinary Officer has been unable to visit the White Nile, where new conditions arising out of the building of Jebel Awliya Dam require special study.' The Principal of the school of agriculture was asked by the District Commissioner for his guidance concerning the prospects of animal husbandry under the new dam conditions and wrote: 'This is the subject on which not only the people need guidance but on which we ourselves need information.[7] It is interesting to note that in the above-mentioned letter the District Commissioner was far more optimistic about animal husbandry than the reality of the situation has since justified. He remarked:

. . . the view has previously been held that the uncertainty of grazing throughout the year limited or forbade any improvements in stock-breeding or dairy work. Now, in addition to the grazing in the rain areas, there is also fodder grown in the Alternative Livelihood Schemes and grazing provided by the falling reservoir during the drought season. The development of mixed farming, stock-breeding and dairy-work will be an important part of village improvement.

Unfortunately this was more 'wishful thinking' than practical reality – for such magnificent projects have never come into being. On the contrary, the post-dam ecological and economic conditions have proved that the District Commissioner was more than short-sighted. The grass of the falling reservoir has proved mostly unfavourable to animal health, and people have not found a suitable substitute for their traditional river grazing alleged to be provided by the falling reservoir. Secondly, the growing of *lubia* as fodder in the schemes came to a halt soon after it was intro-

---

[6] DD/SCR/91, Dueim District Files, 17 July 1948.
[7] DD/1-A-6, Dueim District Files.

duced. People saw it as uneconomic in comparison with growing *dura* or cotton. The government first insisted that *lubia* and *dura* should be grown in equal amounts. It saw *lubia* as necessary, not only as fodder, but for soil conservation. But people constantly cheated by growing more *dura* than *lubia*. The scheme's management was sometimes very embarrassed when some scheme shaikhs were found to be cheating. The scheme shaikhs are the agents responsible for conveying the rules to the individual tenants and keeping a watch on their implementation. In 1945, shortly after the Sufi scheme was built and Abdel Gadier El-Hado was made shaikh of the scheme, he was convicted of growing less *lubia* than *dura* and the shaikhship was taken from him and given to someone else.

However, the government later changed its policy of insisting on the growing of *lubia* especially after the Second World War caused a higher demand for cotton. The growing of *lubia* became optional, and eventually disappeared altogether. The fate of *lubia* was very significant, because it indicated that people were seeking more opportunities for cash cropping and for growing staple foods than for animal husbandry.

Lastly, the development of motor transport in the post-dam period has affected grazing grounds by spoiling tracts of land or by making grazing 'messy' for animals, which were constantly being disturbed by lorries and buses. With the production of cotton and the need for transporting it to ginning factories in Kosti and Dueim, motor transport became necessary and gradually developed on a large scale. Later bus services developed and in 1969–70 there were many bus-routes connecting major towns and villages throughout the district, such as Dueim, Khartoum, Kosti, Abu Quta, Naima, Shigaig, Helba, and Ma'tuq. These factors have greatly affected the prospects of animal rearing as part of a semi-nomadic existence.

For the majority of people, the commoners who have few animals, animal husbandry became largely an indoor business. In the *kharif* when there is abundant grazing in the outskirts of the village, shepherds are hired on a monthly rate of five piastres for sheep and goats and ten piastres for cattle. These shepherds are mostly outsiders, for example, westerners and nomads, but there are some local lineage members among them as well.

The effect on the large scale grazing, characteristic of the ummar, has been even more drastic. Some former owners of large numbers of animals have either abandoned nomadism or have been forced to pasture their animals in distant areas to the west where there is abundant grazing. These measures have had important social repercussions on the role of these owners of large herds.

But the overwhelming majority of the earlier big men have turned most or at least part of their animal wealth into cash and invested it in building small pump schemes for cotton growing. Most of these small pump schemes have been doomed to failure and have actually collapsed with inevitable effects upon the ummar.

CONSOLIDATION OF COTTON CULTIVATION: THE CHANGE TO CASH CROPS

We have to note that although alternative livelihood schemes were planned to grow both cotton and *dura*, national as well as regional conditions in the immediate post-dam period made cotton cultivation unattractive. Firstly, in the interim period, that is, from 1937 to 1943, most people on the west bank were still manipulating the reservoir levels of the uncompleted dam. Many people declined to take tenancies offered to them in east bank schemes such as Fatisa and Hashaba. Thus a governmental report in the early 1940s says

None of these west bank people have benefited to any degree from the alternative livelihood schemes. Owing to the excellent *sufra* crop they have been unwilling to take up the tenancies offered to them, and the enormously wide river has prevented them from sharing the indirect benefits from these developments. That their plight is partly due to their own short-sightedness will not prevent them from suffering great hardships in a few years' time.[1]

Secondly, we have to remember that the interim period (1937–1943) coincided with the Second World War. In this period the demands from national as well as the international textile industries were relatively low while the demand for *dura* as a staple food was high. This was due to two reasons: internationally, western industries were either wracked by war or directed to the production of strategic goods essential for the war. Nationally, the

[8] DD/1–A–6–9/10/1943, Dueim District Files.

Sudan government imposed a 25 per cent cut in cotton acreages
so as to free land for food crops.[9] Thus the exported raw cotton
in the Sudan in 1943 was 38,500 tons while in 1938–9 it had been
62,000 tons (Prest 1948, p. 163).

It is important to note that the international price of cotton was
still apparently gaining at the time because, in economic terms, the
fall in international demand was accompanied by more than a
proportional fall in supply by cotton-producing countries whose
economy became oriented more to the production of food for
their population and fighting forces. The policy of the Price
Stabilization Reserve which was followed by the Sudan government as a counter-inflationary measure, however, had the effect
of making what the tenants received for cotton much less than the
selling price (Prest op. cit., p. 164) and not as profitable as less
controlled products like *dura*. In the Sudan, *dura*, unlike cotton,
had a local market and hence was less under the control of the
government in this respect. The government later intervened to
control *dura* prices on the grounds of moral responsibility for
dispossessed people and of pragmatic responsibility for the protection of its partner in the scheme – the individual tenant farmer.
These measures, concerning the control of *dura* prices, have
greatly affected the big men who basically depended on uncon-
trolled *dura* prices and on the dynamics of speculation in the pre-
dam conditions.

In the post-dam period, western industries recovered and
gradually moved towards full capacity, especially the British
textile industry in Lancashire. As a consequence, cotton prices
boomed and both the government and the people in the White
Nile became very interested in cotton cultivation. Thus many
people from the Amriya lineage on the west bank declined to take
tenancies on the east bank schemes and the acquisition of *hawasha*
in the post-dam period became something one had to strive and
pay for. Some Amriya men paid £S 50 and later £S 100 to get
their deserted *hawashas* on the east bank exchanged for *hawashas*
in the recently developed schemes on the west bank. In general,
the *hawasha* became a highly desired asset and people, even the
chiefs, would go to great lengths to obtain a cultivation plot in the

---

[9] Administrative Files: Governor's office, Gezira Province, Wad Medani –
SCR/91.D.3 – addressed to Secretary, Jebel Awliya Compensation Committee,
Finance Department, Khartoum.

schemes. The chiefs manipulated this situation to acquire power and accumulate wealth which has been used to expand their own schemes.

There were also other economic factors which made cotton very attractive as a cash crop in the immediate post-war period. Both during and after the war there was rationing of important market goods, such as sugar and tea, which constituted significant items in any household budget. To get these goods one needed cash and since a great part of these goods could be sold only on the black market, the price was liable to be very high. By the end of the war, cotton became a more reliable source of cash than livestock since the prospects for grazing deteriorated increasingly.

Finally, the most important factor that led to popular enthusiasm for cotton related to the Korean War (1949–52). The fear that it would develop into a world war caused western industries to accumulate strategic raw materials so that the price of cotton reached a peak. Most of the private schemes built in the White Nile were built during and immediately after the Korean War. Unfortunately, most of these schemes were very small and could not survive the abrupt decline in world cotton prices in the late fifties and onwards. Only the large schemes have managed to survive. There are small pump schemes still existing today but they depend mainly on subsidising themselves with *sargat al-gutum*, or 'cotton theft', from government-owned schemes. 'Cotton theft' means buying cotton directly from farmers at a low price and selling it to companies engaged in cotton marketing who later claim that it is their own scheme's produce. The practice is illegal but it is very difficult to curtail.

By and large, cotton cultivation has become the most attractive economic activity. More people are willing to include their land in cotton schemes, thus changing from semi-sedentary or semi-nomadic farmers into sedentary tenant farmers depending exclusively on these schemes for their living. The scheme has become the source of their economic security and has replaced the total network of arrangements a man had to make with fellow lineage mates to gain a secure living in the pre-dam period.

People are very aware of this replacement of dependency. Thus Shaikh El-Mikashfi, a well-known shaikh in the White Nile, is reported to have said, '*El-hawasha tagbud mab tafik*', that is literally, 'the *hawasha* would tie one to it and one can not escape its grasp'.

The implication is that the concern for the *hawasha* is becoming more than the concern for the wider kin group. This is because a person is forced to give all his time and efforts to the scheme, which in turn supplies the person with what he needs in terms of cash and subsistence. Not only is his dependence on wider kin ties diminishing, but also his dependence on the former security-suppliers – the big men and the shaikhs. Shaikh El Mikashfi, then, is a true spokesman for the ummar and the shaikhs, and his widely quoted statement is meant to discourage people from joining the agricultural schemes as tenants.

6

Agricultural Production and Economic Organization under Agrarian Development

A general description of the agricultural and economic organization of the scheme will be given here. One particular scheme, known as the Sufi-Wad Nimir scheme will be taken as an example. Its organization is typical of all schemes, government owned and private, and in basic respects has not varied significantly since the schemes were first introduced in the White Nile. In this account special emphasis will be given to aspects of the traditional ecology and economy that the scheme and the dam have changed – in particular, the aspects underlying the traditional economic insecurity and the fluctuations of agricultural production.

THE SCHEME AS A PARTNERSHIP

The scheme is based on a contractual partnership between the government and the individual tenant farmer. Most tenants have qualified for partnership through giving up their land for the scheme; accordingly the scheme has given them compensation of one pound per *feddan* of land, plus the allotment of one or more *hawashas* depending on the amount of land a man owned. Usually a scheme allocates land on the basis of a standard compensation rate, for instance the Sufi-Wad Nimir Scheme allocates a *hawasha* of 18 *feddans* for every 60 *feddans* of land a man owns. If a man owns 120 *feddans*, for example, he will be given two farm-plots; if he owns 180 *feddans* he will be allotted three plots and so on. In all cases, the scheme is not allowed to allocate more than one plot for any individual owner under his own name. Therefore, if anyone deserves more than one plot as compensation, he must register the extra plots under other names, those of sons, brothers or any other person. The pattern of plot allotment, ownership and inheritance will be discussed later. But here it is necessary to emphasize the individualistic nature of plot allotment in the scheme and the standing of the individual as a legal partner *vis-à-vis* the government. It is important to understand that the legal right of the individual to his plot does not revert to the government in the case of punishment for failure to fulfil his part in the scheme, but according to the scheme regulations, the plot goes to other members of his family. A family is allowed three chances for internal reallotment, after which the right of ownership passes to the lineage (or shaikhship) and finally goes to the administrative unit, referred to as an *omodiya*, where it becomes the right of the omda to make an allocation to any person he thinks suitable. In the Sufi Scheme I have been able to trace only one case in which the legal right to a plot has passed to the *omodiya* after exhausting all other possible claimants and in this specific case, the right to the plot passed to the omda himself. This point regarding possible claimants, or what we could call 'shadow partners', is significant here because it emphasizes the individual's responsibility and performance as far as the farm is concerned. At the same time, it directly alienates very close kin who have a vital interest in weakening that responsibility. Thus, according to the scheme regulations, if a man fails to come up to standard as a tenant in the scheme, farm ownership passes to one of his sons, then to a brother, if there are no more sons, and finally, to a paternal cousin (FBS). After this, the right goes to the lineage and the *omodiya*. I will consider the handing over of ownership later when discussing some elements of the emerging social organization. One important effect of this law is that it encourages rivalry and competition between very close kin who could be divided into 'partners' and 'shadow partners' – very similar to the government/opposition model of conflict. As a consequence of this, a tenant in the scheme would tend to depend less on his close kin and more upon others, for instance, wage labourers, in his efforts to display the most satisfactory performance possible.

Let me now show what the scheme partnership means. The government, represented by the Scheme Board, provides land, either by releasing its own land or by expropriation and compensation. It is also responsible for irrigation, the provision of technical supervision and management, the provision of agricultural equipment and necessities, and arrangements to provide the farmer with loans to help him carry out the manual labour at the appropriate time and to the desired standard. We shall now examine briefly the different functions of the government in the scheme.

IRRIGATION

We have shown that agricultural production in the pre-dam period depended exclusively on natural irrigation by the river flood and rains, both of which fluctuated unpredictably. The result was that economic production was unstable. In contrast to the natural system of irrigation in the pre-dam period, irrigation in the schemes today is technically controlled and hence artificial. In the scheme, irrigation is mechanized through the use of pumps to draw water from the river. The river flood itself is technically controlled through the system of opening and closing the dam. The dam is closed between July and April every year. The closure is carried out in July so that the flooding waters of the river in the rainy season (July–October) can be stored. In April, the dam is opened so that the water stored can be used for irrigation in Egypt. According to an agreement between the two countries, such a pattern of land use is agreed upon that the period between July and December constitutes a 'free' or unrestricted use of river water for irrigation in the Sudan. The period between December and March is a 'restricted' period and only a certain amount of water is allowed to be drawn from the Nile. According to this agreement and concomitant technical control of the Nile water, irrigation is subject to a fixed schedule to which every farmer has to adapt in order to secure his living under the new conditions.

It is important to give a brief account of the total pattern of irrigation in the schemes today and to show the significance of the various agricultural activities for the people involved. Irrigation in the scheme is under the direct supervision of the scheme inspector. Water is demanded by the scheme shaikhs who know exactly how much water is needed and who needs it. The inspector confirms their demands and gives orders to the chief water guard (*bash-khafir*), as to the amount of water to be allotted to the various shaikhs. Under the *bash-khafir* a number of *khafirs* are responsible for the control of irrigation in the various sections of the scheme. In the scheme, water is controlled by devices known as *khuroum,* (singular *khurum*, literally, a hole). A *khurum* provides a certain amount of water and the amount of water needed by a particular shaikh is converted into a number of *khurum*. The scheme has a main canal (called *tura'*), medium canals (*ummat asharin*); and minor canals (*ummat sita*). *Khurum* control water passing from the main canal into the various medium canals. Each medium canal irrigates a specific section of the scheme, under a shaikh. From the medium canal water passes into minimal canals to irrigate sub-sections known as *nimar* (sing. *nimra*, lit. 'number'). A *nimra* comprises a number of *hawashas*, farms. The minimal canal is accessible to every farm.

Irrigation in every medium canal is supervized by a shaikh who is appointed from among the tenants by the scheme management. Under the shaikh there are a number of subsidiary shaikhs responsible for assisting him by supervising irrigation and other services in the *nimras*.

Irrigation in the scheme is organized into a number of sessions. The scheme fixes a schedule for irrigation sessions according to the

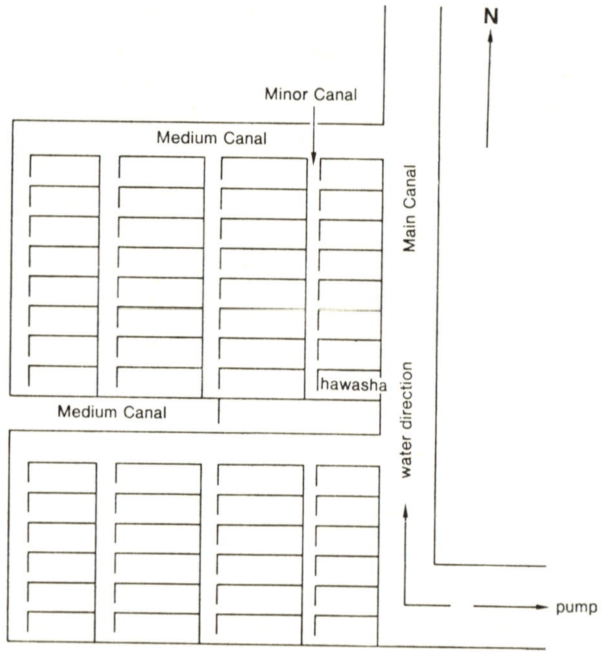

Fig. 11. Irrigation system in cotton schemes

annual plan for crop cultivation. Thus for *dura*, crop irrigation is divided into five watering sessions. Here are these sessions and the stages of plant growth at which they are supposed to take place. (Plant stages are described in local terms and conceptions):

(1) First watering session: On sowing.
(2) Second watering session: On plant reaching the *gidad*, i.e. 'chicken size'.
(3) Third watering session: On reaching the *latib* stage, i.e. 'the early formation of bundles'.
(4) Fourth watering session: On reaching the *shara*, i.e. 'unripe bundle stage'.
(5) Fifth watering session: Reserve session to quicken ripening of crop.

It is interesting to note that the scheme's technical personnel have adopted this native usage regarding the description of plant stages so that communications between the tenants and the technical personnel are harmoniously expressed in a common idiom.

The watering sessions for cotton cultivation are:

(1) First watering session: On sowing.
(2) Second watering session: On reaching *siwsiew* stage, i.e. 'chick or baby chicken size'.
(3) Third watering session: After first clearance known as *tarad*.
(4) Fourth watering session: On reaching *shag-el-tabga*, i.e. 'pre-flowering stage'.
(5) Fifth watering session: On flowering stage – referred to as *shal el-nuwar*.
(6) Sixth watering session: On the boll formation stage, referred to locally as *shal el-durdum*.
(7) Seventh watering session: When the boll matures.
(8) Eighth watering session: When the boll opens up, a stage referred to as *gumriyya*, i.e. 'pigeon'.
(9) Ninth watering session: When the plant is ready for the early picking known as *ash-sharaia el-oula*.
(10) Tenth watering session: During the main picking stage, referred to as *ash-sharaia el-tani*.

K

After the tenth watering session, cotton is referred to as *as-sharaia el-talta*, that is, the third or last picking stage. After this stage follows clearance, pulling up of roots, and setting fire to the land to clear it. All these activities are carried out by the individual farmer helped by the cotton-pickers whom he employs.

The watering session for every farm is arranged every fortnight; so that, in the case of cotton for instance, the ten watering sessions are spread over about 20 weeks or five months from September to February. This period covers the unrestricted Nile water-use period agreed upon by the Sudan and Egypt. Thus for the individual tenant farmer today, the irrigation of his farm is controlled not only by technological mechanisms, but also by the international agreements regarding the pattern of land use in the Sudan. The mechanization, organized control and distribution into standardized sessions according to a fixed schedule has radically changed the earlier environmental factors of fluctuating irrigation. In addition, the rains and riverfloods were controlled by the spiritual mandatory power of the shaikh, acting on behalf of God; the new irrigation system is controlled by the dam, the pump and the *khuroum* worked by personnel provided by the government. The pump has emerged as the symbol of a new economic life and when people refer to their mode of livelihood today, they speak about themselves as 'Arab el-masura', or 'Arabs of the pump'. They say that in the past we were 'Arab bahayim', or 'Arabs of animals', and 'ahal terus', 'or owners of rain cultivation plots'.

FARM TECHNOLOGY AND MECHANIZATION OF
AGRICULTURE

In the pre-dam period manual labour was the basis of all agricultural activities. Today a great deal of these activities are mechanized. In the scheme, ploughing, ridging, ditching, canalization, levelling and rolling are all mechanized. The scheme provides tractors, iron deep-ploughs, ridgers, disc-harrows, levellers, ditchers, rollers and sprayers.[1] It also provides the technicians and operators needed for the maintenance and running of these

---

[1] For more detailed information on the scale of use of these mechanized services in the White Nile and the Blue Nile in general, see *A Report on the Sample Census of Agriculture for the year 1964/65 in the Blue Nile Province of the Sudan*, December 1969, Ministry of Planning: Department of Statistics, Khartoum.

machines. The scheme's management evaluates the services rendered in these spheres for the individual farmer and charges the cost against the common scheme/tenant account. Thus the simple levelling technology of the manual *wasuq* has been replaced by advanced technology provided by the scheme. The *wasuq* was a valued implement. It was bought from the local market and not everybody had one. It also needed three persons at least to work it. These two factors necessitated exchange of the scarce implement and exchange of labour in collective work.

The most significant change in technology has come about through the use of sprayers or pest treatment for crops. I have shown that in the pre-dam period, pest treatment was the monopoly of the shaikhs. With the development of cotton cultivation however, a new technique was introduced. The first instrument used was a manual pump worked by the individual farmer to spray the cotton plant directly. The chemicals used for this purpose are D.D.T., Rogers and other compounds. Then tractors were employed instead of the manual pump. Today the schemes use aeroplanes only. Farmers themselves prefer the tractors to planes and pumps. They say that the last two are less efficient, because the pump takes much time and effort to work while the plane, they claim, spreads the chemicals into the air and little reaches the plant. Moreover the plane costs about £S 23 for an individual farm. The farmers today are very critical of planes and think that their shortcomings are not sufficiently realized by the scheme management. In a questionnaire I tried to elicit the farmers' attitude towards these technological innovations and to see to what extent they realized their advantages. One question in this respect was: 'would you prefer the pump, the tractor or the plane for spreading anti-pest chemicals?' The results are as follows: 23 farmers answered the questionnaire: nine were in favour of the pumps; 14 in favour of the tractor; and none in favour of the plane.

The significance of these answers is two-fold; first, it shows the degree of acceptance by the farmers of new technological tools. They are not critical of equipment but of its performance and efficiency. Cotton cultivation is itself an innovation and its pests were not catered for by the traditional methods of treatment. Secondly, the fact that the farmers not only accept these anti-pest measures but also have their own views on how they can be improved, shows that their old conception of pests as something not directly controllable by man is changing. They are aware that, at least, they are controllable; however, the new pest treatment has not replaced the traditional treatment altogether in the case of *dura* cultivation. Locusts and birds remain an occasional threat to *dura* cultivation, and governmental efforts to combat them have not always been successful. Accordingly, today many people supplement the new pest treatment with services provided by the shaikhs. The new treatment consists of chemicals sprayed by planes onto trees or the more distant hilly areas where locusts breed or concentrate. From time to time the government recruits people from among the various villages and takes them on locust expeditions to wipe out concentrations. In most cases these government efforts have lessened the locust danger considerably. But in many cases where both birds and locusts strike at farms and where no prior efforts have been made to contact the appropriate shaikhs, this failure to do so is given as the cause. For instance, in 1969–70 birds attacked *dura* crops in some farms in the Rahawat-Sufi Scheme. Great efforts were made to spray by attacking the surrounding woods. Eventually they succeeded in eliminating the birds. When I discussed this incident with an informant, El-Tayib Gamilalla, he said:

You know before the birds attacked, a group of us from Humur Garnab section of the Amriya lineage approached Shaikh El-Khalifa Musa, our Shaikh, to write a *waraga* (paper of magical charm) to protect our farms from birds. We gave the shaikh 10 piastres each and promised to give him a *kaila* (a measure) on every *ardeb*, 12 *kailas* if he succeeded in keeping the birds away from our crop. We asked Wad abu-Kuraa', a local Jaa'li retailer, to join us in this arrangement with the shaikh but he did not seem so enthusiastic about the idea and we did not press him further. When the birds attacked last year, he was the first victim. I produced 12 ardebs of *dura* last year. He produced only five *kailas* (that is less than half an *ardeb*). He certainly learnt his lesson.

Thus, in *dura*, the provision of protection against birds and locusts by shaikhs is still in demand, and many people today approach their shaikhs for this service. This is not, however, done on a regular basis, as it was before the dam, and many people have in fact ceased to employ the shaikhs for these services. It is not so much that the spiritual position of the shaikh has survived techno-logical change, as that the secularization of farm technology has diminished his functional position in society, or in Merton's terms, has diminished his role-set (Merton 1949). Nor is it the case that the people believe less in the power of shaikhs, but rather that shaikhs have less to do today. The role-set designating their total functions in society has been narrowed by the taking over of some or most of these functions by the new technology.

INTERNAL ORGANIZATION OF THE FARM

A farm is divided into three plots, referred to as *dawrat* ('rotations'), making for the alternate cultivation of *dura*/cotton/fallow When a plot is cultivated with *dura* in a specific year, it will grow cotton the following year and be left fallow the year after. Each of the three major plots is divided into twelve medium plots referred to as *ingayat* ('sections'). Each *ingaya* is also divided into four minor sections called *arbita* (singular *rubat*, or knot). The demarcation of medium and main plots facilitates irrigation by making possible alternate watering of the different sections of the farm and by solving the problem of uneven levels in the farm by making different levels into separate sub-plots and watering them

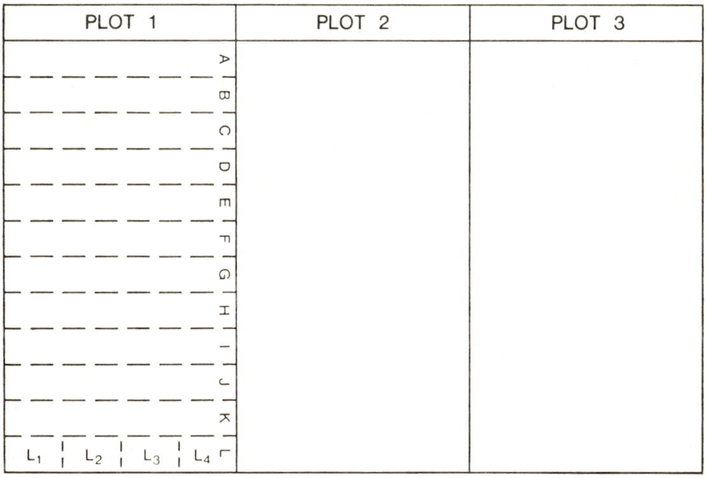

Plots 1, 2, 3 Major plots (making alternate cultivation for durra/cotton/fallow)
A, B, C, D   Medium plots (*ingayat*)
L₁ L₂ L₃ L₄   Minor plots (*arbita*)

Fig. 12. Internal organization of the Hawasha

separately. This is a very efficient system of irrigation and usually makes equal distribution of water possible in the farm. Certainly, it is more efficient than the traditional *hugna*, the reservoir system used for the irrigation of the *terus* cultivation. Figure 12 shows the internal organization of the farm in the agricultural schemes today.

EXTRA-FARM ORGANIZATION

A number of farms form together what is known as *nimra* (plural *nimrat*, literally, 'numbers'). A *nimra* has one common minor canal or *abu-sitta* and thus forms an irrigation unit supervised by a *nimra* shaikh. The *nimra* shaikh is chosen by the farmers from among themselves so as to organize and distribute water between the different farms. A number of *nimrat* together form a shaikh-ship. Each shaikhship is allocated a specific medium canal or *abu-shrin* and so makes an irrigation unit larger than the *nimra*. It is headed by a shaikh chosen from among the farmers themselves. In the past, during the Condominium era, the shaikh was appointed by the scheme inspector and was usually selected on the basis of individual performance in the scheme, for instance, on the record of production and observance of law and order. Since independence however, the shaikh's office is open to competition among all farmers and selection is by secret ballot. The office has not much authority, for the shaikh mainly organizes watering and reports breaches of regulations to the inspector. It is attractive only for the bonus it provides, about three pounds per month. The shaikh is responsible to the inspector for discipline in the shaikh-ship. He takes orders from the inspector and passes them on to the *nimra* shaikhs under him, who pass the orders or information to the individual tenants. As long as the individual tenant obeys orders and follows the scheme instructions, the shaikhs are for him merely messengers. They have only very restricted authority. Thus, in the case of disobedience by a farmer, it becomes the duty of the shaikh or *nimra*-shaikh to report this to the scheme inspector. In all such cases both the *nimra* shaikh and the general shaikh must agree in putting this case to the inspector and later stand as prosecutors in the cultivator's board where disciplinary cases are settled. The board is presided over by the scheme inspector and its membership comprises all the shaikhs in the scheme. The cultivators' board has powers to impose fines of 50 piastres with appeal to the deputy nazir's court: it is thus closely connected to tribal chiefship. Moreover, the cultivators' board deals with disciplinary action regarding technical aspects such as cultivation and water control, while the deputy nazir is responsible for public order in the scheme. Figure 13 illustrates the organizational principles of scheme management and their close inter-connections with tribal chiefship.

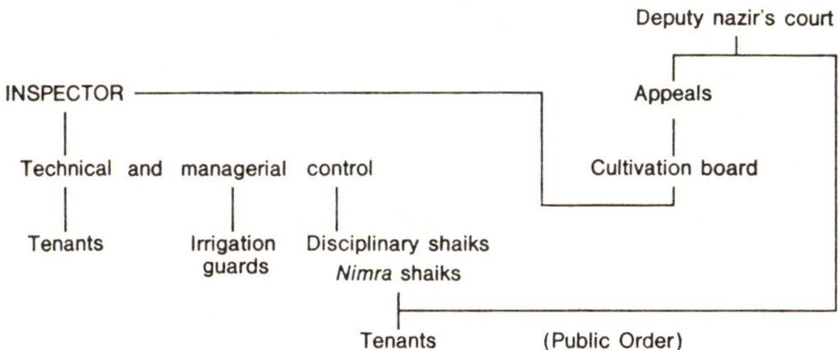

Fig. 13. Scheme management and organization

The Sufi-Wad Nimir Scheme has altogether an inspector, five shaikhs, *nimra* shaikhs, a chief irrigation guard, a number of irrigation guards, and 146 tenants. The distribution of fields (*hawashas*) among the various shaikhships is shown in Table 8.

The scheme consists of 146 fields. Each field is made up of 18 *feddans* thus there is a total of 2,628 *feddans* in the scheme. A field is subdivided into three plots of six *feddans* each. The scheme originally started with only 68 fields in 1943–4, but has been extended since then at least three times. The scheme has also a team of technical personnel. In addition to engineers, machine-operators, drivers, maintenance technicians, etc., there is a Unit of

Table 8. Distribution of fields among various shaikhships

Shaikhship (*name of shaikh*)	No. of hawashas
(1) Muhammad Yusuf	30
(2) Muhammad Omer El Saeid	38
(3) El Mahdi Yusuf	25
(4) Abdallah Mahmoud	23
(5) El Galal Abdel Gadir	30
	146

Plant Protection Department. This unit is responsible for pest combat, soil protection, and supervision of plant growth.

ORGANIZATION OF AGRICULTURE AND LABOUR IN THE SCHEME

The rotation system is meant to maintain the fertility of the soil by the occasional fallowing and the cultivation of two different crops. This sort of rotation is needed more for the White Nile type of soil than, for instance, the Gezira area where the soil is more fertile. The need for fallowing has an important bearing on the size of tenancy in a scheme, for it reduces the number of tenants by at least one-sixth of that in the non-fallowed system. Thus a scheme of 200 fields, for instance, of 18 *feddans* each, could have absorbed another 50 farmers if the fallowed field, 18 *feddans*, was replaced by a non-fallowed one of 12 *feddaas*, making six *feddans* for *dura* and six for cotton. In the pre-dam period, land was cultivated and fallowed according to the variability in the pattern of rainfall and river flood.

There is an annual schedule for cotton and *dura* production set forward by the scheme board. The farmers are kept informed of this schedule through the scheme's shaikhs and asked to act accordingly. The general pattern of the agricultural year is roughly that shown in Table 9.

Table 9. General timetable for the agricultural year

Agricultural activity	*Period*
Dura:	
(a) Sowing (*ziraa'a*)	July–August
(b) Clearance (*hash*)	August–September
(c) Thinning out	October
(d) Harvest (*hasad*)	November
Cotton	
(a) Sowing (*ziraa'a*)	July–August
(b) Clearance (*hash*)	August–October
(c) Thinning Out	October–November
(d) Pest spraying	November–December
(e) Picking	January–March
(f) Clearance of roots (*galia'*) and setting of fire (*harig*)	March–May

TYPE OF LABOUR NEEDED FOR THE AGRICULTURAL ACTIVITIES

Some of these agricultural activities are mechanized. For cotton, thinning-out is done by ploughs and discs. In the case of *dura*, it is done manually. Also the spraying of cotton is done by planes while it is still done manually for *dura*. I have already discussed the other mechanized services in the scheme. The rest of the agricultural activities are carried out by manual labour. Thus the sowing of cotton and *dura* is done by digging small holes by *turiya*, a traditional digging tool, dropping a few seeds in, mostly by young boys or girls, and covering the holes with soil. Clearing (*hash*) is done by hoe. Thinning out and the harvesting of *dura* are carried out with the use of hoe-type tools. For cotton, the picking and clearance of roots is performed manually, directly by hand in the case of picking, and through the use of a certain native tool known as *el-kaggama* (pulling tool for root clearance).

The scheme finances the hired labour needed by the farmers to accomplish their agricultural tasks in time. I have shown that hired labour was extremely rare in the pre-dam period. Most of the labour was exchanged freely between close kin, although in some cases families did supplement free labour with paid labour. The wage labourers in such cases were normally strangers, for instance Jumuiya, Rizaigat, or ex-slaves. Only the very poor lineage fellows were forced to work for money, an activity which was much despised. But today the Hassaniya participate in wage labour at an ever-increasing rate. However, they still do not work for payment for close kinsmen, such as members of a single *khashm-bait*, to avoid manipulation by close kin, whom they may accuse of avoiding the payment of proper wages or of trying to establish authority directly over them. Thus, most of the wage-labour recruited by the Garnab section of the Amriya came from the Ribaihab and other sections. This is, no doubt, a way of avoiding the traditionally despised action of working for payment for one's kinsmen. Some feel that free labour given by close kinsmen cannot be depended upon because they have no interest in making another's career in the *hawasha* successful. The labour needed by the scheme is required at a particular time and must reach a certain standard. It is difficult for a man to go around pushing people to help him keep to schedule; also it is difficult to demand much from a free labour donor, let alone ask him to work with you from dawn to dusk during, for instance, the peak season of cotton picking.

For all these reasons the scheme management itself has encouraged wage labour and has made the job very easy for the tenant farmers by providing them with loans to meet this labour. The scheme even provides the farmers with the money needed for transporting hired labourers from outside the scheme area. It is important to note that the disappearance of free kin labour is also due to the development of markets and a new occupational structure. In the past the Hassaniya had mainly two occupations: cultivation and animal rearing. Today in the market place they work as retailers, tailors, café owners and attendants, sellers of various goods such as grain, animals, firewood for buildings, and so on. Butchery is also very popular and absorbs many people.

The schemes have provided their own occupational opportunities like *khufura* (guards), *muraslat* (messengers) *tulba* (manual labourers) *mekhzangis* (store-keepers) as well as various seasonal jobs such as supervisors on cotton stations where picked cotton is gathered before final transportation to ginning factories and central stores. *Tulba*, manual labourer, is a very important category of employment provided by the schemes because many men are absorbed at one time. For instance, in the clearance of canals, and in the digging and levelling of land when needed. The scheme also needs technical staff such as machine operators, maintenance technicians, drivers, and so on.

The development of the social services in the post-dam period has also created many new opportunities for governmental employment. Many people today work as cleaners responsible for the cleaning of the markets and streets. Some work as guards in schools and markets, and so on. Although in many of these spheres the opportunities have been taken largely by strangers, a growing number of the Hassaniya are entering the occupations that the post-dam development has created.

Table 11 shows the occupational structure of the Sufi village, inhabited mainly by members of the Amriya lineage. The most important fact that the table shows is that the category of *fua'al*, or manual labourers, forms a significant part of the occupational structure among these post-dam settlers.

Table 10. A farmer's account with the scheme (Sufi–Rahawat Scheme 1968/69)

Item	Date	Payment £S.MM
1. Sowing loan	1/9/68	1.200
2. First weeding loan	16/9/68	2.200
3. Second weeding loan	8/10/68	2.200
4. Third weeding loan	6/11/68	2.200
5. Thinning out	6/11/68	1.600
6. Clearance of medium canal	8/1/69	1.000
7. Clearance of minimal canal	8/8/68	0.500
8. Cutting	15/8/68	0.251
9. First mechanized clearance	27/10/68	1.000
10. Importation of cotton-pickers		5.800
11. Credit on produce, first instalment	8/10/69	4.000
12. Credit on produce, second instalment	27/12/68	4.000
13. Transport for cotton-pickers		2.714
Tenant's Share in Common Expenses		
14. 50% of bush clearance		0.722
15. 50% of levelling expenses		2.600
16. 50% of second mechanized clearance		0.800
17. 50% seeds		1.362
18. 50% fertilizers		3.330
19. 50% spraying		13.296
20. 50% cotton sacks		3.003
21. 50% cotton picking		21.853
22. 50% collection points and supervision		2.148
23. 50% transportation of cotton to ginning factories		2.763
24. 50% cotton committee expenses		0.136
25. 50% miscellaneous		0.537
	Total	78.414
Sale of cotton 26 *quarters* 6 rottls		146.753
Loans and expenses		78.414
Tenant's share		68.339
10% reduction		6.834
Tenant's net share		61.505

Table 11. The occupational structure of Sufi village (mostly Amriya)[1]

Occupation	No. of men engaged[2]
(1) Tenant farmers	157
(2) *Fua'al*, or wage-labourers	49
(3) Skilled and non-skilled (*tulba*) schemes employees	26
(4) Retailers	17
(5) Butchers	6
(6) Builders	5
(7) Health and Veterinary Services employees	10
(8) Others	50
Total	320[3]

[1] These figures are computed from a household census survey I have carried out in Sufi village in 1969/70.

[2] Number of men refers to heads of households only.

[3] 320 is the total number of households covered in Sufi village. The survey is carried out as a full census but there is no guarantee that all households are in fact included. For instance, the number of butchers and builders are clearly more than the figures have shown here.

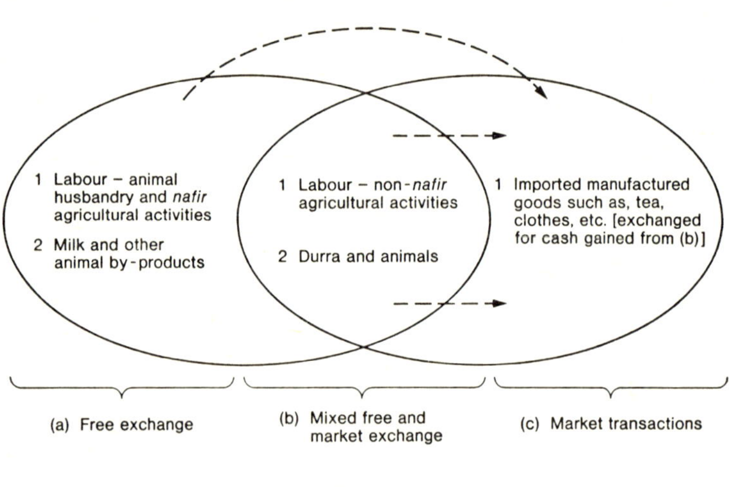

Fig. 14. Changes in the pre-dam spheres of exchange among the White Nile Arabs

7

The Structure of the Lineage in the Post-Dam Period

It has been shown in the earlier chapters that lineage solidarity and corporate unity emerged from the socio-economic necessities relating to the pre-dam ecological and economic setting. The lineage was a wider group to which individuals belonged and which enabled them to maximize their interests and to secure a living. Post-Dam conditions, however, have greatly affected this basis of lineage integration: new conditions of livelihood and new sources of economic security have been provided by the agricultural schemes. The schemes have shifted economic dependency from the wider network of *horizontal* relationships connecting individuals to a more restricted and formal set of *vertical* relationships.

The socio-economic unity of the lineage in the pre-dam period was, as we have seen, based on five premises: (1) the necessary exchange of free labour in an intensively diversified semi-nomadic economy, consisting of both animal-husbandry and subsistence cultivation; (2) the necessary exchange of consumer goods in famine and hardship, common in this environment; (3) co-residence and identification with lineage farming land and pastures as common assets from which the lineage members derived their common livelihood while controlling access to outsiders; (4) the exchange of women in marriage and control of the property exchanged which were reflected in a high degree of lineage endogamy (see Table 4); (5) the focal position of the ummar, the big men, in the social structure and their control of social and political power as a result of the necessary involvement of ordinary people in a wide range of debt – bonds to them. I shall now examine the changes in these factors.

This sphere of exchange has become today the most narrow or restricted one. The decline in animal husbandry as a group activity, and as an essential part of a semi-nomadic existence, has eliminated a very important sphere in which free labour was formerly exchanged between lineage members. It was in animal rearing that free labour was most significant. Many extended families came together in a number of herding partnerships which then united to form a camping unit comprising the overall lineage group. A detailed illustration of the organization of labour in these various units was given in Chapter 2.

The necessary demands of sedentary cotton production, which has become people's basic interest has meant that they can no longer move seasonally with their animals. Cotton cultivation goes on the whole year round and it is not possible in the way it is carried out to fit it into a semi-nomadic existence. I think, therefore that the development of cotton production in the White Nile has, at the least, accelerated the tendency towards the riverain settlement of the semi-nomads. In this respect, Cunnison's remarks (Cunnison 1964) that cotton cultivation cannot automatically lead to the sedentarization of nomads, should be further considered, though one may argue that the semi-nomads/semi-sedentary case may be different and that the reference of cotton cultivation to settlements depends first and foremost on the scale and organization of production. It may also depend on how people evaluate the possible alternatives of investing the income from cotton in buying animals, or in growing more cotton, or embarking on another sedentary form of investment.

It has been shown in Chapter 6 that cotton cultivation has, since the early 1940s, become the most attractive economic activity. Under cotton schemes, people feel that they have more economic security than they used to have. Two questions put to those interviewed in this respect were:

(a) Do you consider that your life after the dam has or has not changed?

(b) If you were to choose again between having or not having the dam built, which would you choose?

The overwhelming majority of those interviewed seemed to think that their life had changed and that they would cast their vote in favour of the dam,[1] it had changed things for the better.

People are aware that they are no longer the united group of kin

---

[1] All those questioned are over 50. Of the 30 questioned, 29 answered both questions positively – only one replied negatively.

that they used to be. They say '*zaman al-mahana fat*', 'the days of compassion have passed', and they also say '*kunna ragil wahid, asa'akulu zoul birgaibtu*', 'we were all as one man; today every one accounts for his own soul!' They are not to be blamed, but rather the *hawashat*, the scheme plots that symbolize the new economy.

In the *hawasha*, labour is either mechanized or paid for with wages supplied by the scheme. Hired labour has become very significant today and a large sector of the population has been transformed into seasonal and permanent wage labourers. At certain times of the agricultural year, the demand for hired labour becomes so acute that it becomes necessary to import labour from the nomadic sector.[2] In the scheme, the farmers follow a fixed annual schedule set out by the scheme management; for instance, the main watering of plants is to be carried out between July and December, for this is the free period for the use of river water set down by the White Nile Waters Agreement, Egypt and the Sudan. The scheme also plans that all clearance activities finish before early winter so that spraying can be carried out. The main enemy of cotton is that known locally as *ad-douda el-masria*, the Egyptian worm, and it attacks mainly in winter so that spraying must be carried out before then. With the total responsibility of the *hawasha* and taking into consideration the technical and managerial problems involved, the tenant farmer has found in hired labour a dependable means of keeping to schedule and fulfilling his obligations and responsibilities towards his farm and the scheme.

People today employ fellow lineage members as wage labourers, but usually avoid very closely related kin such as members of the same *khashm-bait*. Members of the Garnab (Humar) section of the Amriya employ people from the Ribaihab section, but, if possible, avoid employing people from their own section. The exchange of hired labour outside the *kashm-bait* but inside the lineage can be seen as a compromise between a new economic system encouraging hired labour and a former system prejudiced against it. In most circumstances it is the elementary family that is responsible for production in the *hawasha*. This can be explained partly by the conflict inherent in the tenure of the *hawasha* as set out by the

[2] See Abbas Mohamed 1973. 'The Nomadic and the Sedentary: Polar complementaries not Polar opposites', in Nelson, C. (ed.), *The Desert and the Sown*, University of California Press, 1973.

scheme regulations. A farm should be given, or officially recognized as belonging, to one person and not shared. At the death of the owner, a farm goes to his younger son. In the colonial era, it used to go to the elder son, but after Sudanese Independence in 1956, the rule was changed because of cases which arose when the elder son neglected his younger brothers and did not provide them with the necessities of livelihood.

For instance, Abdel Rahim Awadallah had two younger brothers, half-siblings, Bilal and Sulaiman, Bilal being the youngest. Their father died in the 1950s and title to the *hawasha* was in the name of Abdel Rahim. But Abdel Rahim neglected his two brothers so that his stepmother, the mother of the two brothers, made a complaint against him to the Scheme Board. The Scheme Board decided that the farm should be re-allocated to Bilal, the youngest brother, while recognizing Abdel Rahim as trustee: in this capacity his service on the farm ended when Bilal reached adult age. This has since become the general procedure regarding farm tenure. According to this system, the older the son is, the less likely he is to get more than a temporary right to the farm and thus the more quickly he acts to seek an independent source of living for himself and his family. It is possible that it is the older sons who are increasingly being transformed into a group of seasonal or permanent wage-labourers, for by the time they give up their guardianship of the farm they have already gained enough skill in cotton cultivation to enable them to work as wage-labourers in the various agricultural activities.

CO-RESIDENCE AND COMMON SOURCES OF LIVELIHOOD

The post-dam conditions and the rise of agricultural schemes have affected the distribution and social character of the various Amriya lineage sections in this way: in the pre-dam period the Amriya living east and west of the river were economically dependent on each other. Today the Madiab,[3] the Diraia'ab and the Dalwab sections which live mainly on the east bank are separated by a river about four miles wide (see Fig. 15). They derive their livelihood from schemes built on the east bank, namely Fatisa and Gammalab schemes, where they used to have their traditional

---

[3] The nomadic section.

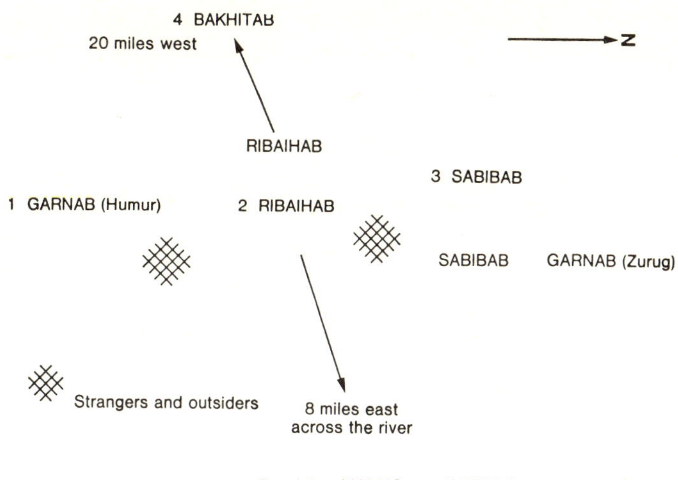

Fig. 15. The core-split: the distribution of the Amriya lineage today

terus land in the past. Secondly, the Amriya on the west bank are themselves distributed among at least three agricultural schemes. Thus 46 Amriya hold their farms in the Sufi Scheme; 170 hold farms in the Rahawat Scheme and 80 hold farms in the Abgar Scheme (see Map 3 for these schemes). Table 12 shows the number of farms held by the different lineage sections of the Amriya in two of the above-mentioned schemes:

Table 12. The number of farm holdings of different Amriya Sections

Lineage section (khashm-bait)	No. of hawashas in the Sufi Scheme	No. of hawashas in the Rahawat Scheme
(1) Ribaihab	21	60
(2) Garnab (Zurug)	15	—
(3) Sabibab	3	20
(4) Madiab*	5	10
(5) Diraia'ab*	2	—
(6) Garnab (Humur)	—	80
(7) Dalwab*	—	—
(8) Bakhitab*	—	—

* Sections which have most of their holdings on the east bank.

L

Thirdly, the nomadic section, the Bakhitab, which formerly interacted closely with the rest of the lineage in its semi-nomadic past, today finds that interaction is greatly affected. It has lost contact with the mother lineage near the river. When I was in the field I tried many times to visit this section but succeeded only once; part of the trouble was that the people near the river seemed to know very little about it. Fourthly, various small groups have dispersed in twos and threes to distant parts of the region, such as the Gezira and Managil. Some, especially owners of large herds of stock,[4] have moved with their animals to the Kosti District and to the western interior to seek richer grazing opportunities.

Some have returned to their lineage homeland after agricultural schemes were built or extended. Thus a group of the Sabibab *khashm-bait* moved to the Kosti District and Turra'a el-Khadra to explore richer pastures for their animals. In the early 1950s when the Sufi Scheme was extended and more tenants were attracted, the majority of this group returned home to take tenancies in the scheme. It is interesting to note that most of them lost a large number of their animals and returned with far fewer than they set out with. Today, this group forms a separate shaikship under Shaikh Wad Ed-daw, whose father originally led the early expedition to the Kosti District.

Some of the Amriya who moved to Dar Kabbabish have returned to take tenancies or to be at home. Others have left most of their animals with closely related people or with hired shepherds while maintaining a kind of semi-nomadic life. Up to the present some of these have their animals listed in Dar Kabbabish. The post-dam development has resulted in the Amriya lineage as a socio-economic unit breaking into various smaller units occupying different sides of the river, deriving their livelihood from different schemes and, in some cases, having different modes of livelihood.

This is accompanied, and partly reflected, in the fragmentation of the lineage or shaikhship into a number of shaikhships or tax-paying groups. The Amriya today are organized into eight shaikhships, each under a separate administrative shaikh. Five out

---

[4] A report in the administrative files at Dueim states that '. . . there will be a drift of the population from the north to the better rain areas on the south (i.e. from Jebel Arashkol southwards into the Kosti District'. (Reference: DD/SCR/2. E.I. – Ref. SCR/(I.A. – Dueim, 2nd April, 1942.)

of the eight shaikhships listed in Table 13 have come into being since the dam. One of these, number 5, was formed in 1943 as a result of the official policy to separate the scheme shaikhship from the tribal shaikhship by organizing the scheme tenants into a tax-paying unit separate from the non-tenant members of the tribe. When the Rahawat Private Scheme was built, in the mid-1940s, the Garnab (Humur) who owned their *hawasha* in this scheme, demanded a separate shaikship modelled on that of the Sufi Scheme. Although the Rahawat Scheme was very small at that time, their demand to have a separate shaikship was met.

The formation of shaikhship No. 1 (see Table 13) took place when Ahmed Ali Ed-daw, the present shaikh, and his group came back from Kosti District to take tenancies at the new extension of the Sufi Scheme. They formed a small group consisting of about 15 men, but owning still a relatively significant number of animals. They now live very near to the traditional cattle-grazing grounds and try to make the rearing of animals a source of living in addition to participation in cotton cultivation. When they first came back from Kosti, they were attached to one of the shaikh-ships but they soon demanded a separate shaikhship. They claimed that their kin, who had already settled, tended to assume that they had more animals than they really owned.

Thus corporate lineage identity in the traditional setting which was exemplified, among other things, by its *de facto* as well as *de jure* characterization as a tax-paying group, has today been greatly affected by the breaking of the lineage into many tax-paying groups.

This process of lineage segmentation may be only partially due to the increase in human population in Dar Hassaniya for, as has been pointed out earlier, the human population of the Dar today is nearly half a million; 30 years ago, it was about 250,000. But the increase in the number of shaikhships is more than proportional to the increase in human population. Among the Amriya, for instance, shaikhships have increased from three to eight, thus making an increase of about 160 per cent. But the Amriya shaikh-ships consist of both riverain and nomadic groups. If we divide the figure of eight among the two groups, we find that the nomadic shaikhships have increased from one to two, while the riverain shaikhships have increased from two to six. The riverain people are more directly affected by the dam, the development of the agricultural schemes and their bearing on the lineage organization.

Table 13. Administrative shaikhships of the Amriya lineage in 1969/70

No.	Name of shaikh	Section	Residence	Tenure of office	Tenure of shaikhship	Camels	Cattle	Donkeys	Sheep	Goats
(1)	Ahmed Ali Ed-dav	Sabibab	Sufi	1966	1966	—	63	16	123	56
(2)	El-amin At-toum	Sabibab	Er-rihaid	1952	old	3	19	20	84	74
(3)	Abdel Gader Sulaiman	Garnab (z)	Sufi	1951	old	1	122	62	179	163
(4)	Muhammad Y. Mishatih	Garnab (H)	H. Ibaid	mid-40s	mid-40s	2	50	83	75	173
(5)	Muhammad A. El Hadu	Ribaihab	Sufi	1943	1943	12	138	90	371	219
(6)	Sulaiman Bakhait	Bakhitab	Pastoral	old	old	87	2	—	14	—
(7)	Bakhait Balal		Pastoral	old	old	72	9	14	377	78

Note: The Amriya on the east bank have their separate shaikhship.
Source: Administrative files at Wad Nimir, the headquarters of the deputy nazirate.

It is also true that the riverain areas have witnessed a greater increase in population than the nomadic areas. There is no statistical evidence for this, for there was no previous attempt to divide the areas into such divisions. But one could easily hold that the increase in human population is, at least partially, due to the development of health services and education. The development of markets and motor transport have helped also in supplying the local population with vegetables and food from other parts of the region as well as from outside it, such as the Three Towns, Kosti and El-Obeid.

The breaking down of the lineage as a tax-paying group into many such units does not necessarily mean that these smaller fragments have an awareness of their corporate identity *vis-à-vis* other units. Shaikhships today are very similar to those among the Kabbabish (Asad 1970), where they emerge as semi-voluntary associations to which attachment is based on choice and interest. Among the White Nile Arabs, the only body that can influence the formation of these units today is the tribal chiefs, members of the Habbaniya ruling section.

The grazing grounds have deteriorated because they have been used as settlement sites and the development of motor transport has also taken its toll. In the new settlements, people of different lineage or tribe are able to build their homes and settle. The expropriation of agricultural land and the taking over of land ownership by the government and its use for building agricultural schemes have combined to undermine the close and relatively exclusive identification of lineages with the land as a common source of livelihood. An agricultural unit is a multi-lineage or a multi-ethnic institution as Table 14 shows.

LINEAGE ENDOGAMY AND CHANGE IN THE PATTERN OF MARRIAGE

I have already noted that preferred marriage was contracted with members of the lineage or the sub-lineage. The new system of tenure, together with competition for farms, produced conflict between close kin, yet people speak as if marriages within the sub-lineage would counteract these conflicts. They argue that if the farm is to be given to one of two or more brothers then its allocation should not be so significant if their children are going to inter-marry and benefit from it later.

Table 14. The distribution of holdings of various Hassaniya, Kawahla and other tribal groups in three neighbouring agricultural schemes

Name of group	No. of holdings in the Rahawat Scheme	No. of holdings in the Sufi Scheme	No. of holdings in the Abgar Scheme
(1) Amriya	170	46	40
Other Hassaniya Groups:			
(2) Imairiya	—	3	15
(3) Gushgushab	60	19	100
(4) Humran	—	—	120
(5) Gur	2	—	25
(6) Nimrab	14	1	15
(7) Dabalab	6	—	30
(8) Akadab	—	5	—
(9) Shamkhiya	2	4	—
(10) Khushunab	13	2	—
(11) Iraifab	—	11	2
(12) Magawir	—	1	—
(13) Salahia	6	8	20
(14) Shigeilab	4	—	10
(15) Gayadab	9	5	—
(16) Siraihat	—	9	—
(17) Maa'galab	—	1	—
Other Kawahla Groups:			
(18) Hissinat	19	15	50
(19) Muhammadiya	4	2	5
(20) Kawahla	2	—	—
(21) Urwab	—	1	—
Other Groups:			
(22) Jummiya	6	—	—
(23) Ahamda	25	—	—
(24) Magdiya	1	1	2
(25) Danagla	2	—	—
(26) Ja'afra	2	—	—
(27) Ja'aliyin	45	8	25
(28) Bidairiya	—	—	15
(29) Diwaih	—	—	15
Total of Hassaniya holdings	333	527	119
Total of Non-Hassaniya holdings	56	32	27
Total of holdings in each scheme	389	559	146

The increase in marriages with FBDS, however, might be due to the fact that many extended families still exist today; such families own enough land and animals to make possible internal 'household integration', based on distributing the various households or elementary families between different spheres of economic activity. Take for instance the following case.

Awlad Yusuf Fadlalah maintain a closely knit group of four brothers and their children. Muhammad and Hammad hold farms in the Sufi Scheme. Mirghani looks after the cultivation of *terus* rainland and a small cheese factory which is held in partnership between himself and Muhammad. Hamid is a retail trader who spends most of his time on the east bank. The four brothers live together in one block surrounded by one *hosh* (outside wall), although each occupies a separate house consisting of one or more huts or mud buildings and a *kashasha* (veranda). The four brothers store their *dura* in one *matmura*, and although each knows roughly how much he has stored, access to the common *matmura* is not checked or regulated. Although each has his own hearth, the exchange of cooked food is very common. Muhammad and Hammad own a respectable number of animals, both cattle and sheep, and they form one herding unit under one hired shepherd. There are many extended families of this kind which are closely integrated, but it is the elementary family which represents the common norm.

THE BIG MEN OR 'WEALTHY TRADERS'

The institution of *ummar gabila*, wealthy big men, had its basis in the pattern of the fluctuating economic production before the construction of the dam. Big men depended on investing their wealth in land and animals, in *dura* marketing and trade. Through speculative storage of goods they received high prices for their *dura* stores. Their capital growth thus depended first and foremost on the existence of fluctuating production together with their power to speculate on the marketing of the essential *dura* crop. Their social power stemmed from the debts others owed them. The greater an amir's capital became, the more he acquired dependants in times of famine and hardship. Attachment to a big man was an insurance policy, a risk-reducing device in an uncertain economy. Apart from the market transactions that take place between the big man and commoner, the relation between the big man and those attached to him – mainly his lineage fellows – is one of patron/clientage in matters of military defence. The significance of these latter aspects was more crucial in the pre-Condominium era when there was little security in the region and tribal warfare was common.

As a patron the big man provides generosity and hospitality. His lavishness reflects his affluence, for only after providing security for himself could he start to provide security for others. In his guest-house (*khalwa*), he entertains his followers, most of whom are close kinsmen – members of his lineage. The function of the *khalwa* as an arena and source of social power is comparable to that of the 'men's house' among the Pathans (Barth 1959). The amir's followers, most of whom are also his core supporters[5] since they are members of the same lineage, enjoy hospitality and provision of subsistence in famine and need. In return they are obliged to give him political support, and also to reciprocate directly by providing free co-operative labour (*nafir*), and by herding his animals. The economic wealth of the big man is not mainly a function of any discrepancy in actual land ownership, but of the built-in potentiality for investing his wealth in a perpetually insecure and fluctuating economy. In this sense, he is a tribal 'entrepreneur'. In the post-dam period the changing economy and improvements in farm technology have had a very significant impact on the contrasting positions and the bond between big men and commoners.

The mechanization of agriculture, especially in the field of irrigation and pest control, has eliminated the two most crucial endemic evils of economic production in the past. This has favoured the commoners at the expense of the 'big men'. The farmer today enjoys a substantial increase in economic security. He provides only his labour and gets in return a reasonable income and extra-bonuses from the scheme. The strong bond between him and his fellow ummar is, therefore, no longer necessary. It has been replaced by a new source of security – the scheme and its management.

The big men have been left not only without people seeking security, but they have also suffered from severe restrictions on opportunities for investment, both economic and social. In the

---

[5] See Bailey 1969, where he distinguishes 'core' as a 'moral' body and not 'mercenary' as in the case of followers.

post-dam period their main investment was in the speculative trade in grain. Today this opportunity has been checked in a number of ways; firstly, by the fact that agricultural production is in general no longer fluctuating. It is fairly evenly controlled by many technical measures. Secondly, the main cash crop is cotton, and cotton-marketing is controlled by the scheme and the government. The government collects cotton from the farmers, exports it, sells it in international markets, and then pays the farmers. Big men have no chance to invest in cotton marketing. This has not only deprived them of new sources of wealth, but also direct contacts or involvement with the farmers whom they could have manipulated as sources of power and authority.

The government has also intervened more actively to protect the farmers as its partner in the scheme by assuming responsibility for providing the farmers with *dura* which is either bought locally or imported, and, in cases of shortage, charging the farmer either from the sale of his cotton crop, or later, when it is convenient for the farmer to pay. At the same time the government, through rationing and direct seizure of crops from the local traders, has forced the big men to accept standardized or fixed *dura* prices. The relevance of these developments to the position of the ummar and to their relations with commoners is that they have given the average peasant increasing security while at the same time severely restricting the opportunities of rich men for economic and social investment.

THE SHAIKHS (MEN OF GOD)

I have attempted to account for the impact of technological development on the traditional sources of economic and social power which were monopolized by the shaikhs. The position of the shaikhs has been shown to have changed from that of mediators and peace-makers to competitors involved in sectional conflicts mainly because traditional roles did not seem to pay off. In this connection, I. M. Lewis (1966) has offered an interesting approach in setting out to examine the impact of wider agricultural settlement and the accompanying distinctive features of social organization . . . on the position of the men of God in northern and southern Somalia. He concluded that in southern Somalia in secular affairs, and inter-clan politics, particularly, Muslim influence is more pervasive than in the north. Similar tendencies appear to have taken place among the White Nile Arabs. Shaikhs have lost much of their power and have tried to compensate for this by identifying themselves with sectional interests. But sectional interests have become very blurred for it is the individual interest that has become paramount. This is why the shaikhs have not succeeded in gaining power through this move. In this context, however, I am concerned only with giving an outline of the way in which the post-dam economic, techno-logical and other changes have acted negatively on most of the sources of power on which the shaikhs formerly relied.

First, the mechanization of irrigation and modern pest treat-ment have undermined the people's dependence on the religious shaikhs for influencing rain and river flooding and for keeping away birds and pests. Second, the development of veterinary services has provided the inhabitants with new means of securing the health, fertility, and well-being of their animals. Religious shaikhs are scarcely consulted today in this respect. Third, the progress in health services has encouraged more and more people to seek the advice of modern doctors. In certain health problems, for instance madness, shaikhs are however, still consulted and in some cases more favoured than modern medicine. Nevertheless, people are accepting modern treatment to the extent that they demand new dispensaries and health centres despite the presence of at least one of these services in almost every big village (see Map 3. Fourth, the increase in the number of schools together with popular realization of the advantages of modern education has had a drastic effect on the importance of the traditional Quranic schools (*khalwas*). This is not only because disciples of the *khalwas* in the past formed a major category of the followers of shaikhs who were dispersed among different lineages and ethnic groups, but also because scholars at the *khalwas* formed an impor-tant core of free labour which the shaikhs utilized for cultivation and animal husbandry.

The main demand in every village today is to have an elemen-tary school, a dispensary and a veterinary unit. To have these services allows the villagers to depend less on the shaikh and more on those whom they contact to get these services – the tribal chiefs who have effective control over these services, both in the Native Administration and the NWNRC, the main body of the local government. The tribal chiefs hold the key-positions in the

NWNRC, viz. that of president, vice-president and head of the financial committee (responsible for the allocation and organization of financial resources throughout the North White Nile).

The fact that modern social services have become popular has meant that their provision has become an important source of power for the tribal chiefs, at the expense of diminished dependence on the shaikhs. In addition to this, like other ummar, the shaikhs have been affected by the general post-dam economic development which has meant virtually complete identification with, and dependence on, the agricultural schemes. Again, the tribal chiefs hold the most important positions in the management of these schemes which provide them with direct economic sanctions over individuals (see Chapter 8).

Thus the lineage has become a fragmented, disorganized unit of self-asserting individuals competing with each other and endowed with friction and tension more than unity and harmony. What united them in the past was the congruence of individual interest and group interest, and since that congruence no longer exists it is the individual interest which has precedence in action.

CONCLUSION

The post-dam economy has provided individuals with new sources of livelihood and replaced the network of what élite theorists have called 'horizontal relationships' by binding lineage members together through a more precise and specific set of vertical relationships with the scheme and its management (Parry 1969). In the scheme management, and especially in the allocation of resources, the tribal chiefs have a great measure of authority. The economic sanctions which the tribal chiefs can assume in these spheres are explained in more detail later. It is important here to see that there is an inverse correlation between the magnitude of horizontal relationships between individuals, and vertical ones between individuals and the scheme. In the final analysis, most vertical relationships are controlled by the tribal chiefs. If one is to follow Bailey's distinction, what have usually been seen as normative or moral bodies, such as lineages, might be seen equally as simply amalgamations of individuals which emerge as a result of individuals' choices and interests, with little or no moral context. The lineage among the Kawahla is a case in point. It is the élite theorists' assertion that 'horizontal contacts between members of the society break down and are replaced by vertical contacts between atomized individuals and the élite' (Parry op. cit., pp. 55–6) that aptly reflects the economic and social changes that have taken place among the Hassaniya and other Kawahla. In this chapter it has also been illustrated, especially with reference to taxation and courts, that the more individuals relinquish their collective security, the more dependant they become on chiefs, and hence the more they become dominated by them.

8

Administration and Tribal Politics in the Post-Dam Period (1937–69)

A brief discussion of tribal and administrative politics in the pre-dam period was presented earlier in Chapter 4. The basic features of the system are as follows:

(1) Major politics and decisions affecting entire tribal populations in the region were formed in the meglis, a 'quasi-parliamentary' institution, and thus were not taken alone by the tribal chiefs or even by the government.

(2) The high degree of political autonomy of what might roughly be designated as the federal unit, the lineage. The lineage acted as one tax-paying group and the lineage's leaders were responsible for its administration. Internal social control was managed by the ummar and shaikhs.

(3) The hierarchical structure of tribal administration was a lesser source of power for the nazir and his deputies, or the administrative shaikhs or omdas under them. The latter officials depended on the backing of their lineages and *de facto* recognition of them as lineage leaders or co-leaders.

The post-dam political and administrative centralization has radically changed the nature of tribal politics. Not only have the tribal chiefs, members of the ruling section of the Habbaniya, consolidated their administrative power in the hierarchical structure of the Native Administration, but they have also manoeuvred successfully to attain the top positions in other administrative spheres, in local government, and in other key institutions such as the economic institutions and party political machinery. The fact that they were able to attain supremacy in all these institutions, is an indication of both the absence of competition or resistance, and of an added source of political power.

THE NATIVE ADMINISTRATION

Since the establishment of the Native Administration in the 1930s, the Habbaniya family has had a monopoly of the senior administrative offices and has been able to turn their position in this structure, which was formerly hierarchical only in appearance, into one of dominance. This involved the bureaucratic transformation of their status *vis-à-vis* omdas and shaikhs. Today, they control the omdas and shaikhs and have a greater say in their appointment and in the formation of the subordinate units.

In 1938 Abdel Gadir Idris, the nazir, retired voluntarily to give the office to his elder son, Idris, who remained in office until 1967 when he died after 29 years of rule. There was no tribal consultation or summoning of the meglis to back this appointment. On his death, the office was competed for by Idris's elder son, Omar, and his paternal uncle, Yusif, who had been a deputy since the 1930s. Yusif succeeded in getting the position, and Omar became a deputy. This incident caused for the first time a serious split in the ruling family, but it was quickly resolved after Omar became the Principal of the Executive Rural Council, responsible for the administration of the local government body, NWNRC. Both parties then realized that to carry the conflict any further would inflict irrevocable damage on their monopoly of the Native Administration. There was no competition from outside the Habbaniya, and the decision has become a *de facto* as well as a *de jure* concern of the Habbaniya alone.

Not only did the Habbaniya family retain the office of nazir, but also the three deputyships and major omdaships. Throughout this time, the offices were passed over from one generation to the next, or exchanged and distributed within the family to the exclusion of all other claimants. Thus, for instance, after the death of Haj Omar, the deputy of the Hassaniya East, in 1945, his office was taken by his brother, Idris, until 1949, and then by his brother, Khogali, until 1969. Throughout this time these offices have remained an exclusively Habbaniya concern.

THE LOCAL GOVERNMENT

The NWNRC (the North White Nile Rural Council), established since the early 1940s under formal Warrant as a Local Authority, has a separate budget. The Council budget is the responsibility of the Executive Council which will be discussed presently, but its implementation is the direct responsibility of an Executive Officer who is a Local Government official.[1] Council expenditure covers such aspects as sub-grade education, sanitation and projects concerning security, development and renewals.

THE EXECUTIVE COUNCIL

The development of social services such as education, health services, and sanitation, mainly in response to the post-dam conditions discussed in Chapters 6 and 7, entailed the development of local government services in the mid-1940s to take over part of their responsibility from the Native Administration. The tribal chiefs, the Habbaniya, acted quickly to take the initiative in the formation of the administrative bureaucracy. They pressured the government to create a mediatory role between the Native Administration and the NWNRC, called *wazir*, or minister, referred to officially as the Minister of Dar Hassaniya,[2] and to assign that role to Shaikh Ibrahim Habbani, the son of the first nazir. This role was instituted and Shaikh Ibrahim Habbani actually took over the responsibilities of the Executive Officer which were and still are assigned to trained local government officials.

By the late 1940s the Executive Council was formed and the tribal chiefs were given three important positions on it; the presidency, vice-presidency, and headship of the financial committee. Other members of the council were nominated by the government from among the other Native Administration ranks such as omdas and shaikhs. Thus A. H. Marshall (1949, p. 10) reports on the local government in the Sudan in this period:

... the local authorities are really the native authorities operating under the umbrella of a warrant. . . . The councils are composed of nazirs, omdas and shaikhs.

The report continues:

... most of the executive work being done by the tribal hierarchy, who regard the council meetings as gatherings of tribal functionaries. . . . In

---

[1] After the Native Administration was abolished in 1969–70, two branches of the NWNRC were established at Abu-Gata and Wad Nimir to take over administrative responsibilities from the deputy-nazirs.

[2] To the best of my knowledge, this sort of office has not been instituted in other parts of the Sudan.

such authorities nazirs, omdas and shaikhs – all paid servants – sit on the council to decide the policy, which they will subsequently execute. . . . As the judiciary is largely manned by the same personnel there is thus a complete blend of judicial, legislative (or policy making) and executive functions in the same persons.

This did not change much until 1969–70, when the Native Administration was abolished. Even when some elections were held for the membership of this council during the 1960s, the tribal chiefs of the Hassaniya ruling family sat as *ex-officio* or nominated representatives of the Native Administration.

I have said that public services such as dispensaries, schools, and wells, have become desired public utilities. To obtain these, people have to contact the Habbaniya, the senior tribal chiefs. For the Habbaniya, the control of the provision of these services has become an important source of power and means of recruitment of support. In the 1950s, for instance, when the first general elections were to take place, Ibrahim Habbani, Minister of Dar Hassaniya, managed to get funds from the NWNRC to build at least thirty concrete-based wells for drinking water, and as a result has always succeeded in becoming the representative of one of the east bank constituencies in the National Assembly.

The tribal chiefs, the Habbaniya, have managed to take up these new positions of authority without tribal consultation or summoning of the meglis. Not only have the tribal chiefs obtained all the new offices but they have even created new offices themselves so as to find jobs for unemployed members of the ruling section. As we have seen earlier, the institution of *wazir*, or minister, in the mid-1940s was mainly due to pressure from the Habbaniya upon the government to find a suitable job for Shaikh Ibrahim Habbani.

TRIBAL CHIEFS AND THE POST-DAM ECONOMY

The major source of living for the majority of people today is the agricultural schemes. The individual today depends on the *hawasha* and gives it most of his time and effort. The network of relationships that traditionally bound him to his lineage members has been replaced by formal relationships binding him to the agricultural scheme. The management of the schemes has two important aspects both of which bring the individual into contact with tribal chiefs and their authority. These are (a) allocation of *hawashas*, and (b) disciplinary measures regarding the settlement of disputes and the checking of tenant performance in the scheme. Both of these aspects are controlled by the Scheme Board which consists of three officials; the inspector, the nazir or his deputy, and the omda. In the allocation of farms, the power of the board is most significant in cases where an individual's land is not large enough to qualify him for a farm-plot. The board has the right to allocate a certain number of plots to individuals whom it defines as poor, having little or no land. Such individuals have to contact the nazir, the deputy and the omda to get their support before the board holds its meeting. These contacts are usually accompanied by presents in cash and kind. I have not attended any allocation of plots for no such occasion arose while I was in the field. But it is usually the case that about one-quarter of the plots in any governmental scheme are allocated to non-landholders or holders with very small pieces of land.

It has also been pointed out in Chapter 6 that the board holds the right to take away the plot from a farmer in case of proven negligence on his part. This gives the tribal chiefs, the Habbaniya, direct economic sanctions over individuals although these sanctions are not unlimited. A farmer must be referred to the board by the scheme shaikhs and usually it is only after a number of warnings that the board dismisses him. Even so the plot goes to one of his near kin before the omda or nazir is entitled to give it to whomever he wants. Thus, we have seen in an earlier case in Chapter 6 that the omda allocated the plot to himself after three successive tenants failed to cope with its cultivation.

In the scheme, quarrels between tenant farmers and breaches of the regulations concerning watering, clearance, and other agricultural activities are very frequent. These are normally settled by the disciplinary committee which consists of the inspector, the omda and all the scheme shaikhs. Appeals from this committee, however, go to the deputy court, which the scheme charter refers to as the 'ultimate body responsible for the maintenance of social order in the scheme' (see Fig. 14). This pattern of organization continued until 1967, when the system, following national pressure upon the Native Administration, was changed and the nazir and omdas no longer sat on allocation or disciplinary committees, although disciplinary cases were still referred to the deputy court in cases of appeal.

M

PRIVATE SCHEMES

In the White Nile there are about 17 large schemes and innumerable small pump schemes.[3] Private schemes are similar to governmental schemes in every aspect except that the licence is held by an individual entrepreneur. Out of the 17 large agricultural schemes, the central tribal chiefs own 14, a list of which is given in Table 15. Most of these schemes were built in the early and middle-1950s.

The building of large schemes depends upon many factors. It depends firstly on the ability of the licencee to release land from as many prior owners as possible; secondly, upon his ability to get a licence from the Nile Pumps Control Board; thirdly, on his provision of the capital needed to institute the scheme and to meet the running cost of machinery and production; and fourthly, on his acquisition of outside contracts to arrange for the ginning and marketing of cotton. In all these spheres it is the tribal chiefs who have succeeded in mobilizing their resources and relationships to

Table 15. *Large private pump schemes owned by members of the Habbaniya section*

Scheme	*Name of owner*
(1) Rahama	Yusuf Habbani
(2) El Khanger	Idris Habbani
(3) El Magam	Ibrahim Habbani
(4) El Bushra	Bushra Habbani
(5) El Mabrouk	Khogali Habbani
(6) El Mungara	Haj Ali Habbani
(7) El Bara	Khalifa Habbani
(8) Ed-dubasi	Khalid Y. Habbani
(9) Esh-shatawi	Sayid A-E Habbani
(10) El Wasim	Mahdi A-E Habbani
(11) Habbani	Tibaira I. Habbani
(12) El Nagma	Idris Habbani
(13) Ahad	Idris Habbani
(14) Abu Araki	Shelai Habbani

Note. There are only about three large schemes owned by non-Habbaniya. But there are about 150 small pump schemes in the White Nile owned by different people.

[3] Small pump schemes refer to those of 4″ to 6″ size and consist of about four to six farmers; large pump schemes refer to those of 10″ and above and may consist of 200 tenants or more.

meet these prerequisites, for they can influence people and induce them to give up their land. Through their connections with the local and central bureaucracy they can obtain licences, approval and co-operation from the Survey Unit, and the Registry Office. They can provide the capital either from their own resources, or by the exploitation of their official positions from salaries, taxes, and presents, or through outside commercial support. It is interesting to note that the most important commercial company which provides loans for the White Nile private scheme is the Mahdi Commercial Company. The official agent for this company is Bushra, from the Habbani section. This makes it easier for the tribal chiefs to get loans for their schemes and gives them also an important source of power over the owners of small pump schemes that the company supplies with loans. For instance, in the 1967 general election some of the owners of these schemes campaigned for Dr Omar Nur El-dayim who was the rival to Bushra Habbani in the Hassaniya west constituency. The first thing Bushra did was to withdraw loans from some of these people which resulted in the destruction of several small schemes.

An owner of a scheme can have great influence over the tenants, for the tenant depends exclusively on the farm, yet can be sacked by the scheme owner. It is true that a tenant has freedom to leave the scheme if he wishes, but this leaves him without an alternative means of support.

The loans given to the tenants during the agricultural season have sometimes been used by the tribal chiefs to influence people and recruit support. In 1966, for instance, there were local elections for the Rural Council. One of the candidates was a member of the Habbani section and to make sure that he would get the backing of the people, he directed a member of his section who was the owner of the Khanger Scheme to pay a loan for the farmers before its time, on the eve of the election. The payment was made, and with it the owner, who was in fact his representative, asked every tenant to swear on the Quran in the presence of a very respectable religious shaikh to give his vote to the Habbaniya man, who then succeeded in overcoming the other candidate.

THE ANSAR BROTHERHOOD AND THE UMMA PARTY

Most of the White Nile Arabs were devout followers of the Mahdist revolt in the last century (see Chapter 4). Following the re-occupation, the Mahdists' activities were strictly banned, but in the 1920s the government changed its policy and gave Sayid Abdel Rahman El Mahdi, a son of the Mahdi, the right of free movement and religious activity. He moved to the White Nile at Aba Island and began reviving Mahdist missionary activities.

The tribal chiefs of the Hassaniya, the Habbaniya, are connected through marriage to the Mahdi's family since Idris Habbani, the first nazir, married the widow of Sayid El Fadl, another son of the Mahdi's, and begot Yusuf, Ibrahim and Bushra. Accordingly, they quickly associated themselves with the new religious revival. Thus, in the early thirties, Shaikh Abdel Gadir Habbani, the nazir at the time, went to Aba, met Sayid Abdel Rahman there and declared his *baia'a* (religious support).[4] He came back and began contacting some of the big men of the Hassaniya and Hissinat, giving them news from Aba, where Sayid Abdel Rahman lived, and encouraging them to go and declare their *baia'a*. Some important leaders, for example Shaikh El Hadu and Fekki Muhammad Ali Kurtumun, went from among the Amriya lineage.

Political developments in Khartoum, especially the rise of the Graduate Club, and the emergence of its role in the national movement, caused Sayid Abdel Rahman to move there. This halted the organizational activities of his missionaries in the White Nile. By the late 1940s, political parties had emerged. The Umma political party was formed to mobilize the support of the *Ansar* (Mahdi supporters).

In the White Nile, the religious and political leadership of the *Ansar* began to crystallize also in the hands of the tribal chiefs. Until that time *Ansar* leadership was diffused among many shaikhs and other notables. Most of the shaikhs belonged to both the *Ansar* Brotherhood and other religious orders and there was no official organization or ranking. But by the early 1950s, Idris Habbani, the nazir, became the chief representative of the *Ansar* brotherhood, and consequently of the *Umma* political party. Shaikh Yusuf, the deputy nazir, emerged as a self-styled president of the party branch in the White Nile. He organized a committee consisting of notables from the various tribes and tribal sections to

---

[4] Nazir Abdel Gadir was so enthusiastic about this movement that he retired in 1938 so as to free himself for the mission. He was a very politically-minded man and was trying to unite his policy with a religious cause.

deal with *Ansar* affairs. But the committee rarely met, had no statutory power, and most of the policy decisions are actually made by the Habbaniya family.

In any case, the Habbaniya's monopoly of the *Ansar* Brotherhood and the *Umma* Party in the White Nile is both a clear reflection of their ability to move freely and to act quickly without effective competition or opposition and is also an added factor in the consolidation of their political dominance. In such a political field, where a small cohesive minority faces a scattered majority of self-asserting individuals, the control of a top position at one or more levels would lead automatically to the control of other top positions. In other words, power would increasingly create power.

As a result of all these factors regarding the dominant position of the Habbaniya in most of what élite theorists such as Burnham and C. W. Mills have called 'key institutions' (Parry 1969), they emerged as the body primarily responsible for decision-making, which resulted in the incipient dissolution of the tribal council. The power and ability of the Habbaniya to take the initiative in all important matters affecting the entire region is illustrated in the following cases.

(1) *The appointment of Nazir after Shaikh Idris' death in 1967 and the Habbaniya Split*

Nazir Idris died in 1967. The office of nazir was competed for by Omar Idris, the nazir's elder son, and Yusuf, the nazir's paternal uncle who had been a deputy since 1930. The competition was so fierce that for the first time it split the ruling family. The division was accentuated when the *Umma* Party itself split into two factions, that of Sadiq and of the Imam. Among the Habbaniya, the Yusuf faction identified itself with the Imam faction while the Omar faction identified itself with Sadiq's.

The most interesting thing about the course of this competition was not so much the split of the ruling family, as the fact that no one else tried to manipulate that split to produce an alternative outcome. Both Omar and Yusuf managed to mobilize people and to make the split a total division of the regional population into two parts. Omar led his supporters in a demonstration at Khartoum and Dueim; Yusuf summoned the omdas, his juniors, briefed them on the issue and told them, 'This young chap is not after the Nazirate, he is a communist – he is against the Nazirate altogether!'

The government, led by the Imam faction of the *Umma* party at the time, conferred the office on Yusuf, justifying this on the basis of omda backing. But it was only when a truce (*sulh*) was declared between Yusuf and Omar that the administrative machinery returned to normal. This case showed two new phenomena in Hassaniya politics: the absolute lack of opposition to the chiefs and the high degree of mass mobilization the Hassaniya chiefs could enlist.

(2) *Dispute over the Khanger Private Pump Scheme (1966)*

The Khanger Private Pump Scheme was established in the late 1950s. Shaikh Idris Habbani, the nazir, was the scheme licencee and Abdalla Wad Farah a financier. Most of the tenants in the scheme belonged to the Dabalab lineage. A dispute developed between the licencee and the financier over the scheme, when it became clear that the financier was trying to put the farmers against the licencee on the occasion of the expiry of the licence in 1966. The financier tried to get the support of the Dabalab tenants by promising them more *hawashas* and a greater share in the profits than the nazir gave them. He also exploited the tenants' feeling that the nazir had tipped their shaikh, Wad El Khanger, the most celebrated religious leader among the Hassaniya, by giving him more *hawashas* at the expense of the rest of the people.

A small group of militant Dabalab led a revolt against the nazir by attacking the scheme's tractors, destroying them and injuring their operators. There were many sympathizers from the Dabalab who expressed their wish to back Wad Farah against the nazir, but the nazir and his family acted quickly to suppress this move. They imprisoned most of the militant group and declared that since the shaikh, his family, and many other Dabalab supported the nazir, those Dabalab who wanted to support Wad Farah would have their *hawashas* separated from the scheme. This would mean that they would have to establish their own scheme from scratch. To start a new scheme needed time and effort and also meant that the separatist farmers could not cultivate their land for some time. In addition to this, the nazir, through his close contacts with the Survey Department, was able to get a statement from the Survey Unit to the effect that the only part of the scheme land which could be separated as a convenient block to make an independent scheme would be difficult to irrigate from a separate pump because of the difficulty in digging a canal to the river at this point. The issue became so desperate for the separatists that the nazir and his group won. From that time on the nazir expelled Wad Farah and replaced him with Diarat El Madhi from the Mahdi's Trading Company, as a financier. This event was celebrated in a few lines of song composed by a former woman slave of the nazir:

> *Mashurunna Mabingalia*
> *Wad Farah Ingaria*
> our scheme will not be taken away,
> Wad Farah, keep away!

(3) *The 1953 General Election and the conflict between the Tribal Chiefs and Shaikh El Wasila Es-Samani*

In 1953 the first general elections were held prior to national independence which took place in 1956. Dar Hassaniya was divided into three constituencies, one on the west bank, and two on the east bank. The tribal chiefs who dominated the *Umma* party, to which most of the White Nile Arabs belonged, nominated three candidates: two from the Habbaniya ruling family, Shaikh Bushra Habbani and Shaikh Ibrahim Habbani, and one from the Central Party Committee at Khartoum, Shaikh Abdalla El Fadil El Mahdi, who was a half-sibling of Shaikh Yusuf Habbani, the deputy-nazir, and well connected through marriage to the Habbani ruling family.

Shaikh El Wasila went to Yusuf Habbani and told him that he intended to stand as candidate in Hassaniya West. He told Yusuf that this was not his personal wish but that of many of his followers. Yusuf Habbani first tried to object diplomatically, saying that politics is a dirty game and not suitable for pious shaikhs, but failing to convince El Wasila, he addressed him, 'Look, I must make it clear to you that there is no chance of your candidature. This is Hassaniya land, and you are not a Hassani. A candidate must be a Hassani. You are our guest here. I must tell you that we have already appointed the candidate for the West bank constituency. He is my brother Shaikh Bushra. I think it would be much better for you to go and relax in your *Khalwa* (Quranic school)'.

Shaikh El Wasila was very offended and felt humiliated at what he conceived as rising tyranny. He led a strong campaign depending mainly on non-Hassaniya, especially the nomadic tribal groups in the west interior, such as the Magdia, the Kurtan, the Shiwaihat and also the Hissinat. Because the *Umma* party machinery in the White Nile was controlled by the Habbaniya, he left the *Umma* party and joined the *Ashiga* party and later became a Unionist. He won the election and defeated Shaikh Bushra.

In the 1956 general elections, however, the tribal chiefs directed all their power and efforts to defeat him. They built a number of agricultural schemes for the people and many modern wells for the nomads in order to win their support. In addition to this, because of their access to the local bureaucracy and national party machinery, they were able to gerrymander in the constituencies by including some riverain groups from the east bank in the west bank constituency. People referred to this section of the constituency as '*El amyana*', the blind, meaning that the people there were blind because they knew only one thing – that they were there to vote for the nazir. Shaikh El Wasila was defeated and the tribal chief, Yusuf Habbani, won by a large margin. Habbaniya dominance had been re-established.

(4) *The Hissinat 'Men of God' revolt against the Hassaniya chiefs*

Throughout the pre-dam period the Hissinat shaikhs refrained from accepting the administrative offices of omdas introduced by the Condominium government. When their tribal kinsmen claimed a separate nazirate or deputy nazirate, the shaikhs mediated to suspend this claim rather than identify themselves with sectionalism. The dam and the new life under the agricultural schemes, however, affected the positions of these shaikhs very greatly, putting their economic position into decline. People also were beginning more often to take their disputes to court and were becoming more and more dependent on the scheme and its technology. At the same time, their kinsmen, who had followed their orders to move from their traditional homeland near Jebel Awliya Dam and settle at Abdel Magid scheme, had suffered having found that of the scheme built on Hissinat land the Hassaniya had obtained nearly half.

In 1949 the shaikhs, caught up in their own cause, tried to take advantage of their kinsmen's suffering and told them that it was time to revolt against the Hassaniya chiefs. They actually led a revolt and demanded a separate deputy-nazir. The revolt was led by Awlad Shaikh Dafalla and Khalifa Muhammad Abdel Magid. Armed with spears, guns, wood and iron bars, the Hissinat attacked the deputy-nazir's court and attempted to kill the Hassaniya deputy-nazir. When he fled, they occupied the court building. Later, Khalifa Muhammad Abdel Magid, a highly-respected and pious man was charged with attempting to kill the deputy-nazir.

At the same time, the Hassaniya gathered together to muster their forces and there was a critical confrontation between them and the Hissinat. The Governor at Medani and the District Head-quarters at Dueim were informed by the local police, and soon armed police were moved to the scene to separate the Hassaniya and the Hissinat. It was, however, the nazir who acted quickly with wisdom and foresight, ordering the Hassaniya to disperse and telling the Hissinat that, since they did not want a court, he would transfer it to Geteina, and that he would replace Shaikh Idris, the deputy-nazir, with Shaikh Khogali, his brother and the deputy on the west bank. The Hissinat dispersed but made it clear to the nazir that they would not accept anyone but a Hissinawi deputy. But among the Hissinat Aramab section themselves there were factions and rival leaders. For instance, Wad Saghayroon, a conspicuous leader from the Aramab who belonged to a small Aramab section, allied indirectly with the Hassaniya nazir by declaring that if the other sections of the Aramab were given a deputyship, he would also ask for a separate one. He benefited more from a Hassaniya deputy who treated the different leaders and sections of the Aramab equally, than from having a Hissinawi deputy who, through his knowledge of the details of the internal affairs of the Aramab, treated him as a minor leader belonging to a minor section.

The nazir ignored the Hissinat claim and instituted the deputy-ship at Geteina. He told the Hissinat that if they needed the court they should go to Geteina; if they did not need it, no one would compel them. But Hissinat unity, disregarding the Wad Saghay-roon faction, was only situational. They soon engaged in internal disputes which they were compelled to take to Geteina to settle. They soon found the frequent journey to and from Geteina tiring and time-consuming. At last they begged the nazir to bring the court back to Abdel Magid and agreed to subject themselves to the Hassaniya deputy-nazir.

THE TRIBAL CHIEFS, THE HABBANIYA, AS A CORPORATE GROUP

The Habbaniya consist of people related within four to five generations to Idris Habbani, the first nazir during the Condominium. They are about 5,000 in number. They live mainly at Naima, the headquarters of the Nazirate, Wad Nimir, the headquarters of one of the deputyships, and Dueim, headquarters of a deputyship and also the headquarters of the NWNRC.

Most of them, especially the younger generation are well-educated: eight have acquired a university education and some are pursuing further studies in Europe. In contrast to this, the Hassaniya are limited mainly to elementary and intermediate education. Pursuing higher level education is very expensive, and requires release from helping their families to gain a living. It also requires contacts with the government at Khartoum and considerable effort to find scholarships abroad. In contrast to the fragmented, scattered and egalitarian character of the overall Hassaniya and other Kawahla groups, the Habbaniya ruling family, to which the tribal chiefs belong, has maintained a close-knit corporate and cohesive character similar to that among Awlad Fadlallah of the Kabbabish (Asad 1970).

Their corporate unity is based on the common interest of the group and its monopoly over the desired public utilities. It is only through this corporate unity that they act quickly, communicate more easily and keep basic information away from the rest of the people. Through their contacts with the bureaucracy, central government and political parties they become well-informed about political realities, agrarian development and the marketing of crops. To keep this basic information to themselves they maintain secrecy and pass information on incorrectly to others. Thus for instance, after the October revolution in 1964, there was a National Front formed in all parts of Sudan. One of the main aims of the National Front at the regional level was the abolition of the Native Administration and the taking over of private agricultural schemes by the government. The branch of the Front formed at Dueim had two members of the Habbaniya in it, and one was selected as the link between the committee and the rural areas.

One of his main functions was to help in establishing branches of the Front in the rural areas. But the information passed to the rural areas was that the main aim of the Front was to raise funds for those who died in the October revolution. Ordinary people were not so enthusiastic about the idea and branches were never formed in the rural areas.

CONCLUSION

The basic features of tribal and administrative politics in the pre-dam period have changed. In the earlier period, the power of the chief family, the Habbaniya, was largely curtailed, or at least balanced by the power of the corporate lineages and their representatives, the ummar, who used to sit in council to determine major policies and decisions. The Habbaniya depended more on the backing of the colonial government and the inevitable compromises they made with the semi-sovereign, semi-autonomous lineages than on the authoritative power embodied in the formal hierarchy they occupied. Indeed, the system was only superficially and formally hierarchical.

Today, the position of the Habbaniya is different: they are the decision-makers, the policy enacters, the top entrepreneurs, the controllers of economic institutions and party-political machinery. The consolidation of Habbaniya supremacy in all these spheres is expressive of two basic social characteristics: their own distinctive, cohesive unity, and the fragmented, disunited and egalitarian character of the rest of the tribal population, which is itself a function of post-dam economic and social changes.

9

Conclusion

In this book I have attempted to give an account of the ecological and economic factors which affected the changing pattern of socio-political relations of two interlocking structures, the lineage and the polity, that accompanied the inauguration of the Jebel Awliya Dam Development Scheme in 1937. I have found it essential to give priority to ecological and economic factors as determinants of individual loyalties and interests,[1] rather than to the normative or ideological representations which are cast in the idiom of common genealogies and agnatic kinship. Within this framework, I have analysed the forces that have led to the increasing centralization of the former loosely structured polity of confederated lineages which arose from an emergent cohesive leadership and weakened lineages.[2]

Leach (1961, p. 7) has convincingly argued:

If anthropologists come to look upon kinship as a parameter which can be studied in isolation they will always be led, by a series of strictly logical steps, to think of human society as composed of equilibrium systems structured according to ideal legal rules. *Economic activities come to appear of minor significance and the study of social adaptation to changing circumstances is made impossible.*

But an alternative possibility is to regard economic relations as prior to kinship relations. In this case the continuity of the kinship system need not be regarded as intrinsic; it is, at every point in time, adaptive to the changing economic situation. [My italics.]

Cunnison has demonstrated that despite the strength of the dogmatic mode of kinship among the Baggara, adherence to the

---

[1] For by emphasizing individual interests, social change may not be seen as disruptive but mainly as indicating a shift of individual interests from one sphere to the other.

[2] Cunnison's study of the Baggara Arabs (Cunnison 1966) has clearly demonstrated the tendency for lineage autonomy to be weakened in response to stabilised power positions, despite the ideological strength of the dogmatic rule of the 'brotherhood of the closest'.

dogmatic mode in explaining political behaviour 'tends to lead the investigator astray' (1966, p. 188). For members of agnatic groups, he argues, are 'swayed by other diverging interests . . . (they) have little time for single-minded pursuit of the interests of their lineages . . . (1966, p. 189). In fact, as I have argued in the Introduction, the priority of kinship can only be a function of the lack of alternative provisions for individual action and interest. It is only by emphasising economic priority that individual interest can best be met. Individual interest and economic priority are therefore inseparable. In the analysis of social change I have given an emphasis to the individual's interest and what, as Lewis puts it, 'serves his interest in a fashion which, in the circumstances, he regards as most advantageous' (Lewis 1968). This approach, to my mind, would inevitably elevate the status of ecology and economy, from the background to the backbone; from their conventional position in the introductory chapter, where, whatever significance is consequently attributed to them they still remain on the periphery of the frame of reference to a place as recurrent, dynamic and sequential elements in a pervasive theme. Accordingly, I have tried to relate and to account for socio-political change at all levels of analysis in terms of 'grass-roots' changes in economy and ecology which inevitably direct the individual's interest in a manner different from what it was before. Thus it has been a main pre-occupation of this analysis to show that the lineage is a corporate and differentiated structure, incompatible with centralized or dominant political power, with its basis in the environmental context, ecological and economic, which made co-operation necessary and wider group loyalties indispensable. Lineage viability remained during the major part of the Condominium (1900–37) despite the imposition of formal hierarchical administration, precisely because the ecological and economic foundations of the lineage did not change much.

Élite theorists have demonstrated that the emergence of dominant centralized power, the 'élite power group', is not compatible with the existence of viable corporate groups. The question then becomes, as Asad (1970) has put it, one concerning the social circumstances that give rise to and consequently ascriptively maintain an élite power group. It is the élite theorists' insight that élite power can only mushroom as corporate groups decay that has led me to see in the disintegration of lineages embracing the

Kawahla polity an explanation for and prerequisite of the relatively recent development of centralized political leadership under the Habbaniya chiefs, similar in many respects to the recent development of such political domination among the Kababish under the Awlad Fadlal'ah as analysed by Talal Asad.

The lineage was a corporate unit that emerged out of a process and action on the part of individuals to organise themselves in extended families, herding partnerships and camping units to exchange labour and goods in a diversified semi-pastoral economy. Individuals had to belong to wider groupings to insure against the contingencies of famine and hardship. Lineage solidarity was both reflected in and promoted by its acting as a tax-paying group, a vengeance group and an endogamous unit. In this respect its structure and significance recall the *hamula* among the Arab border villages in Israel in the early phase of the development which Cohen (1965) calls the 'Joint-Estate Period'.

The same conditions that necessitated lineage solidarity also promoted differentiation where the ummar and shaikhs acted as *foci* for lineage unity and corporate political action. Their leadership was necessary both inside the lineage and outside as delegates in the tribal congress – the main decision-making body catering for lineage interests. Cunnison (1966) has argued for the Baggara:

> In the old days political association under leaders was an answer to various challenges, for warfare and enemy raids were common occurrences, while slave-raiding and elephant-hunting were profitable pursuits that needed numbers, leadership and organization. . . . What kinds of interest now compel men to follow leaders and associate politically?

What, then, happened after the dam?

I have shown how the dam and the agricultural schemes changed those factors underlying the traditional fluctuating pattern of agricultural production by making them, through technology, more controllable (Chapter 6). The traditional risk-reducing devices such as attachment to lineage members and wealthy men, and the constant redistribution of subsistence goods have become redundant through the direct economic planning of the government in the scheme and its management.

In the scheme, today, productivity is controlled and calculated. Plant technology is used to improve both the quality and the quantity of the product. Plant protection units assume responsibility for combating pests, birds and other enemies of fertility and conservation. The individual interests and contacts are more and more identified and restricted to the agricultural scheme. In the process, the scheme has shifted economic dependency from the wider network of kin relationships to a more restricted formal set of relationships with its management. I have referred to the former set of relationships as 'horizontal' and to the latter as 'vertical'; these may also be distinguished roughly as 'formal' and 'informal' relationships. The horizontal relationships binding lineage members together in the pre-dam period, involving the exchange of labour, consumer goods, land rights, marriages and a wide range of debt bonds with the wealthy big men, have been greatly undermined. I have shown that it was in animal husbandry that the exchange of labour was most significant, and that its decline as a group activity and essential part of the semi-nomadic economy has eliminated a very important sphere in which free labour was formerly exchanged. Cotton cultivation has become the primary interest, and the demands of its sedentary cultivation have meant that people can no longer move seasonally with their animals. In the scheme, labour is either mechanized or catered for by cash workers supplied by the scheme. From the point of view of both the scheme and the tenant farmer, hired labour is found to be more efficient and dependable. In this way the elementary family has emerged as the basic unit of production.

We have also seen how post-dam conditions have broken down the lineage into various smaller units, occupying different sides of a wide river, deriving their livelihood from different schemes and, in some cases, having different modes of livelihood. This has also accompanied the division of the lineage as a tax-paying group into many such units. The expropriation of land and its use for building agricultural schemes which emerge as multi-ethnic institutions, has further undermined the relatively close identification of lineage with land as a common source of livelihood.

All these factors have altered lineage structure, solidarity, and the privileged position of its leaders, the ummar and the shaikhs, who have been greatly affected by the secularization of agricultural production, its mechanization and its technology. Signs of lineage disintegration are found in many spheres: in the frequent conflicts and disputes between its members, in the taking of these disputes to courts, in the relatively narrowed conception of closeness as reflected by prevalent modes of marriage and last, but not least, in the inability of lineage leaders to mobilize support for common political action. As Cunnison (1966) has said of the Baggara who still, however, employ kinship relations in some respects, lineage members 'have little time for the single-minded pursuit of the interest of their lineage'.

The change of the Kawahla lineage from a viable corporate group into a disintegrated unit, as horizontal relationships binding constituent members are swayed by other diverging interests, which may be referred to as 'vertical' or 'centrifugal', as against 'centripetal' interests which can bind lineage members in a common cause, is similar in many respects to the change which the *hamula* has undergone in Palestine during the shift from the Joint-Estate Period to the Mandate Period. In the first period, the *hamula* 'played important collective roles in the economic and political, as well as the kinship spheres, and *hamula* organization provided the basis of political organization in the village (Cohen 1965, p. 4). For then '. . . the men of the *hamula* held the land jointly and co-operated closely in the agricultural production (Cohen op. cit., p. 6). Later, however, certain external factors, namely, European influences and internal factors, the most significant of which were the break-up of the joint estate, the conversion of land to private property, and the emergence of landless tenants, lost the *hamula* its economic basis. 'The new lines of stratification cut across the *hamula* boundaries and tended to disrupt the *hamula*. . . . Thus the *hamula* as a political organization dwindled in importance . . . (Cohen op. cit., p. 8).

But the disintegration of the lineage among the Kawahla is only one side of the picture: the concomitant repercussions of this on the polity embracing the lineages are also significant. I have shown here that the polity gradually changed from a loosely-structured confederation, run by the tribal congress as well as by the chiefs, into a centralized polity, as one function of an emerging dominant political leadership. As contacts and bonds between lineage members broke down, they were replaced by vertical relationships with controllers of the agricultural schemes and other desired public utilities. The tribal chiefs who occupy, or more correctly who have manoeuvred successfully to occupy, the top formal positions responsible for managing these aspects of public life have thus gained control over individuals upon whom they never previously exerted direct economic or other political influence. In the pre-dam period, relations between the central chiefs and the individual tribesmen were channelled through the lineage big men. Today, ummar power can be overlooked, and the more individuals depart from traditional loyalties, the more they depend on the central tribal chiefs and hence the more they come under the latter's control. Socio-economic change has thus produced two different and basically incompatible forces: the individualization of economic and political action on the one hand, and the inevitable attachment of the individual to new forces with which his interest is most closely identified, and, ironically, to which it is most clearly subordinated.

The undermining of corporate groups has weakened any effective opposition or resistance to a dominating power; and the chiefs not only consolidated their power positions in the hierarchy of the Native Administration, but they also occupied key-positions in other key-institutions in the local government, economic institutions and the party-political machinery. Their power in any sphere leads to power in other spheres. They have become an emerging power élite. I would like to limit my final remarks to this phenomenon.

Talal Asad (1970) set out to explain the dominance of the ruling élite among the Kababish, the Awlad Fadlalah, in terms of this dichotomy, between a corporate minority versus a fragmented and egalitarian majority, which is derived from early élite theory such as that put forward by Mosca, Michels, James Burnham, Pareto and C. Wright Mills. Asad's thesis is a pioneering attempt in the serious application of élite theory to small-scale tribal communities. Unfortunately, however, Asad has not included the élite theorists' dichotomy between 'vertical' and 'horizontal' relationships in explaining the dominant position of Awlad Fadlalah in relation to the entire Kababish. Thus he was unable to provide an account of what I have called 'horizontal' relationships among the masses, that is, the Kababish as a whole, and went straight on to explore the differential characteristics of Awlad Fadlalah as a corporate group without showing systematically (except in a general and implicit manner), the sort of vertical relationships which existed between the rulers and the ruled. Asad's book has two parts, one on domestic and one on political authority, which

N

although in some sense interconnected, are substantially autonomous. This, to my mind, is the main reason why Asad has emphasized only the dominance aspect of the relations between rulers and ruled. Thus, while Asad acknowledges Mosca's influence, he has not paid much attention to Mosca's rigorous and systematic thesis that, as Bottomore puts it (1964, p. 13) 'there is an interaction between the ruling minority and the majority, instead of a simple dominance by the former over the latter', and also the fact that Mosca is much more aware of "interests or social forces which are represented in it . . . of its intimate bonds with the rest of the society. . . " In accounting for the emergence of the Habbaniya as an élite power group among the Kawahla, I have emphasized the dual representation of interaction and domination as characteristics of ruler/ruled relations. I have also attempted a synthesis of what most of the élite theorists have to say about the prerequisites for élite rule.

Parry (1969, p. 35) has summarized the élite theorists' point of view as follows:

. . . Mosca and his disciple Michels, held that an élite owed its power to its organizational abilities. . . . James Burnham, attempting a marriage between élitism and Marxism, saw the power of the élite as a consequence of its control of economic resources, and finally C. Wright Mills similarly explained the élite's dominance not as a product of the personal qualities of its members but of the positions they held in a number of key institutions within the society.

The growing dominance of the Habbaniya can be explained in terms of most or all these factors:

(1) Organizationally, they have been able to form a coherent, cohesive, self-conscious group with a common will to action.

(2) In the Marxist sense employed by Burnham, Habbaniya power has its roots in the developed control over the chief means of production, the agricultural schemes.

(3) In C. Wright Mills's sense, Habbaniya dominance is to be explained in the total context of the changing social structure. In all spheres of life, it has been shown how the tribal chiefs have managed to occupy the key positions in the key institutions.

The Native Administration, Local Government, the *Ansar* Brotherhood, party-political machinery, and agricultural schemes are the kind of institutions which Mills saw as having pivotal importance in society. The Habbaniya who occupy the upper ranks in these institutions are by definition the occupants of Mills's 'strategic command posts of the social structure' (Mills 1959, p. 4).

We have to emphasize that these features are the very ones élite theorists have seen as characteristics of the élite. These theorists, and my study, agree that for such an élite to develop, the masses (the subjugated majority) must first experience a state of fragmentation, disorganization and atomization as individuals, all of which in the Kawahla situation have accompanied the inauguration of the Jebel Awliya Development Scheme. The emergence of the power élite is thus a result of the socio-economic changes that have taken place among the Kawahla Arabs of the White Nile.

Appendix I

The Genealogies of the Gushgushab and other Hassaniya Lineages

The Genealogies of the Gushgushab, as given to me by Muhammad En Nur (El Ka'ab) of the Gushgushab lineage.

Kahil	1	(founder of the Kawahla
Khalifa	2	(founder of the Khalayfa)
Hassan	3	(founder of the Hassaniya)
Muhammad	4	
Shash	5	
Imair	6	(founder of the Imairia)
Hamid	7	
Abdel Rasqul	8	
Gushgush	9	(founder of the Gushgushab)
Keiwat	10	
Hamid	11	(founder of the Hamdab *Khashm-bait*)
Muhammad	12	
Sulaiman	13	
Bilal	14	
Muhammad	15	

(Note: no mention is given of Teifay here and surprisingly the name given next to Hassan is Muhammad which would suggest that there are Gena Muhammad.)

Another version excludes the Gammalab and Shamkhia from Gena Teifay, and is usually given like this:

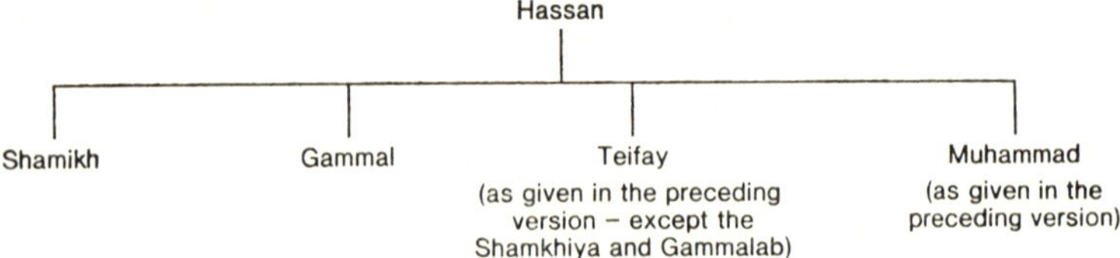

The Gammalab and Shamkhia strongly adhere to this version. They say we are *kubra* to others, that is, genealogical seniors.

Another version agrees with this and the preceding one as far as Gena Muhammad are concerned but excludes another lineage from Gena Teifay, in addition to the Shamkhia and Gammalab.

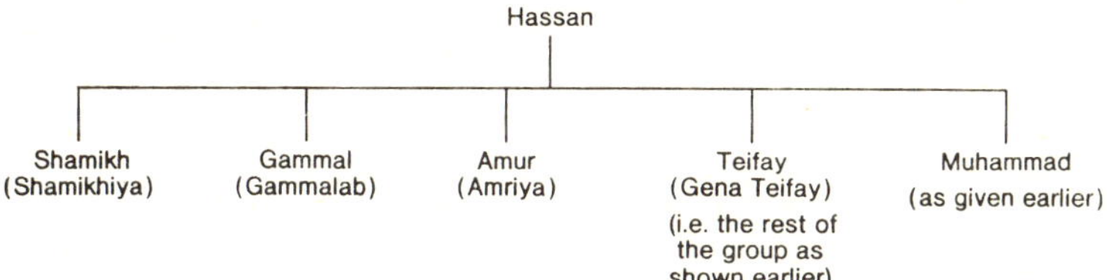

This last version is often confirmed by a mythical story stating that Gammal was killed by another tribe, or was taken as a hostage by that tribe. Shamikh, the elder of his brothers led the 'vengeance group', consisting of the other brothers. Either they succeded in freeing their brother or in revenging his death, and on their way back, Shamikh asked God to make certain wishes come true:

For Muhammad he said: '*inshaa'ala salih o'falih*'. Literally, 'if God wishes be pious and learned'.

The myth tells that other wishes were for Amur and Teifay and that these wishes were addressed to God by Shamikh after he became aware of the personal characteristics of his brothers during their vengeance expedition. The informants usually ended this myth by the comment – 'See how these wishes have come true!'

Appendix 2

A list of Important Historical Events and Dates among the White Nile Arabs [1]

Name of Year	Meaning of name	Arabic date	English date
Sanat Um-Kiwaisat	A famine year – a measure used for measuring out the *aish*	1301	1883
Sanat el-aish el-kariemi	Red dura imported from Gedarif	1303	1885
Sanat el-dieg-Sanat el-goua'a	Famine year	1306	1888
Sanat el-tarhiela	Year of abundance	1308	1890
Sanat Niel Fadl el moula	A *dervish amir* – a high flood year	1312	1894
Sanat Um-Sikaikoun	Plague of small grasshoppers also called 'fly-by-nights'	1318	1900
Sanat el saila	High flood	1319	1901
Sanat el Saffaya	*Habboobs* and hot winds destroyed crops	1322	1904
Sanat um-saffaya	A year of hot *habboobs*	1329	1911
Sanat el-habour	Widespread cattle disease	1332	1914
Sanat um-dahab-	Famine year. Gold paid for *aish*	1332	1914
Sanat aish el Hind– or Sanat um *rotl*	*Aish* brought from India to relieve distress. The *rotl* used here for the first time	1332	1914
Sanat Wad Land	Woodland D.C. Dueim, obtained *aish* and distributed it, paying for a great deal of it himself. One of the most popular figures there has ever been in the White Nile	1332	1914
Sanat ed-douda	Maggots destroyed crops	1334	1916
Sanat el bahar el kabir	A high river	1335	1917
Sanat el khairan	Very low river only filling *khors*	1336	1918
Sanat um dahab or Sanat abbarbaein	Famine year. Gold paid for *aish* which reached £4,000/mms. per *ardeb*	1337	1919
Sanat el aish el kateir	High river and plenty of *aish*	1338/39	1920/21

[1] Reproduced without change from administrative files, Dueim District.

Appendix 3

The Kawahla Pedigree

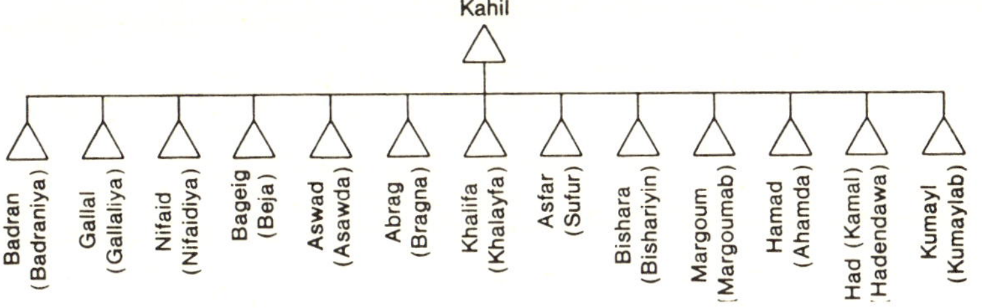

LIST OF WORKS CITED

ASAD, T., 1970. *The Kababish Arabs: Power, Authority and Consent in a Nomadic Tribe*, London.

BAILEY, F. C., 1970 (2nd impression, originally 1969). *Stratagems and Spoils: A Social Anthropology of Politics*, Oxford.

BARTH, F., 1959. *Political Leadership among the Swat Pathans*, London School of Economics Monographs on Social Anthropology, No. 19, London.

—, 1968. 'Economic Spheres in Darfur', in *Themes in Economic Anthropology*, ASA Monographs No. 6, London.

BOTTOMORE, T. B., 1964. *Elites and Society*, Penguin Books.

CARR, E. H., 1964. *What is History?*, Penguin Books.

COHEN, A., 1965. *Arab Border-Villages in Israel*, Manchester.

—, 1969. *Custom and Politics in Urban Africa. A Study of Hausa Migrants in Yoruba Towns*, London.

CUNNISON, I., 1966. *Baggara Arabs*, Oxford.

—, 1962. 'Some Social Aspects of Nomadism in a Baggara Tribe', in *Nomadism and Economic Development in the Sudan* (Proceedings of the 10th Annual Conference of the Sudan Philosophical Society, Khartoum, 1962).

EMMET, D., 1960. 'How Far Can Structural Studies Take Account Of Individuals?', *JRAI*, 90, pp. 191–200.

EVANS-PRITCHARD, E. E., 1940. *The Nuer*, Oxford.

—, 1949. *The Sanusi of Cyrenaica*, Oxford.

FOX, R., 1967. *Kinship and Marriage*, Penguin Books.

FREEDMAN, M., 1966. *Chinese Lineage and Society*, London School of Economics Monographs on Social Anthropology, No. 33, London.

FRIED, H. M., 1967. *The Evolution of Political Society: An Essay in Political Anthropology*, New York.

HASSAN, Y. F., 1967. *The Arabs and the Sudan*, Edinburgh.

HOLT, P. M., 1961. *A Modern History of the Sudan*, London.

LEACH, E. R., 1961a. *Pul Eliya: A Village in Ceylon*, Cambridge.

—, 1961b. *Rethinking Anthropology*, London School of Economics Monographs on Social Anthropology, No. 22, London.

LEWIS, I. M., 1961. *A Pastoral Democracy*, Oxford.

—, 1965. 'Shaikhs and Warriors in Somali Land', in M. Fortes and G. Dieterlien (eds.), *African Systems of Thought*, Oxford University Press for the International African Institute.

—, 1968a. 'Contrast and Conformity in Somali Islam', in *Islam in Tropical Africa*, London.

—, 1968b. Introduction to *History and Social Anthropology*, ASA Monographs No. 5, London.

—, 1969. 'Tradition and Transition in East Africa', in P. H. Gulliver (ed.), *Studies of the Tribal Element in the Modern Era*, London.

—, 1971. 'Nomadism, An Anthropological View', Paper given at an FAO Conference in Cairo.

LLOYD, P. C., 1967. *Africa in Social Change: Changing Traditional Societies in the Modern World*, Penguin Books.

MACMICHAEL, H. A., 1912. *The Tribes of Northern and Central Kordofan*, Cambridge. (1967. New Impression, Frank Cass & Co Ltd.)

—, 1922. *A History of the Arabs in the Sudan*, Cambridge (2 vols).

MANGAR, N., 1961. Al-Rahhalah Jun Bitrik, Part 3, *Accounts of Three Travellers in the Sudan in the Nineteenth Century*, Arabic Text, Cairo.

MARSHALL, A. H., 1949. *Report on Local Government in the Sudan*, Khartoum.

MERTON, R. K., 1949. *Social Theory and Social Structure*, Free Press.

MILLS, C. WRIGHT, 1956. *The Power Elite*, New York.

—, 1959. *The Sociological Imagination*, New York.

MINISTRY OF PLANNING, Department of Statistics, Khartoum, 1969. *A Report on Sample Census of Agriculture for the Year 1964/65 in the Blue Nile Province of the Sudan*, Khartoum.

MOHAMED, ABBAS, 1971. 'Political Neutrality and Commitment of the Men of God: Politics in the White Nile, Sudan', paper given in Politics of Africa Seminar in the London School of Economics (unpublished).

—, 'The Nomadic and Sedentary: Polar Complementaries, not Polar Opposites', in Nelson C. (ed.), *The Desert and the Sown*, California, 1973.

MUHAMMAD, AWAD M., 1951. *Al-Sudan al-Shamali Sukkanuhu wa qa-balluha, The Peoples and Tribes of Northern Sudan*, Arabic Text, Cairo.

PARRY, G., 1969. *Political Elites*, London.

PAUL, A., 1954. *A History of the Beja Tribes of the Sudan*, Cambridge.

PETHERICK, J., 1861. *Egypt, the Sudan and Central Africa, with Exploration from Khartoum in the White Nile Regions of the Equator*, London.

PETHERICK, J. and MRS PETHERICK, 1869. *Travels in Central Africa and Exploration in Western Nile Tributaries* (2 vols), London.

PREST, A. R., 1948. *War Economies of Primary Producing Countries*, Cambridge.

REID, J. A., 1930. 'Some Notes on the Tribes of the White Nile Province', in *Sudan Notes and Records*, vol. XIII, part II, Khartoum.

ROSENFELD, H., 'Social Factors in Explanation of the Increased Rate of Patrilineal Endogamy in the Arab Villages in Israel', n.d., unpublished manuscript.

SALIH, H. M., 1971. *An Ethnographic Survey of the Hadendawa*, M.Sc. Thesis, University of Khartoum.

SAHLINS, M. D., 1965. 'On the Sociology of Primitive Exchange', in *The Relevance of Models for Social Anthropology*, ASA Monographs No. 1, London.

SHIBAIKA, M., 1964. *Mamlakat al Fung al Islamiyah, On the Islamic Kingdom of Fung*, Arabic Text (Ma'had a l-dirasat al-Islamiyah), Cairo.

SMITH, M. C., 1960. *Government in Zazzau*, International African Institute, London.

WEBER, M., 1947. *The Theory of Social and Economic Organisation*, translated by A. M. Henderson and Talcott Parsons, London.

GLOSSARY

afu: pardon
awgad: arbitrator
baia'a: religious support
baraka: religious blessing
bash-khafir: chief water guard
birak: pools
dahawa: morning herding session
darat: post rain period
diya: blood money
duhriya: afternoon herding session
dumur: permanent dwelling centres
dura: sorghum
durdur: half straw-mud hut
fitna: intrigue or feud
fursan: horsemen
furua: lineages (branches)
ghufara: guards
goz: sand dunes
guttiya: straw hut
hawasha: farm
hikir: right of land use
hugna: reservoir
karama: sacrifice
khairan: watercourses
khalwas: Quranic schools
kharif: rainy season
khashm-bait: lineage section
khat: Turkish administrative unit

mareesa: local beer house
masmir: commissioner
matamir: harvest storage pits
meglis: tribal council
merkaz: subdistrict headquarters
mihaya: holy water
muhafzin: messengers
murah: herding unit
nafir: collective labour
nas-el-shura: people of consent
nazir: paramount chief
nimra: member
rushash: early showers
saif: summer
sarba: night herding session
sha'ar: wool hut
shita: winter
shorab: grazing land
shukkab: straw hut
tarha: veil
terus: rainland
tin: fertile clay soil
tulba: manual labour
ummar: big men
ummar gabila: well-to-do tribal elders
wakil: deputy
warga: charms
zariba: fenced enclosure